What people are sa

Being still whilst the rest of the world is spinning is hard but essential. The world is complicated, but you're not alone. This guidebook shows how to create positive relationships with yourself and others to help navigate decisions and move forward in a way that is meaningful for you – even when everything else in life is in flux.

Richelle Schuster
Head of Innovation – Programmes and Impact, Leeds City Council

Helping people of any age; taking a moment to reflect, rationalise and apply effective tools and thinking to their own development is such a valuable resource. This guidebook has the potential for helping young people build confidence and, ultimately, solve problems they previously felt were unsolvable.

Joe Gaunt
Founder and Chief Executive, Zeno (Zeno health group.com)

In the history of humankind, there has never been a more difficult and challenging world. The pressures of society are immense. Health, happiness and love are the things we strive for most, but acquiring these qualities seems at times an impossible journey which can result in us doubting our behaviour. This insightful and perceptive guide helps navigate this path, written by a man who believes in the potential of every soul he meets. Years of experience mentoring young and hungry minds provided him the knowledge and certainty to embark on creating a guidebook that will inspire and help drive forward the goals of future generations.

John Macintyre
Sales and Marketing Director FMCG

Tony has brought his many years of teaching experience and skills and created this interesting and enlightening guide to assist in the challenges of the dynamic workplace. This guidebook will help all people, but especially those with new careers or entering or re-entering the workforce. It combines good information and colourful storytelling to create a roadmap to help the reader navigate the evolving world of work. Furthermore, it serves as a useful reference guide that can be used later for clarification and assisting with new work challenges. It is an interesting read for all.

Denise Chong
Interim Chief People Officer

The last few years has changed us all in ways that we'd never have anticipated; what is important to us as human beings has sharply shifted, although the what, when and how we navigate the changed world are still up for debate. This guidebook is a great way to help feed that narrative. For some, it may seem common sense; for others, it may stretch the realms of our consciousness. Either way, having more of an understanding of ourselves and what we need – whilst understanding more about those around us and what they need – is a sure way to ensure that you are playing your part in helping the human race navigate this complex world that we all inhabit.

Alex Naylor
Co-Founder and Chief People Officer – Gravitas

For my dearest loving parents, who always encouraged me to think freely, fearlessly and creatively in the pursuit of my dreams.

.

Contents

Excursion Two
The E in LEAD – EMOTION – 231

Excursion Three
The A in LEAD – ACHIEVE – 253

Excursion Four
The D in LEAD – DESIRE – 307

Foreword

Unearthing treasure was my pervading perception while reading and absorbing the rich and life-enhancing messages in this unique guidebook. It has just the right blend of vision and practicality to make it a genuine benefit that will enable young people to explore and envision for themselves a different, sustainable and more fulfilling future.

Tony has an understanding of and empathy with young people, derived from years of working closely with them – not just as a teacher but also as a mentor, coach and guide. This is matched with his more recent experience and success in innovation and creating a small to medium-sized enterprise (SME). The result is a powerful blend of synthesised thinking and impactful practical application that provides accessible and nuanced guidance and direction for young people, not just those who might be struggling to explore and understand their options for the future but also as a checklist for those who think they have this sorted.

Regardless of their starting point, Tony's perceptive and comprehensive process for negotiating and navigating the 'jungle' will ensure opportunities for positive and beneficial outcomes. It provides young people with thinking and decision-making processes that, when taken to their inevitable conclusion, give assurance and confidence in the substance of the steps they then take for themselves. It provides assurance that they're well thought through and fully resolved.

Realisation of our full potential in life is a laudable self-affirmation aspiration. Far too few of us achieve this. This guidebook is an invaluable tool for getting as close to this as anything else I've seen to date.

Roland Meredith
International Education Advisor

Introduction

Storm clouds

To what extent will you grant yourself permission to fully stoke the glowing embers within so they transform into a raging fire that might inspire and light up the outside world?

Gorfesiw (whom you'll meet later in this book)

Welcome.

It's a jungle out there, and it's being compounded by relentless storms of global upheaval and change that can overwhelm your ability to navigate work life confidently.

Are you struggling and in need of inspiration or a more holistic perspective to help manage this problem? If your answer is yes, then your wake-up call for personal transformation simply can't wait any longer.

This is why you have this guidebook in your hands; it's a much awaited ally that's stepped up to accompany you on your journey through the crossroads of life, and it has the sole purpose of helping you to release the sense of discord and draw all your frustrations to a close. You're about to embark on a unique adventure in which you'll understand more about yourself and uncover the solutions you so deeply desire!

How you choose to think and feel as you navigate today's turbulent world is more important than ever before. Looking ahead, the only thing we can know for sure is that there will be uncertainty. We can't control uncertainty, but we can control how we choose to think.

At this point in your journey, you may feel somewhat isolated or at a crisis point in your life, but fear not, your struggle is justified, and you're certainly not alone. There's a silent cry within so many, and at its core is an urgent desire to temper feelings of anxiousness or demoralisation. So many people are searching for greater perspective, self-worth, balance and positivity.

The problem is that, when you're so deeply lost in the jungle, no one can hear you calling! Your guidebook is here to listen, and it understands your cries for freedom.

Do any of the following themes resonate with you?

→ A desire to break free of negative thought loops, financial insecurity or job uncertainty

Do you find it difficult to maintain a balanced mindset when faced with a crisis, an upheaval or a transition? Whether you work for yourself, within an organisation/business or for frontline services, are the demands becoming intolerable? Do you automatically think the worst under these circumstances and so are held captive by fear, phobias, catastrophising or unworthiness?

Do financial pressures weigh heavily on your mind as the monthly bank statements continually reinforce the idea that you're not really in control? Do you feel as though the harsh outside world (with its poor economy, rising inflation and societal upheaval) has control over you?

Do you feel increasingly expendable at work? Do you worry that your work position could completely disappear overnight, never to be replaced?

Do you succumb to victimisation as bad experiences from your past haunt you, preventing you from thinking clearly? When you attempt something new, are old habits released that immobilise you, accompanied by that uncomfortable feeling of dread that you'll not hit the mark?

Do you suffer from anticipatory anxiety, loss of control or a lack of ability to move through challenges with focus and resilience?

How often do you repeat the phrase 'I don't need negative people around me right now,' only to realise you unwittingly attracted them into your life in the first place?

→ A desire for more confidence or an ability to combat feelings of overwhelm or anxiety that prevent you living a life in tune with your true values

Are you at a loss when trying to forge the right coping strategies to combat anxiety, worry or stress? Do you dwell on the damaging long-term effects that these emotions place on your health?

Stress can result from a range of situations, including an unrealistic workload, a lack of time, poor relationships or leadership, and keeping up with a fast-paced technological world. Do you yearn to turn this situation around and replace it with a more caring and fulfilling life?

Do you find yourself increasingly numbed, irritable, distracted or unable to appreciate joy in the present moment? Do you find it difficult to concentrate while navigating the hustle and bustle of work life?

These feelings of worry, doubt and fear that seem to form a low background vibration only serve to compound your inability to live purposefully and energetically. Do you find it difficult to address sensitive mental health issues within your work environment? Do you long for somebody to step into your life who really understands and cares about how you're feeling? Does the appeal of downtime or receiving a good dose of positivity rank highly on your wish list?

→ A desire for greater holistic meaning, purpose and fulfilment

Does life thrill or threaten you? You may dream of rising each morning with a buzz and living a life congruent with your true values and aspirations. Do you recognise this longing as another painful realisation that something is missing and there seems no immediate answer to soothe it? Do you long for a fairer and more just world in which truth and transparency prevail?

Are you relatively comfortable financially and have all the possessions you require, but you recognise you harbour an unfulfilled inner world that's void of purpose? You buy the new car, the new house and book the exotic holiday, but several weeks later, you still feel dissatisfied.

Are you becoming increasingly confused with what a lifestyle that's balanced and considers your well-being means exactly? If only there were more space and more time to gain perspective and come up for air! If only you could unravel the secrets to managing time effectively and avoiding feelings of guilt arising from focusing on certain areas in your life while neglecting others. Do you yearn for opportunities to nourish your soul with a deeper spiritual (formless power) connection? When you eventually stop and pay attention to what that quiet inner voice is saying, does the experience suddenly feel rather unsettling? This voice reminds you that holistic well-being isn't just about one-off yoga classes, colour-therapy sessions, green smoothies and evening meditations but is also the subtle way you appreciate the everyday unfoldment of life. Simple gratitude for what's directly in front of you and being present also matter. How on earth do you get your head around that one?

→ Freedom from feeling ignored, harassed or undervalued

Do you find it difficult to manage your emotional reactions or coping strategies when you're stuck working alongside people or environments that are far from ideal, oppressive, frustrating, or far too big or powerful for you to change?

Examples could include the following:

- A lack of recognition from those around you for the work you humbly and diligently accomplish, while those who exert their ego and shout the loudest receive all the attention.

- Feeling constantly on edge while managing your own business in a harsh and often unforgiving world.

- Working in environments in which your leaders, employers or people you serve show very little compassion or interest in you.

- Working within an unhealthy work culture entrenched in outdated practices that claim to have your well-being at heart.

- Poor communication in which you're rarely listened to or consulted by management when decisions are made that may affect your workload. Inadequate or insincere support for your health and fulfilment.

- Poor delivery of Health and Safety Executive standards from the organisation you work for.

- Being unable to feel psychologically safe (working within an organisation that respects your autonomy and provides you with regular opportunities to ask questions, raise concerns, and share ideas or suggestions, free from the fear of ridicule, rejection or embarrassment).

→ An escape from feeling cut off, detached, lonely or disconnected

Maintaining a close family or friendship circle of support may be a number one priority for you right now, but do you feel frustrated about how much time you can spend with them practically? Have the choices you once had regarding your time management been removed or placed under threat?

Through no fault of your own, have you lost critical social support hubs within your workplace? Has a community you once enjoyed sharing time with been fragmented? You may have relied on these hubs as a sounding board and a place to go when you needed a listening ear throughout periods of challenge, transition or crisis.

Honest human interaction at work that involves humour, eye contact, warmth, compassion and humility may seem in short supply. Does your work environment neglect the most basic of human desires for trust, belonging and appreciation? Do you find it draining having to work your way relentlessly around work politics? All of these scenarios create a state of fear and constant self-protection that's emotionally debilitating.

→ A desire for more independence, opportunity, personal transformation or freedom from authoritarianism

Is there an entrepreneur, writer, global business owner, innovator or activist seeking expression within? Do you feel discomfort that you're wasting your life while a higher cause within you beckons quietly? Do you desire to participate and serve more, stand on your own two feet, and immerse yourself in what you truly love? Do you wish you could steer increased environmental change, social inclusion, equality awareness or reform? Does your work support or hinder personal growth and expression?

If you're already an entrepreneur or small-business owner, do you feel stuck and frustrated while you're struggling to create the big break and deliver the fantastic pitch that could open the doors to greater success and prosperity?

→ Freedom from technological information overload, the rise of virtual work or the always-connected culture

Do you feel in control of your ability to monitor your health and well-being while immersed within a technologically driven world? Technology alone isn't the problem: it's the loss of control that blurs the line between your work and leisure time that troubles you the most.

Do you succumb to the urge to continue working on your devices right up until bedtime? Do you resent the intrusive, always-on technological culture that invades your life continually? Do you find it increasingly difficult to switch off mentally after enduring a whole day of back-to-back virtual work meetings delivered to your home office? Do you continue working even though you're unwell (presenteeism)? With Wi-Fi connections available virtually anywhere, do you find yourself working outside contracted hours and using allocated time off, or non-working days, to complete tasks (leaveism)?

Is your virtual world of communication via email, texting or blogging beginning to numb your connection with what it means to be a social human being? Do you find you get fed up trying to figure out what people really mean in an email and just wish you could hold a clear, face-to-face conversation to avoid misinterpretation? Do you find the majority of your email activity revolves around replying to others' needs, rather than instigating ideas or creating new opportunities? Last week, you were on a downer because the internet connection was down, and you felt a failure for not completing a work project (which should have been left at the office and not taken home in the first place) because your laptop hard drive failed.

Do you have an inseparable relationship with your smartphone? This addiction occasionally troubles you, but it's subsequently replaced by the excuse: *Hey, we all do it!* You wonder if using your smartphone in bed is adding to your insomnia. Furthermore, there's the allure of the text message ping from your phone right in the middle of a business meeting or having a coffee out with a friend or your family. Should you reach across into your coat pocket, take your phone out and read the message while pretending to be still engaged in the conversation? *Will it look bad?* you ask yourself, but of course, you so often give in to the temptation.

Are you held hostage by the addictive rush of dopamine you experience every time your 'like' stats grow on one of your social media posts? As you climb down from your temporary high, you feel even more helpless and manipulated.

→ A desire to escape a manic or impulsive lifestyle driven by force and competition

Spending too much time submerged in our own thoughts or

working in isolation can encourage our own self-importance to take centre stage. Do you ever feel driven to get ahead and agitated, pushing others out of the way and only ever associating the feeling of satisfaction with winning? Does your ego continually seek being anywhere but here (the grass is always greener on the other side) or do you fall into self-pity or victimisation traps? The opposite of an ego-driven existence is living more attentively within the present moment. How good are you at creating space for peace, contentment and surrender?

Get clear on your wishes

Another way for you to summarise the problems we all face in today's world is to review the following statement and highlight any of the following key words that apply to you:

I wish for more...

- energy
- confidence
- resilience
- good news / change of fortune
- time
- vision
- choice
- focus
- identity
- hope
- money
- business
- mindfulness
- control
- freedom
- ease
- peace
- opportunities to serve
- opportunities to make a difference
- drive
- spark
- purpose
- contentment
- authenticity in my behaviour
- meaning

And so the list goes on.

Ask yourself these questions:

» *Am I living out the best version of myself?*

» *Am I being true to my value set and my family?*

» *Am I living a life of balance, ease and flow?*

» *Is my focus generally empowering and meaningful?*

How you react to or navigate the themes outlined earlier obviously determines how you show up in the world, the decisions you make and the types of relationships you forge. Taking this idea a step further, your self-concept (that is, what you think of yourself) will ultimately affect your beliefs about what's possible for you to achieve in life and, subsequently, your view of reality. Above all, one overriding truth prevails: you're either stepping backward from growth, experiencing lack or despondency, or advancing confidently toward an expanding and liberating future through acts of fulfilment. This advancement requires a broad and balanced range of behavioural skills and attitudes, which are often referred to as a 'growth mindset'. A key element associated with such advancement is the ability to take full responsibility for the outcomes in your life by conducting an honest self-review of how you manage your time and energy. The Swedish psychiatrist and professor Marie Åsberg developed a concept called the 'exhaustion funnel'. Her model highlights the danger of continually following the urge to pursue just one particular venture, which merely depletes our natural resources and results in burnout. We fail to achieve healthy and fulfilling lives when we neglect our responsibility to satisfy our broad bedrock of key psychological and emotional needs.

> *Not all storms come to disrupt your life,*
> *some come to clear your path.*
> **Paulo Coelho**

The map analogy

Have you ever had that stressful or bewildering experience of finding yourself lost, running late or behind schedule, trying frantically to navigate your way through an unfamiliar environment such as a busy city centre, complex airport terminal or crowded theme park? Under these circumstances, if there's no one immediately available to ask for help, you'd more than likely do one of two things: pull out your smartphone and activate some form of GPS app to receive route guidance / directions, or locate a public information board or street map and start searching for that reassuring arrow highlighting 'You are here!' In either example, once you've successfully pinpointed your location and begun following the correct guidance, there's always that sense of relief because you can relax for a moment, divert your focus away from panic and confusion, and place your trust in the fresh routes revealed to you.

Introducing the five essential components

While bearing this map analogy in mind, enough of the negatives: how about taking your focus off the narrow road of worry and frustration, instead elevating your view slightly to reveal the crossroads ahead that could alter your direction toward fresh insights and solutions?

You now hold a guidebook that can accompany this journey, but there remains one final question for you to consider: are you willing to make changes and leave the familiar behind?

If the answer is yes, take a moment to review these five essential **components** that are necessary for planning a successful travel excursion into the unknown and notice how they share a similarity with the preparations required for embarking on a successful journey of self-improvement:

Component One

Be clear on your objective in selecting a new map, such as identifying your preferred destination and fresh places to explore en route that may inspire or inform (you've already identified new directions are required to improve certain aspects of your work life and selected this guidebook as a means of mapping these out), so consider this one done!

Component Two

Set a series of **Route Guidances** or key stages that unfold progressively throughout your journey to help guide you forward (in this guidebook, these routes set out instructions, insights or information that build on each other, directing you safely to your destination: liberation). So by having acquired this book, this component is done too!

Component Three

Consider the **vectors** associated with the route you intend to follow. In map reading, the term 'vector' refers to a quality that has magnitude (size or extent) and direction, such as a course or compass bearing. In this guidebook, these vectors are a series of important growth mindsets, attitudes, thought directions or qualities of mind that, if considered carefully, will help improve the calibre or course of your thinking, which will enable you to get the best experience from your guidebook. These include taking care of yourself during your journey and remaining open and receptive to new learning or fresh perspectives designed to empower you. (We're going to be looking at this next, in Route Guidance One.)

Component Four

Select your companions to help invigorate your adventure. Who might be the ideal people to accompany you on your adventure who will enhance the experience and, inevitably, help embellish the narrative you share with your family and friends upon your return? In this guidebook, you'll be accompanied by fictional but highly likeable characters and a narrative designed to invigorate and augment your experience of travelling along the path toward liberation and greater fulfilment. (We'll be introduced to these in Route Guidances One and Two.)

Component Five

Review your itinerary and familiarise yourself with the outline or stages of your journey. In this guidebook, your journey toward greater fulfilment is split into four **excursions** (liberate, emotions, achieve and desires) to take you progressively through a series of ideas that will empower you, liberate you and also expand your awareness.

Now before we go any further, let's also take a moment to understand what else is needed to make fundamental changes in our jungle of work-life exploration.

Liberate your emotions

Never disregard the power of your emotions – they hold the key to unlocking your potential. Although you may be unaware of it, you exist in a responsive, vibrational universe in which your feelings or state has a direct effect on the circumstances or people you attract. In other words, change begins as an inside job, and we must start by adjusting our perspective or feelings about some of the circumstances in our work life that are simply too big to change. Trying to fix the outside world without first fixing yourself is a misguided assumption. Looking outwards for answers rather than within is the penultimate definition of short-sightedness. How do you feel about this idea?

What you resist, persists.

Carl Gustav Jung

At first, embracing this heightened level of responsibility for choosing the right moods and feelings, as a force in governing what turns up in the outside world, can feel somewhat at odds with how we were traditionally taught to regard the workings of the universe. We spend most of our childhood being constantly reminded by our parents and teachers about our fragility and subservient relationship with physical matter or circumstances. However, we can also recognise the impact or ripple effect we can have on those around us and, indeed, the wider world simply by pushing out specific emotional expectations or behaviours.

We can all recall those moments when we felt uplifted, connected or at ease. Subsequently, the day just seemed to flow more effortlessly – we inhabited a world in which we could put no foot wrong. Caught in this state, it often appears quite natural and obvious to us that things should work this way, but when the table is turned, it's not always as easy to assume such responsibility regarding the control we have over our thoughts. Here, we find ourselves at the opposite end of the spectrum, perhaps closed off, deflated, withdrawn and sluggish. Stuck in this emotional vibration, everything seems to feel at odds with us. We've all encountered moments when we're lost in thoughts of self-doubt or worry. Have you ever experienced that awkward moment during a team meeting or social engagement when you've mentally drifted away and someone has needed to pull your presence back into the room with *'Hello! Knock knock. Earth calling... Anyone in there? Are you still with us?'* This withdrawal into this inner box of negative emotions or self-condemnation is the misuse of an ultimate power that, if deployed correctly, holds the key to releasing your highest aspirations on the path toward liberation. You may be asking, 'What is this ultimate power?'

Dare to believe in the reality of your assumption and watch the world play its part relative to its fulfilment.

Neville Goddard

The first step in the art of living an enchanted life full of wonder, abundance and possibility begins by raising your level of awareness, understanding the power of imagination, granting yourself permission to dwell there positively and purposefully as often as possible, and finally, by tracing all your circumstances that ripple back from this creative first cause.

The importance of mindset

You may be familiar with the terms 'intellectual intelligence' (or 'intelligence quotient' [IQ]) or possibly 'emotional intelligence' (or 'emotional quotient' [EQ]), which are a set of key behavioural skills, knowledge and attributes that a person can develop to help them communicate, flourish and progress, thus confidently navigating the challenges of modern work life.

However, there's a new kid on the block that supersedes these intelligences and represents a set of highly favourable behavioural competencies that are advancing rapidly up the scale of critical employee skills most sought after by employers when searching out new employee talent: 'motivational intelligence' (or 'motivational quotient' [MQ]).

This refers to an individual's competency in exercising an open, proactive and highly adaptive mindset while navigating periods of immense change or upheaval. You'll find out more about this quotient and how to develop these skills and attributes fully later in your guidebook (in Route Guidances Eight and Sixteen).

Proceed to the highlighted route

As this guidebook was written with the intention of offering complete explications of the skills and perspectives required to navigate the challenges of work life successfully, it would be incomplete without exploring thoroughly the furthest summits of wisdom and insight.

Just like the image implies on the cover of this guidebook, this path of learning requires an elevated perspective; it's less conventional than what you're probably used to, but nonetheless, it's yours for the taking. The further you ascend this spiralling path of learning and the more you engage with the suggested exercises and tools within your guidebook, the closer you'll get to grasping the penultimate level of awareness, which is encapsulated by a term unique to this guidebook: 'meaning intelligence' (or 'meaning quotient' [MeQ]).

It's only through a complete and thorough exploration of this elevated behavioural aptitude that you can truly transform your personal feelings of demoralisation and uncertainty into heartfelt states of encouragement, fulfilment and peace of mind.

- It's this aptitude that millions were forced to consider while locked down and cut off from the normal distractions of day-to-day life during the 2020–2022 Covid-19 pandemic.

- It's this perspective and experience of life that continues to gain urgency among the minds of so many people who are navigating a world that's blinded by fear and uncertainty.

- It's this quality that supersedes all other intelligences, and once mastered, it releases capabilities beyond your wildest dreams.

- On imagining yourself lost in a dense jungle at night, it's this animate intelligence that acts like the fireflies' glow to continually illuminate your path of escape from despair and bewilderment.

To summarise

In this introduction, we've clearly defined the elements of dramatic change, uncertainty and discord being forced upon us in the outside world. All these challenging pressures and distractions can make it difficult for us to map out our life's purpose, maintain perspective, think clearly and positively adapt our behaviours accordingly to successfully navigate the jungle of work life.

We've raised the importance of growing more aware of how our habitual emotions, beliefs and self-concept can affect our ability to unlock our true potential and thus become more resilient or fulfilled. This shift is an inside job and has to begin by us taking greater responsibility for how we choose to think, raising our level of awareness and understanding the power of imagination.

To help liberate and empower us to operate more freely from the obstacles of the jungle of work life, we've examined what's meant by the terms 'growth mindset' and MeQ and we've mapped out five essential components, or fresh and insightful perspectives, that are necessary for planning a successful trip into the unknown.

Next, in Route Guidance One, you'll explore ten essential **attitudes** or qualities of mind, which you're encouraged to develop, that can greatly support your ability to get the best out of your guidebook and the adventurous journey that awaits you. You'll discover the vital part that narrative-based content has in providing you with even further subtle wisdom or truth as well as giving you delightful and entertaining fictional companions to accompany you on your quest. Finally, you'll be introduced to the four key excursions within your guidebook, which progressively build upon each other to help you arrive at your true north – your point of liberation!

Route Guidance One
Exploring the components of a successful excursion

*I can't understand why people are frightened of new ideas.
I'm frightened of old ones.*

John Cage

Having already completed Components One and Two – mapping out your objective (holistic solutions to help you navigate the jungle of work life) and getting your hands on a guidebook packed full of route guidances designed to help direct this journey – let's examine in greater detail the remaining three components as outlined in the introduction.

Component Three: The ten vectors to help you get the most out of this guidebook

A quick reminder of what's meant by 'vectors': they're a series of important growth mindsets, attitudes, thought directions or qualities of mind that, if considered carefully, will help improve the calibre or course of your thinking, enabling you to get the best experience from your guidebook.

Vector One: Take care of yourself at the core of your shell

We're living in unprecedented times in which a fundamental shift in human consciousness is taking place, which will impact how we'll work, relate to each other and survive. If there's one urgent lesson humanity has learnt recently, it's how we go about caring!

The years from 2020–2022 marked a transformation point. The Covid-19 pandemic crisis, and the record temperatures logged in Europe and western North America in the summer of 2023 woke millions up to the fragility of the earth and the responsibility we all have to care for it, as well as creating an opportunity to truly pause and reassess our role or purpose within our work life. There was very little that was 'normal' about our world pre-2020. The frantic manner in which we navigated work life on autopilot – taking so much for granted while ignoring the nurturing of our planet, and indeed ourselves – resulted in an environmental and societal ticking time bomb. The global Covid-19 crisis gave rise to workplace change faster than at any other time in history (that is, the great resignation, with employees rethinking their jobs and careers).

However, more and more people are waking up to embracing the idea that from crisis bursts forth the seed from which we'll evolve our behaviours and act with more humility. We're guests on Planet Earth, and as our focus gravitates toward greater responsibility and compassion, so too will the nature of work and how we coexist. In order to manifest a more compassionate and empathetic world, we first have to be able to embody these qualities within ourselves before we can see them in others. Right at the forefront of this spiral of change rests the necessity of caring about how we each think and apply our mind.

The word 'care' lies at the heart of this guidebook, and it's developed further in the following image.

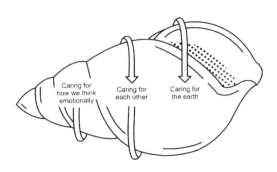

Have you ever peered into a conch shell? What did you see? There's a spiral radiating out from deep inside that grows in size the further it gets from the centre.

The three stages of care highlighted in the image are these:

1. Caring for our emotional stability, caring how we think emotionally, and promoting continual lifelong learning or higher-order thinking (a growth mindset, raising awareness, positive self-talk, vision, creativity, mindfulness, etc.)

2. Collective kindness: caring for each other, cooperation, inclusive culture and communities, and global awareness

3. Caring for the earth, the environment and nature

The latter point explains why the narrative sections of this guidebook are respectfully embedded in a natural ecosystem. More about this later (see Route Guidance Two).

Your personal growth has to begin at the core of your shell with a careful self-analysis of how you think emotionally and the assumptions you make about what and who you are. You can then become more conscious of the thought patterns that may spiral outward to influence your actions within the wider world.

Sticking with the image of the conch shell, we all know what it feels like when negative energy prevails. It draws our attention into a narrowing vortex of emotions that, ultimately, incapacitate us or limit our potential. Positive emotions, however, grow and spiral outward, stimulating greater well-being, productivity and self-respect. Grant yourself the space to foster some self-respect, because personal growth relies on this delicate and fragile foundation to blossom fully and grow. Much like the surface of this precious shell, self-respect can easily be crushed by relentless tides of self-doubt or ridicule from a harsh and sometimes unforgiving world.

If caring how we think serves as the starting point, then what exactly does this entail? The answer lies in these three steps:

1. Taking command of the thoughts and emotions you entertain. Manifesting fresh opportunities and improved fortune by embracing more-empowering thought processes relative to the situation you find yourself in.

2. Grasping the idea that the only way you can grow and resolve the negative situations in your life is by raising your level of awareness, even during challenging times. You must choose to move away from negativity and embrace a bigger focus on positivity.

3. Exploring the idea that you're an unlimited spiritual consciousness at the centre of a meaningful and connected universe in which every thought affects your outer world. This also includes growing more aware that you're connected to all of your fellow human beings. Finally, although you possess unlimited spiritual potential, you still need to take care of your physical health and well-being.

Vector Two: Take gentle steps through the jungle

One step at a time is good walking.
Chinese proverb

The study approach required to get the most from your guidebook relies less on haste or force, but more on exercising steady steps of open-mindedness and self-reflection.

Whatever you're doing and wherever you are right now – at work or home – you can begin preparing for this by remembering this two-step discipline.

Step One: Reframe, focus and pause. Step back a little before venturing forward. Listen and review, rather than reacting blindly. This seemingly simple act is one of the key behaviours that define critical thinking.

Step Two: Take a moment to consider whether you're applying the faculties of your mind (memory, intuition, reason, perception, will and imagination) in a manner that truly serves you. You'll discover more information on this topic later in your guidebook (see Route Guidance Thirteen).

There's no need for rash decisions; the answers you seek are contained within a gradual process of personal unfoldment. To add elastic energy to a rubber band, you first have to warm it up and stretch it out gently before you let it go – but not so far that it snaps! Your journey of learning how to think in such a way that you transform your mind is very much the same: small, incremental steps at a pace that suits you – one gentle stretch at a time! There's no need to take one huge aggressive leap.

Possible? Achievable? Yes!

Vector Three: Take caution looking backward while en route

The negative thoughts and circumstances that currently surround your life are merely reflections of the choices you've made in the past. You could look at these reflections as the 'old you'. Forging a more-empowering future relies on you entertaining the idea of developing a 'new you'.

Continually immersing yourself in disempowering thoughts from the past (note the use of the word 'yourself', which is separate from 'your thoughts') creates self-destructive habits. In this state, you're operating in negative overdrive, and your roadmap toward greater freedom is continually held hostage. It's really important to ask yourself right now if these thoughts are serving you. Do these thoughts bind you or liberate you? Do they actually solve anything?

In this moment, can you consider letting go of these old thought patterns and instead entertain fresh perspectives that could ignite a new beginning?

With all of this in mind, don't be too hard on yourself – you aren't alone. Retain some self-compassion, and it's worth remembering the following quote:

No real growth occurs without first experiencing some limitation at one's core.
Robert Kegan and Lisa Lahey (2016, p.92)

Vector Four: Remember small shifts in course = a new you

A dear friend and mentor of mine always says, 'Well done, you!' every time she congratulates someone for reaching a small milestone toward a goal. But at the core, this is what that statement means:

- You're always a success if you're willing to learn, remain flexible and open in your thinking, grow, and accept help.

- You're always a success if you embrace the challenges life delivers and do so in a calm, reflective and patient manner. It's really important that you rise above these challenges and learn.

- You're always a success if you truly value your unfoldment while staying the course, understanding Rome wasn't built in a day!

- Remember that it's often true that success arises from events that may have initially been regarded as unfavourable. Many give up just before the door to success is opened for them.

- Your story is unique and isn't about continually comparing yourself to the success of others.

- Finally, you're a success if you remain honest, truthful and authentic with the people in your life – becoming a reliable beacon of light for others to warm to.

Don't underestimate the power of making small changes in the way you think. Small shifts in perspective create new horizons, and new horizons transform your personal evolution.

Examine the following statement; it's related to finances, but the root of this statement can apply to any situation: *Even an increase of £100 in your monthly income creates a new version of you!*

The phrase 'a new version of you' explains the way in which you can willingly transform your self-concept at the drop of a hat, just by experiencing a small, favourable change in your outward circumstances (receiving a compliment, winning a prize, having an extra day off work, etc.). We can all relate to this temporary rush of excitement.

However, how much of a responsibility do you take for managing your lesser moods and feelings following a knee-jerk response to something the external world delivered to you that you deemed unfavourable at the time? In this example, it's less a case of willingly transforming your self-concept and more about forgetting your true power and handing over subserviently the control of your emotions to whatever negative events are taking place in the outside world. These automatic responses to life are a lot harder to control.

There is, however, another way to create a new you that doesn't simply rely on abiding by these automatic emotional responses delivered by the outside world. You do this by guarding your thoughts carefully, applying the power of imagination positively and focusing your mind constructively on your preferred reality; then you take the necessary actions required to move yourself closer to your ideal. Now you're creating your reality from the inside out! Only in this way can you truly create a new you, liberate your mind, and scale new and exciting heights of awareness.

Vector Five: Prepare to hike to new mountain heights to gain perspective in creating a new you

Do you think it's possible there are multiple versions of you, waiting to be discovered and celebrated, that exist untethered to the constraints you presently perceive are out there in the world? Can you imagine entertaining new empowering ideas and transforming these ideas into small behavioural tweaks over a period of time, which will ultimately create a fresh you and a new reality? Did you know you can mould a new brain and rewire a new identity or self-concept by learning and applying the process of neuroplasticity (more about that later in Route Guidance Thirteen)?

Do you think the overburdened you whom you drag to work every day is the same as the excited, lighthearted you who's packing clothes to go on holiday? In this sense, you become aware that your state is changeable and you have the power to adopt different versions of yourself. Could you evolve your thinking, imagine the extraordinary and believe this inner state can be reflected in your outer world? Can you consider what it might mean to you to reverse the statement 'My outside world governs how I feel' so it reads 'My feelings and assumptions ultimately govern what turns up in my outside world.'

Every state is already there as 'mere possibilities' as long as we think of them, but as overpoweringly real when we think from them.

Neville Goddard (2010, p.18)

This alternative mode of thinking isn't always easy to embody, as forces within you – such as self-doubt or low confidence – will attempt to keep you on safe and familiar ground. You'll find out later (in Route Guidance Four) why this conditioning isn't your fault and why the education system and script of life, to some degree, ill prepared you. This is why it's vital throughout your journey to consider every new thought perspective that serves to empower you to be a mini victory and one step further away from bondage.

When you question the old and replace it with the new, you're growing. You're now mirroring the behaviour of the brave and fearless, shifting from your comfort zone into the elevated realm of liberty and self-awareness!

Remember that it takes courage and responsibility to face the thoughts and behaviours you wish to improve.

Also, honest self-reflection and openness precede freedom and fulfilment.

Now consider this:

- Your birthright is to enjoy harmony in life
- Your birthright is to grow and flourish
- Your birthright is liberty
- Your birthright is to love your work
- Your birthright is to stand tall, be confident and be authentic
- Your birthright is to discover who or what you *really* are

Vector Six: Be careful how you frame your current work situation

I overheard someone once say that work was just something you did to pay the bills. It was something to endure before real life began when you did nice things with your family at home at the weekend or on holiday.

Really? Perish the thought!

Work, or what you spend your days doing, should be a privilege! It should enrich and satisfy you. Let's be honest, you spend most of your time there!

Let's now clarify exactly what the term 'your work' means within the context of *this* guidebook, bearing in mind that so much of 'life' is often carried over into work.

Your work

Put simply, the term 'your work' encompasses the environments you frequent and the activities you complete that define your typical day. Alternatively, you could consider the images that come to mind if you were asked to summarise 'a day in the life of [insert your name]'. These work activities, which fulfil a specific responsibility and/or provide an income, could include the following:

- Studying in the work/home office space
- Crafting or designing in the workshop
- Caring for another
- Looking after children
- Working outdoors
- Working from home
- Forging ahead with entrepreneurial activities
- Studying/education
- Transporting goods or providing a service
- Teaching, coaching or instructing
- Managing a team, project or environment
- Serving in hospitality
- Participating in a group project
- .... (fill in your activity)

Many people define themselves by the roles, tasks or jobs they carry out – which are separate and somehow incompatible with their authentic self.

For many, work can also represent a rather stressful or intimidating environment that's far removed from the ideal circumstances they secretly desire. In this sense, work represents an inconvenience that's obscuring the roadmap toward fuller meaning or fulfilment.

This limiting form of self-prophecy can seem undeniable and fixed, as if the power to lift us to greater heights resides somewhere 'out there' and is held captive by circumstances beyond our control. Although rare, the jungle out there can throw us the occasional curveball of good fortune (that big break to allow you to escape the mundane), but the truth of the matter is that the transformative power so many desire is readily accessible and resides a lot closer to home – deep within *you*! However, there are two critical considerations you'll have to contemplate before you can free this force and initiate the change you so deeply desire:

1. Honour your time in the jungle of work life. It's important to acknowledge that you only ever consciously exist in the present moment – the eternal now. It's from this perspective that fresh seeds must be sown from which a new narrative concerning the future fortunes of your life can emerge. Centre your attention and gratitude on honouring the precious time playing out immediately in front of you – it's the only experience of time you'll ever have!

When we fail to remain present, we lose the ability to focus our talents, receive inspiration, allow our best self to surface, direct our learning and appreciate the process of unfoldment.

2. Honour your place in the jungle of work life. Whatever your current situation, like an actor on a stage flanked by scenery and props, you have to deliver your first line of adventure relative and attentive to where you are – the current backdrop of your life. Never underestimate the assumptions you make concerning the current circumstances and people in your life. Are the people and events around you there to be ridiculed, avoided or feared? Or could they represent opportunities for growth, humility or deeper connection? These assumptions have a huge bearing on the theme and direction you're subconsciously weaving into the adventure script of your future self. Making peace with circumstances isn't simply about giving up intention or desire. It doesn't involve huge self-sacrifice or personal upheaval. Instead, as with any peacemaking process, it involves gradual bridge-building from old to new foundations.

Consider the activities you execute daily and then define which ones are *enablers* and which activities constitute *goals*. What you want isn't simply money – money is an enabler not a goal. The real question is what sort of life do you want to create for yourself and others? If you don't have the answer to this question, then start with what you don't want – the rest is simply a process of elimination.

Can you entertain the idea that your work could also incorporate what you feel most passionate about? You don't need to quit your job immediately to experience the new you. First, start where you are right now, honour what you already have around you, and then take a leap later, if necessary.

However, all that being said, the mastery of life isn't simply a case of honouring the present moment or remaining attentive to where you are – emotions matter too. It's extremely difficult not to get wrapped up in the drama of life or swamped in our own self-importance. However, it's this impetus – how you think and feel moment to moment – that's vitally important in determining the ease with which you'll travel this new path of self-discovery.

Unlike the machines or technology that inhabit our work spaces, we still turn up to work as emotional human *beings* carrying all our worries, fears, hopes and dreams around with us. If our transformation relies on modifying our emotions, we can evolve wherever we are. We always have the choice to share our warmth, talents or abilities with the people in our immediate environment, and unless you can do this, you'll never be prepared to share what you have with the wider world! Remember to honour the present moment because it's only from here that a new thought or condition can manifest.

The old world view assumes employees must somehow leave who they truly are at home before stepping into the world of work. We'll explore what this means later (see Route Guidance Sixteen) and how some leading organisations are challenging this paradigm.

True story

Ella worked as a front-of-house assistant at a restaurant. She was much loved by all the customers as she carried out her role with a cheerful optimism and an upbeat attitude. Her beaming smile, authenticity and warmth brought a reciprocal smile to whoever had the good fortune of sharing her company. Despite earning only a modest wage, Ella was reliable, honest, trustworthy and accommodating. Her presence radiated such a glow that it wasn't unheard of for new customers to approach her with their requests, assuming she was the manager. Ella's consistent approach (although never manipulative or assuming) to making her customers feel at home paid off eventually. She found herself being headhunted by other local employers within the catering and hospitality industry, and she was even offered a pay increase if she stepped up to a managerial role within her current workplace. Ella's energy and attitude made her simply irreplaceable, but more importantly, highly likely to succeed in whatever she set her mind to in the future, because she appreciated that every day was an opportunity to shine even brighter.

Now go back and consider which of the points made earlier within Vector Six Ella applied as she went about her daily activities.

Vector Seven: Increasing your self-awareness creates ripples through the jungle

It takes very little effort to cast a pebble into a body of water and generate a ripple that grows continually and expands outwards, eventually impacting the sides of the bank or shoreline.

In a similar way, one of life's biggest joys lies in our ability to share the very best we have with the people or things closest to us, creating a positive impact that subsequently expands and ripples outward into the wider world. Behaving in such a natural and symbiotic manner and resisting the urge to force ourselves on the world allows more ease, harmony and serendipity to show up in life.

Curiosity and speculation are very often the states that kick-start the quest toward a higher degree of freedom and empowerment. You must begin by asking questions. For every question you ripple out into the universe, there must be a corresponding answer (by law), but you have to be prepared to remain patient and listen! On the other hand, life isn't linear but is full of limitless possibilities. Your truth and direction isn't always about 'this or that', but it's an appreciation that solutions are organised more along the lines of 'this and this and this and this...' In other words, allow the universe to reveal plentiful options for what works, as opposed to how you think solutions should arrive. To put it another way: get out of your own way and stop trying to force or control everything in your life!

Whatever your circumstances are right now, this is your opportunity for a fresh start; it's your point of impact on dipping into an ocean of possibilities through the power of intention. You don't need to go anywhere, force an issue or create a huge noise in the outside world, because everything begins and ends within the silent realm of the imagination!

Subsequently, the only requirement demanded of you is to become more aware of your beingness, and this is made up of all your beliefs, behaviours, thoughts, feelings and actions. Keep your willpower close to home in the pursuit of wisdom, and keep your affairs sincere and noble.

Wisdom is the principle thing; therefore get wisdom: and with all thy getting get understanding.
Proverbs 4:7 (King James Version)

Vector Eight: Consider the colours you share in the jungle of work life

Picture a peacock boldly displaying its colourful plumage for all to see; what colours do *you* reveal in your work? Are you behaving congruently around other people? 'Congruence' describes an authentic state in which you behave in a way that's aligned with your true values, beliefs and purpose.

Transformation begins with awareness, and you must begin by performing an honest self-review of your thought habits that run throughout your day and noticing which category – constructive or destructive – each one falls into. The next step is to open up, examine fresh perspectives and replace any negative habits with new empowering ones. Finally, you inject this new awareness into everything you do – including your work and the people you spend time with! If executed correctly, you'll soon notice certain events, coincidences, new acquaintances or opportunities gradually entering your life in a spirit of harmony and flow.

Despite how uncomfortable it may prove to be, honesty is critical during any path of self-development.

In order to explore the issue of congruent behaviour, we have to start by asking ourselves searching questions such as these:

- » *Am I sharing or protecting myself from the world?*
- » *Do I rehearse how I'll behave and act around others to build relationships, harmony and authenticity?*

» *Depending on the situation, do I hide nervously behind a mask or share my character and talents wholeheartedly?*

» *Am I self-accepting, fulfilled and willing to persevere?*

» *Do I undertake honest self-review and check my motives are aligned with my purpose or beliefs?*

» *Have I paused recently and examined my conduct or integrity?*

» *What limits do I impose on myself? And do I draw any connections between this attitude and my interplay with the outside world?*

Vector Nine: Step boldly through the jungle but remain aware of the predators closer to home

Empowering information can be temporarily uplifting, but unless these ideas are fully internalised and translated into tangible actions, little can change. Realising we should change and actually transforming this into tangible action are two entirely different things.

Unfortunately, we're all occasionally susceptible to falling victim to a multitude of habits that can hold us back from change and keep us firmly seated in the familiar or known circumstances. *This fear that inhibits and controls is called a 'paradigm', and it resides within you* (don't worry about that just yet – more on that later in Route Guidance Five). It will try to convince you that you're wasting your time. It will urge you not to unsettle the status quo, step outside of your comfort zone or try something new.

Human behaviour is driven by habit, and breaking free of habits is hard. More often than not, we all tend to do what we did last time and leave it at that! We feel safe in familiar worlds or following the herd when everyone is doing what we're doing.

In reality, we can only experience true change and growth when we embrace the unknown, but it's one of the hardest things to initiate.

With expansion comes risk. Some days flow better than others. Situations can arise that throw you off track. Don't beat yourself up if one day feels harder than another – that's life. The key to your journey of growth is to maintain a consistent, positive vibration over a period of time, rather than getting stuck in emotional peaks and troughs.

Think of life as a roller-coaster ride. Sometimes, you can feel like you're zooming ahead with your goals, but at other times, you find everything an uphill struggle. The main thing is that you remain secure in your vision and stay strapped in your seat. Enjoy the ride and keep going – it's a process! Aspiring to achieve specific goals or ambitions is all well and good, but remember that many lose their focus on the process of becoming. There should be as much, if not more, joy experienced through working on each small, manageable, incremental step than in the final promise of the big win at the end of the journey. The big win is always fleeting and soon replaced by new desires or goals. Furthermore, our sense of meaning is very often revealed steadily; it's woven into the fabric of our journey of unfoldment. An all-or-nothing attitude focused merely on the allure of some distant big win is neither healthy nor meaningful, and it's the main reason so many give up on their dreams. When you discover meaning in your journey, you're far more likely to retain your enthusiasm and stay the course.

Vector Ten: Choose wisely whom or what you listen to while en route

There are some people who live in a dream world, and there are some who face reality; and then there are those who turn one into the other.

Desiderius Erasmus / Erasmus of Rotterdam

Very few people truly study and internalise the sorts of subjects revealed in this guidebook. It stands to reason, then, that you're probably going to face a few rapids along your journey. As you study further, you may feel at odds with what's mainstream. You may attract a little intrigue or even ridicule from your friends and family ('What are you doing that for?'), and this can feel very unsettling. What actually matters is that you hold your course, so it's worth repeating the point: wherever you are and whatever you're doing, you're either stretching out into fields of growth or stuck playing it safe within familiar and well-rehearsed routines.

We often adhere to certain societal assumptions: 'There's a limit to what we can achieve' or 'Life's a bitch and then you die'. These limiting, status quo views can suffocate our ability to try new things and stretch our full potential. It makes sense, then, to choose wisely whom you discuss your goals with. Avoid wasting time seeking approval from the grumpy next-door neighbour, as they're more than likely to pull you back to the 'known' and reinforce the idea you don't have what it takes.

When confronted with a negative or disempowering conversation, listen to your intuition (that is, your inner voice of wisdom or caution) and ask yourself, *Is that person really happy? Do they exhibit a zest for life? And is this advice leading me to where I want to go?* Remember that it's only the people who have neglected their natural connection to abundance and personal fulfilment who will advise you to stop reaching higher. These people have shortage, blame or fault-finding consciousness, and it's highly toxic. Have you ever shared your heartfelt hopes and dreams with someone, hoping for support and camaraderie, only to receive that classic sceptical reply: 'There's a limit to what's possible... That's just how it is, and anyway, who the hell do you think you are?'

The next time you encounter this statement, remember the following: even the tiny blades of grass continue stretching upward in winter toward the light, despite being blanketed in relentless waves of frozen hail and snow. It's the way of the universe for you too to stretch, forge courage, challenge assumptions and originate ideas that, up until now, were deemed impossible. If you're offered an opinion or advice that feels heavy or manipulative, then it's probably not going to serve you. Remember that weeds grow low down and in poor soil that's rarely tended! Attend to your own affairs, lighten your load and elevate your consciousness toward abundance. Abundance is your birthright! Focus instead on planning more time with those who encourage or inspire this quality.

Amalgamating all ten vectors

All ten vectors are aimed at helping you prepare a new set of attitudes or mindsets that will support your ability to remain receptive to new information as you progress through this guidebook. When we amalgamate them, we explicate a secret formula:

Liberate your perception of self and unlock the control of your emotions, and then you'll achieve your desires.

You'll discover exactly what this means as you progress through this guidebook.

Let's now examine the fourth and fifth components necessary for planning a successful excursion: selecting the right companions to accompany you on your journey and reviewing your itinerary.

Component Four: Select your companions to share in the narrative

To sit alone in the lamplight with a book spread out before you, and hold intimate converse with men of unseen generations – such is a pleasure beyond compare.

Kenko Yoshida

Can you recall your favourite childhood fables or fairy tales? Rekindling the sense of mystery and enchantment portrayed through such stories is a fantastic way to stimulate your own creativity and imagination. When you take that journey into the world of fantasy, you grant yourself permission to break free from the stresses and strains of everyday life and revert to a childlike state in which you become more amenable to comprehending some of life's subtle wisdoms or timeless truths.

Truth and wisdom skilfully woven within the fabric of a story can have a greater long-term impact upon the quality of the reader's learning than merely relying on a simple presentation of facts and figures alone.

People think that stories are shaped by people.
In fact, it's the other way around.
Terry Pratchett (1992, p.8)

In Route Guidance Two, you'll be introduced to Dael (pronounced like the male name Dale and from the ancient interpretation meaning 'valley' and the letters 'lead' reversed), a troubled lizard who struggles to find fulfilment within the jungle of work life. Luckily, one day, he bumps into Lead (pronounced as in the beginning of the word 'leader', from which it's derived), a thriving female chameleon who takes Dael under her wing and mentors him while sharing wonderful secrets and insights to life. Lead's behaviour epitomises a broader awareness concerning care and empathy toward people and the wider world, as highlighted earlier with the image of the conch shell. Her zest and curiosity for inspiring and imparting knowledge concerning the skills and approaches required for achieving fulfilment in life stems from working for a value-based-learning organisation.

LEAD   DAEL

You'll notice that the further you delve into this guidebook, the more the non-fiction format slowly gives way to an ever-increasingly narrative-based style of writing. This isn't accidental, as you'll be encouraged to unearth ever-increasing meaning and significance in your life, which will subsequently reveal more of the hero's journey embedded within your own life adventure!

Alternatively, Dael's adventure story may encourage you to identify and appreciate certain forgotten strengths within you that were forged as you navigated your way through a past challenge or crisis. Although difficult to manage at that time, these events ultimately led you to a point of personal clarity or transformation. In this sense, life may indeed make more sense looking backward than forward (see if you can spot a similar pattern encrypted within the spellings of the names of each animal character encountered in Dael's story.)

Component Five: Review your itinerary

There are four excursions to this guidebook:

Excursion One: Liberate

- You'll examine the shortcomings of an outdated education system and the impact this can have on your way of thinking later in life. You'll uncover the vital decision you must make to allow your personalised curriculum to take effect. The advantages of lifelong learning and techniques you can adopt to make study easier will be revealed.

- You'll learn to identify and build techniques to overcome distractive and disempowering thoughts – such as fear, self-doubt, low self-esteem and poor confidence – which inhibit constructive thinking.

- The characteristics of resilience will be explored, as well as the skills of concentration, decision-making and focus.

- You'll discover empowering information and specific tools to help you act with more confidence when faced with a setback or challenge, enabling you to press on with your goals.

- The current trends and challenges concerning the development and well-being of people within work will be explored.

- You'll uncover how an understanding of the lifestyle and activities of our ancient ancestors as they worked and survived in the natural world can help explain why millions of people feel discord or struggle in trying to get ahead within today's modern world of work.

- You'll explore some highly innovative worry or stress-management exercises that you can apply at any time of day to help you develop greater balance and peace of mind.

- You'll gain clarity concerning exactly what constitutes the key characteristics of well-being and vitality, and you'll acquire access to practical ideas to help you maintain a more holistic and incremental approach to improving your health and fitness levels.

- You'll examine the topic of 'authenticity at work' and why so many feel they need to hide this quality within the workplace.

- You'll uncover thirteen critical competencies that can help you flourish within the world of work (character, empathy, emotional intelligence [or emotional quotient (EQ)], motivational intelligence [or motivational quotient (MQ)], humility, mindfulness, resilience, authenticity, twenty-first-century work skills, diversity awareness, inclusion awareness, effective leadership and entrepreneurism) and learn how to develop and apply them to your advantage.

- You'll learn how to gain more confidence and resilience by studying and forging seven fearless mindsets.

- Finally, you'll become more aware of the unique unlimited power within you, the natural abundance in your life and the importance of simply being yourself.

Excursion Two: Emotions

There can be no transforming of darkness into light and of apathy into movement without emotion.
Carl Gustav Jung

This section begins with an examination of the emotional thought processes that hold many people back from achieving their full potential. There's only one avenue through which to understand and modify our emotions: the art of self-awareness. This is why this guidebook is grounded in education, a word derived from the Latin *educere*, meaning 'to develop or draw out from within'.

This section examines the fact that, whatever your current situation, you can't instantly change your physical circumstances, but you do possess the power to change how you emotionally think and feel about them, which allows you to recalibrate the world you perceive.

- You'll examine the habitual manner in which so many search and fail to discover true happiness and fulfilment, not realising that what they seek actually resides a lot closer to home.

- You'll examine the importance of growing more aware of your sense of 'I-ness', or your emotional state, when making judgements or assumptions about your outside world.

- You'll learn how the manner in which you observe the outside world has a direct effect on many of the circumstances that are reflected at you.

- You'll learn what's meant by 'being lost in an emotional state' and the 'thought–feeling emotional feedback loop'.

- You'll learn how to release yourself from being suffocated by ongoing negative emotions through applying the 'flip it', 'step on it' and 'lead emotion' techniques.

- You'll learn about 'emotional leverage': your ability to monitor, select and raise your emotional state toward more-empowering emotions that can help improve your day.

Excursion Three: Achieve

In this section, you'll examine many of the psychological and behavioural aspects of your personality that can be transformed to help move you closer to your goals or objectives.

This primarily involves the following:

- You'll come to understand the role of your conscious and subconscious mind in relation to influencing your behaviour and the results in your life.

- You'll examine the idea of neuroplasticity.

- You'll come to understand the hold paradigms have over many of our decisions or actions.

- You'll learn how to apply the art of creating empowering affirmations, vision boards, kinaesthetic techniques and reverse psychology to help improve the results in your work life.

- You'll explore radically new ideas and perspectives on the notion of time and space, with the intention of revealing new ways of allowing your dreams or goals to manifest in your outer world.

- You'll learn to fully appreciate and work within the beauty of the present moment, to help unleash a more grounded or spiritual approach toward problem-solving or for use while searching for deeper insight or inspiration.

- You'll learn how to reconnect with the greater force and wisdom within you, which – once acknowledged and revered – can completely change your perception of the outside world, as well as your results.

- You'll explore the idea of the universal subconscious mind and the connection this has with your individualised mind in relation to achieving results in your life.

- You'll learn how to achieve more freedom and fulfilment in life by specialising in the art of purposeful manifestation by obtaining a thorough and complete understanding of the process of primary causation.

- You'll liberate your self-belief and ability to achieve your dreams and goals by examining the law of vibration, the power of imagination and the notion that creation is already finished from a quantum perspective.

- You'll learn how to assert your true state of being and the power of affirming 'I am' as a means of gaining greater clarity regarding the purpose of your life and your position along the path of enlightenment.

Excursions One, Two and Three then unlock...

Excursion Four: Desires

Without giving too much away and spoiling your adventure of navigating your way through your guidebook, the final section, entitled 'Desires', pulls together all the learning from the previous sections. You'll be dropped into a value-based-learning organisation in which you'll uncover the holistic mindsets and approaches that wonderful leaders deploy in developing thriving and fulfilling work environments for people to work in.

You'll uncover what the best leaders do to inspire confidence, trust and loyalty among their employees. You'll also uncover how they do the following:

- innovate or approach problems;
- discover their purpose and create a legacy;
- remain self-motivated and confident;
- maintain a growth mindset to help reach their full potential;
- engage others and open doors of opportunity for them;
- actively develop others and help them feel psychologically safe;
- remain adaptable and navigate uncertainty;
- develop their confidence and resilience;
- exemplify humility and empathy;
- develop team coherence by communicating effectively; and
- approach the development of diversity and inclusion awareness within the workplace.

The ideas in this section may encourage you to consider how you might become a leadership ambassador, sharing the skills outlined in the previous lists, and demonstrating integrity and wisdom in guiding others through change.

Choose your intention

Finally, before we embark, let's summarise this section with a wonderful quote. It's probably from a deeper perspective than you're normally used to, but it's guaranteed to stretch the imagination. There is, however, a reason it appears so early in this guidebook – it will either confuse you or inspire you! Either way, this is good, as both states will induce curiosity. Shortly, you'll discover this is where it all started for Dael, when he met Lead for the first time. He asked questions, engaged in excellent meaningful conversations, but most importantly, exercised fresh thinking.

Everything you could ever ask for, you could ever have now, or ever ask for in the future, you already have right now. You already have all of it; you are simply not experiencing it. Because everything that has ever happened is happening now, and ever will happen is happening right now. And so, it is for you merely to reach into the sea of infinite possibilities and call forth the reality you choose now to experience.

Neale Donald Walsch (Martina Désirée, 2008)

Route Guidance Two
Dael's world

*Do not go where the path may lead.
Go instead where there is no path and leave a trail!*

Ralph Waldo Emerson

Your jungle companions

Once upon a time there lived a neotropical ground lizard called Dael. Every morning, come rain or shine, Dael walked his familiar jungle pathway to work. During his journey, he'd repeat the same gloomy thoughts:

Is this it? Where did I go wrong? Why does nobody care about my ideas and dreams? I just wish I had more self-worth and could kick-start a new way of viewing life. I wish I felt more empowered and confident. What must it feel like to receive recognition, feel less detached and strive to be better? I just wish I could escape or find someone who could show me a new way.

His little heart sank with dissatisfaction, and a sense of hopelessness engulfed him. He had forgotten what it felt like to be passionate, energised or driven. He found the activities he endured at work and the lizards who worked alongside him draining and uninspiring. His leaders never showed any interest in his well-being or asked how he was doing. Dael spent most of his energy and time at work hiding or playing it safe.

Dael did have one escape, though: a fascination with botany and the healing characteristics of tropical plants. In the jungle, there was a wealth of exotic foliage, but few realised the health benefits these plants could bring. If he'd worked harder at school or maybe chosen different career pathways, he might be doing more of what he loved, but now it just felt too late. There was never time to develop this passion, and it was pointless mentioning it at work as nobody really cared. If no one showed any interest, why bother? Instead, Dael just dreamt of what it might be like to share this passion with the world one day.

When the working day was over, he avoided questioning his life any longer and chose instead to relax by the pond, catching fireflies. Eventually, this numbing activity would cause him to fall asleep (as well as rewarding him with sore lips and indigestion), which was a respite before the whole familiar routine would be repeated the next day.

A year previously, he had become so disillusioned and stressed that his tail had fallen off! Most lizards possess the ability to detach their tails voluntarily, at weak points called 'fracture planes', when cornered by a predator. A lizard tail will continue to wriggle for minutes after detachment and serve to distract a predator long enough to allow a hasty escape. A new tail can take many months to grow back, but being formed from cartilage rather than bone, it's never as resilient as the old tail. A lizard only has a limited number of opportunities to replace its tail, and the loss is so public and humiliating. Dael had reached the lowest emotional point in his life, but it was the implication this had on his very survival that worried him most. When neotropical ground lizards reach an emotional low, their skin loses its camouflaging abilities, making them highly vulnerable to attacks from jungle beasts. Dael was exhausted by constantly keeping watch for the most dangerous creatures of all: the feathered birds of prey. What was this poor reptile to do? Would there ever be a happy conclusion to his story? Would there ever be an end to the pain?

Despite everything that Dael had gone through, nothing could have prepared him for what happened in the spring of that year. A huge tropical storm ravaged the jungle for weeks on end, and all the jungle animals took refuge in their homes. Simple acts, such as meeting friends and family outdoors, were far too dangerous, and the only way to remain safe was to lock down and stay indoors. While some of the jungle animals tried to do their best, continuing their affairs by communicating via the jungle web, some simply chose to escape and return to hibernation.

The storm was devastating, but even after it had eased, it led subsequently to years of intolerable hardship for the inhabitants of the jungle, who had to endure financial and well-being deprivation. No one knew if jungle life would ever return to normal.

Meanwhile, Dael's path to work, which was normally flanked by huge palms protecting him from the prying eyes of flying beasts, was damaged and dangerously exposed. To remain safe, he selected an elevated, narrow track that ran up a hill and skirted high above the exposed treeline. This new route became increasingly comforting for Dael as it provided him with time alone to view his journey to work from a fresh perspective where nobody could bother him.

One morning, as Dael climbed the new path to work, a chameleon (which was quite rare in those parts) came suddenly bounding past, displaying a variety of vibrant colours. To Dael's surprise, the chameleon stopped and smiled.

Chameleons are generally regarded by the lizard community as quite mysterious creatures. Luckily, Dael had been taught by his uncle not to fear them, as chameleons also possess several favourable traits:

- Contrary to popular lizard belief, a chameleon's outside environment has little influence over their choice of skin colour. The colours they choose aren't intended as camouflage. They change colour depending on their chosen emotion, and they're not ashamed to share it. They move through the jungle, anticipating *their day and openly displaying the colours they wish others to benefit from. They understand that, by choosing new emotions, they can attract what they want, including a mate. If a chameleon is ever pale, it's a sure sign it's unwell.*

- *The word 'chameleon' comes from the Latin phrase meaning 'lion of the ground' as the head crest of a chameleon somewhat resembles a lion's mane. Just like a lion, these little creatures certainly don't lack resilience and courage. They move through life with focus and stay calm under pressure.*

- *Chameleons can communicate with each other using vibrations that travel through solid objects, such as tree branches. They understand the power vibration has in attracting an equivalent energy in the outside world.*

- *Chameleons are highly focused, but they never take themselves too seriously. Being able to orientate their eyes independently through 360 degrees, they know how to add a little fun and perspective into their day. By adopting this technique, they exemplify resilience, carefully directing the lens through which they view the world or their circumstances.*

- *They have a quantum perspective of the world that comes from viewing distant objects then magnifying the image inside their brain. This makes them great visionaries.*

- *They never stop growing throughout life: chameleons are lifelong learners!*

Normally, Dael would hide his face and ignore anyone who had the audacity to travel to work in the morning with such vigour, but for some reason, he chose to acknowledge the chameleon's friendly glance. What followed was unprecedented: Dael found himself standing in the middle of the jungle holding a conversation with a complete stranger. Chameleons are somewhat complex conversationalists; however, the interaction between the two lizards marked a moment that changed Dael's life forever!

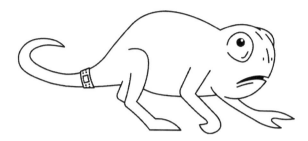

The chameleon uncurled her tail and introduced herself as 'Lead'. Immediately, Dael found himself completely engrossed with Lead's energy, warmth and lively conversation. He was unsure exactly where Lead had come from and whom she worked for, but it was clear that, wherever that was, something special was going on.

Dael was captivated by Lead's energy and enthusiasm. She shared personal stories of struggle in which she explained how she discovered the secret of fulfilment. Lead went on to describe her journey to work and how it provided her with the perfect opportunity to take stock and plan or review the day. She exuded a deep gratitude for the people in her life, the learning and the unfoldment. Lead explained how she was fascinated by lifelong learning and the meaningful coincidences that popped up from time to time. For Lead, life was a thrill!

Throughout the conversation, Dael noticed how Lead's eyes twinkled with charm and warmth. There was conviction and authenticity in the way she spoke.

Lead went on to explain that eye contact was a fantastic happiness transmitter that developed 'mirror neurons' inside a lizard's brain, leading to increased releases of serotonin (a natural chemical release inside the brain that helps send messages between nerve cells and that affects mood). There was no escape from Lead's engaging energy: it was infectious and it brought immense relief to Dael's current predicament.

At one point, both lizards rested on a rock as Lead looked deep into Dael's eyes as if she could mysteriously read how he was feeling. She uncurled her tail again and, using the tip of it, etched the following words into the sandy jungle floor:

Our world is complex, but we possess a power far greater!

What followed was a conversation so enthralling that Dael felt compelled to listen for even longer. Lead went into much detail about the change required within the leadership of people at work. She explained how important meaning, purpose, trust, honesty, teamwork and belonging are in cultivating a healthy and thriving work environment. All of these fascinating facts, however, were somewhat superseded by the information she began to share concerning the potential power locked up in every creature, which could create startling results in the dreams and goals of every living creature in the jungle.

The conversation was so enthralling that Dael lost track of time and, consequently, had to apologise for bringing the meeting to a close or he'd be late for work.

They agreed to meet again at the same spot the next morning before work.

As the two lizards said their goodbyes and went their separate ways, Dael thought how best to record future conversations.

Of course, *thought Dael,* a diary. What better way to mark each meeting?

That day was a special day: someone had stopped and explained to Dael why modern jungle life was so hard, but also that all was not lost. Now he'd found a truly authentic lizard to trust and learn from, maybe there were solutions toward gaining greater freedom and hope!

For the first time in Dael's life, he felt a real connection with a new acquaintance and a subtle shift in his personal awareness. Dael had sometimes heard the phrase 'meaningful one-to-one conversation', but he'd never really understood what it meant. Now everything had become clearer; a unique friendship had been forged that was less about what the two lizards had in common and more about what could be shared.

As Dael went about his day, he wondered if Lead would keep her promise and meet him the next morning. If only Lead had been around earlier in Dael's life, maybe things would have been a bit different. It was as if he'd got everything the wrong way round in his life, but this could now be the opportunity to change direction and turn things around. He thought back to his school days and the missed opportunities so as to find the answers that really mattered most: how to get on and find fulfilment early in life. He felt let down; education had ill-prepared him for adult life.

As for his experience at work, everything centred on simply clock-watching, keeping out of trouble, enduring micromanaged directives and stressing over job security, all while never trusting his leaders.

Route Guidance Three
DAEL VS LEAD

Liberate | Emotions | Achieve | Desires

*To deny the connection between feelings and performance
is a finite-minded way of looking at leadership.*

Simon Sinek (2018, p.108)

In this section of your guidebook, we're going to examine how highly effective teachers and leaders communicate successfully and inspire others with confidence and loyalty, so they bring out the very best in the people they lead and serve.

But first, let's contrast two very different management approaches or processes of thinking (summarised with the acronyms DAEL and LEAD) that a leader can deploy to achieve this aim.

There's good reason why we're spending this time examining the DAEL and LEAD acronyms, as it will help you appreciate and prepare for the style of teaching, approaches, tools and activities that appear throughout your guidebook.

DAEL

Desire | Achieve | Emotions | Liberate

A lead in the wrong direction

In an ideal world, the educational or work environment should provide the perfect opportunity for the people who reside there to foster greater confidence, meaning, opportunity, self-worth and fulfilment. Unfortunately, a dominating paradigm can exist within an institution's leadership approach that can actually negatively impact the confidence, security and autonomy of the people who work there. We're going to refer to this poor style of leadership using the acronym DAEL (desire, achieve, emotions, liberate).

The DAEL acronym can also be used to summarise a set of shared thought processes or feelings expressed by individuals working within an organisation toward the people or processes that are supposed to manage, direct and serve their best interests.

As you review this section, consider how this model of leadership may surface within your current work environment. If your current work activity sits outside of these scenarios, then imagine yourself enrolling on a new mentorship or coaching programme that requires your engagement with unfamiliar or challenging learning content, and ask yourself which of these leadership approaches intuitively feels the most supportive for you as a new student. Alternatively, as you review each model, you could think back to your past experience in education or possibly consider the negative experiences your colleagues may express concerning the quality of communication or management approaches inherent in their work environment.

A poor model of leadership

Referring to the elements of the DAEL acronym (desire, achieve, emotions, liberate), a traditional employer's, leader's or teacher's perspective or attitude toward their students, apprentices or employees could look something like this:

D – Desire

*I wish my cohort arrived at work with more **desire** or drive. This would mean I'd get more from them so I could meet my targets quicker. They should understand they're here to work, and I don't owe them any favours – period! I've earnt my position, and I'm not here to look out for anyone. Meeting my objectives has to be my main concern, despite the* *fallout it might create among the people I lead. I'll keep my distance and micromanage, monitor and implement performance-related spot checks, exams or ongoing assessments to help remind them who's boss and keep them driven and in check.*

A – Achieve

*Then they'd **achieve** more by knuckling down and meeting my objectives or the demands of the organisation as a whole.*

E – Emotions

*This stability would force them to even out their **emotions** and get on with what they're supposed to be doing, and I'd have to do far less to sort out their problems and be able to get on with what I have to do.*

L – Liberate

*They'd then be far more likely to **liberate** themselves by standing on their own two feet, and they'd refrain from exercising a deflated and apathetic perspective of life. They could then replace this feeling with finding deeper satisfaction in work and behaving appropriately by displaying greater loyalty and respect toward my objectives.*

An employee's or student's perspective

Again referring to the DAEL acronym, a student's, apprentice's or employee's perspective toward their work or education culture or environment might look something like this:

D – Desire

*I wish I had far more **desire** and drive at work.*

A – Achieve

*If I could fix this problem, then I'd **achieve** more, my attitude would improve, and I'd feel more resilient and fulfilled.*

E – Emotions

*This would lead to a growth in my **emotional** resilience and capacity to cope with the daily challenges thrown at me.*

L – Liberate

*Finally, if I were somehow able to find a way to sequence and internalise all these mindset skills, I could unlock my journey of personal growth and then **liberate** and improve my self-concept, allowing me to find greater satisfaction in my work and my relationship with my organisation.*

Why DAEL doesn't work

The DAEL approach toward leadership and the everyday management of human resources inhibits the genuine, sustainable and holistic development of people. It negatively impacts opportunities for innovation, creativity and agility within organisations. It stifles employee relationships, communication, trust, compassion, retention and loyalty. Ultimately, it prevents the development of the whole person: the foundations from which authenticity, self-responsibility and confidence can grow.

If the only experience people have of work is simply clock-watching, hiding behind a mask, enduring micromanaged directives and stressing over job security, then the trust between, empathy with and humility of those at the top and those on the frontline can fracture. People can't feel psychologically safe operating under such circumstances. Do any of the previous scenarios resonate with you?

> *Employees will respond negatively to well-being initiatives if they believe they are merely being implemented to get them to work harder.*
>
> **Professor Sir Cary Cooper CBE, Professor of Organizational Psychology and Health, Manchester Business School (Stevenson and Farmer, 2017, p.58)**

To help embellish this idea, picture a teacher receiving their new class at the beginning of the academic year. If they adopted the DAEL leadership model immediately, what might the long-term implications be on the confidence and growth mindset of their students? Would they feel inspired, valued and self-assured? Would creativity, cooperation and transparency truly flourish? Would the students' initiative, optimism and self-belief grow? Put simply, would the best in all students be nurtured and revealed?

What's hiding behind the curtain?

An organisation's mission statement that proclaims to place its people at its heart with an emphasis on well-being, trust and personal development is meaningless unless it's valued, embedded and celebrated within the teams that reside there. The best way to measure the impact of such initiatives is to examine the extent to which the recipients exercise loyalty and trust toward the organisation or people appointed to lead them.

The true picture of what underpins the beating heart of an educational establishment is often referred to as the 'hidden curriculum'. It's these cultural values and beliefs that, ultimately, spiral downward from those in positions of leadership and, subsequently, permeate and impact the thoughts, feelings, moods and actions of the people who operate under their direction.

If you find this concept confusing, the following analogy may help. Imagine being interviewed for a new job that you secretly know isn't right for you. You need the cash and convince yourself there's no harm in gaining the work experience, so you arrive at the interview armed with what you think are all the right answers. No matter how hard you try to convince yourself and the interviewer that you're the best person for the job, your inner belief of 'I'm not really committed and don't really want this job' becomes the predominant intent you communicate subconsciously. In other words, you're saying one thing, but the person listening to you is picking up an entirely different set of messages delivered subconsciously. This is where the saying 'I can read you like a book' comes from.

> » *What hidden messages might exist within the environments you work or study in?*

» *Do you know someone who works or studies within an establishment that's struggling with a negative reputation that, despite all efforts to counteract it, was still picked up subconsciously by the general public in much the same manner as the hidden curriculum?*

» *Could poor cultural practices or beliefs exist within your work environment that operate below the surface and, ultimately, negatively affect your level of confidence, performance or self-belief?*

» *Can you relate to a personal experience in which somebody in a position of authority whom you worked for promised one thing publicly, but they then went on to operate in a completely opposite manner behind the scenes?*

The ideal model of leadership

Leaders need to be flexible and think 'outside the box' to work with team members to develop innovative strategies for achieving their goals.

Ronald E. Riggio (2023)

The shortfalls of the previous model of leadership explain why the great teachers or mentors whom we never forget and who encouraged us to think positively about ourselves resist the DAEL leadership approach. Put simply, they built trustworthy environments in which people felt safe and valued under their direction and guidance, and they did this by deploying a thorough understanding of emotional intelligence (or emotional quotient [EQ]). They understood the power of developing learning built around creative and meaningful environments filled with positivity and purposefulness.

> *... the teacher who can inspire the children with the faith and purpose of the advancing life... will never be out of a job. And teachers who have this faith and purpose can give it to their pupils. They cannot help giving it to them if it is part of their own life and practice.*
>
> Wallace D. Wattles (2007, p.81)

It's within this work or education culture that individuals have a far larger chance of experiencing giant shifts in confidence and self-belief that, ultimately, aid their personal transformation and performance. In the end, the significant benefit to all concerned can be summarised as being the maximisation of potential or the realisation of our best self. This is the LEAD approach.

LEAD

Liberate | Emotions | Achieve | Desires

Turning things around

> *Putting resources into employee development is an essential way to demonstrate both respect and recognition.*
>
> Ronald E. Riggio (2023)

Returning to the acronyms, watch what happens when we turn the DAEL approach around and apply the letters in reverse: we LEAD!

A good model of leadership

The best leaders liberate people by helping them understand and manage their emotions as a pathway to improving their achievements, which in turn fulfils their desires.

This model of leadership epitomises the qualities of integrity and authenticity we seek most when selecting the right coach or mentor to take the lead, helping us to fulfil our deepest dreams or desires or to equip us with the right skills and attitudes to overcome a personal challenge or obstacle.

Referring to the words represented by the letters LEAD, an employer's, leader's or teacher's perspective or attitude toward their students, apprentices or employees could now be this:

L – Liberate

The development of people matters, so let me **liberate** *my cohort by inspiring them with enlightening information about themselves and their personal goals, which I'll deliver consistently over a period of time, and that goes beyond the immediate needs of the organisation. This approach will encourage people to thrive – alongside providing them with greater meaning, authenticity and self-respect – and to like a little more of themselves. Let's develop loyalty and engagement by showing them how they're valued and protected. Let's work together and involve everyone in planning how best to forge ahead fearlessly into the unknown future, both personally and as an organisation, by remaining agile and adaptable.*

E – Emotions

This approach would help the people I serve unlock empowering **emotions**, *which would serve to help them build greater resilience, self-confidence and self-belief. If my cohort are emotionally empowered and self-aware, they're far more likely to support each other, trust each other and communicate openly, including asking for help.*

A – Achieve

Then they'd **achieve** *more, which would benefit their attitude toward themselves and what they do. The experience of achieving a personal milestone would result in the formation of more self-responsibility.*

D – Desires

By delivering the preceding stages, the people I lead would have a larger capacity to arrive at work with increased **desire**. *This would impact their* *sense of direction and drive. This would encourage them to be at their best. People that are driven by desire are self-motivated and far more willing to share, communicate freely and formulate innovative ideas. This then increases the level of trust people feel working together within a strong community where everyone feels safe and empowered to contribute. People working within an environment with this culture are far more likely to remain open to new ideas and to initiate and sustain their own path of personal development.*

An employee's, student's or apprentice's perspective

An employee's, student's or apprentice's perspective of work life following the LEAD approach would develop into the following:

L – Liberate

*I can **liberate** myself because I'm supported, inspired and engaged. This level of care and the approach to learning helps me understand and appreciate the endless potential I have within me, and this includes the opportunities available within my current environment. Ultimately, this impacts how I share my time and talents with the people I work alongside, as well as what I give back to the world. Furthermore, I feel motivated to remain loyal to and supportive of the leaders who liberated and inspired me. I can now act with more authenticity and confidence.*

E – Emotions

*This liberated state of self-awareness and a deeper sense of personal meaning naturally leads to a growth in my ability to handle my **emotions**. This helps me to develop my EQ and my capacity to thrive with increased resilience.*

A – Achieve

*After passing through the previous growth stages, I now **achieve** greater competency and ease in coping with challenging everyday situations. My productivity improves.*

D – Desires

*I have more **desire**, drive and direction at work and in life in general. This desire helps me make the best of each day, dwell in a state of gratitude and stand on my own two feet. My self-motivation and initiative have improved, and I'm increasingly keen to support those around me. I have a bigger desire to contribute ideas that could help my organisation move forward.*

Not only do I have increased drive in these areas but I'm also more able to fulfil these desires as part of my work life and elsewhere.

Lead the way

> *Companies can and should take on the onus of training talent... and instilling cultures of continuous learning.*
>
> **Bernard Marr (2022)**

The LEAD formula, whether exercised at a one-to-one level of mentoring or delivered across a large group, encourages people to foster greater self-confidence, self-belief and resourcefulness. Armed with these skills, individuals are more likely to navigate the challenges life throws at them and initiate their own personal growth path to developing some of the more-complex soft (critical) skills currently in such high demand in today's ever-changing world of work.

The LEAD approach lies at the heart of the teaching contained within your guidebook. It's the enduring beacon that helps you navigate your course through the jungle of work life. What follows is a mantra that will grow ever more familiar to you as you journey through your guidebook:

***Liberate** your perception of self
and unlock the control of your emotions,
and then you'll achieve your desires.*

Finally, note how the letter pairs 'DA' and 'EL' within the DAEL approach represent two sets of words led by nouns ('desires' and 'emotions'), as opposed to the LEAD model where the letter pairs 'LE' and 'AD' represent two sets of words led by verbs ('liberate' and 'achieve'). Poor leadership is passive and inert compared with outstanding leadership, which is dynamic and active. In a similar manner, from your very first step forward on your journey through the jungle, the tools and suggestions contained within your guidebook abide within an action-led methodology.

Let's embark by examining the Excursion One section of your guidebook and begin to scale new heights of understanding and self-awareness!

It is not enough to stare up the steps, we must step up the stairs.

Vance Havner

Excursion One

The L in LEAD
LIBERATE

*It's not who you are that holds you back,
it's who you think you are not.*

Denis Waitley

Route Guidance Four
Curriculum bearings

*What we need is not evolution,
but a revolution in education.*

Sir Ken Robinson (TED, 2010)

Backtracking the education trail

To kick-start our journey studying the **liberate** stage of the guidebook, let's first pause, take a look back in time, and consider the critical role that traditional education plays in shaping many of our ideas and assumptions concerning our potential and place in the world.

Prior to work, the established institutionalised education system had the responsibility of preparing you for the world of work. Consider if this system adequately prepared you to do the following:

✓ move confidently through the jungle of work life;

✓ find fulfilment or self-worth;

✓ fully utilise your talents to do more of what you really love;

✓ discover what you could offer your community as well as the wider world;

✓ develop initiative and operate in a financially independent way; and

✓ specialise in creative techniques to empower your mind in supporting the accomplishment of your goals.

This section of your guidebook delves deeper into reviewing these questions. We'll examine the topic of education from past, present and future perspectives.

First, we'll explore some of the shortfalls of the education system that are partly responsible for bringing about the lack of confidence and low morale currently experienced by millions of young people entering the jungle of work life.

Next, we'll take a peek at some of the values young people carry over into work and the sorts of challenges they can encounter. This section reveals eight curriculum **foundations** that could be embedded at the heart of education to help equip young people with the psychological skills and attitudes needed to thrive in the modern world. This section concludes by revealing the most important curriculum foundation, which is not only consistent with the LEAD approach covered earlier but also provides the key to unlocking all previous eight foundations: *know thyself.*

Finally, we'll leave the past behind, swing the focus back to *your* current situation and apply the LEAD approach to setting you a new bearing toward exploring the fresh ideas and tools that will establish your personalised education roadmap to liberation.

Obviously, we all have different narratives concerning our journey experiences through the maze of established education, and for many of those for whom academia and studying subjects are important, the current system remains relevant and is designed for them.

It's also important to stress that the ideas in this chapter don't nullify the obvious fact that children should always retain the right to receive a state education that equips them with the fundamental competencies and knowledge necessary to operate successfully in their work life (for example, the application of number skills;

engagement with the creative arts, other than just English literature; reading; science; digital technology; physical fitness; and health education).

However, looking beyond these core subjects, it's impossible to predict the exact nature or content of the knowledge demand that an ever-changing world may throw up in the future. For this reason, we'll focus in on examining the critical life skills and attitudes of mind, or thinking approaches, that are often missing from education but will always remain pertinent in supporting an individual's ability to sustain self-discipline and responsibility, without the need to relinquish their ability to think big and find fulfilment or self-worth.

As you read on, consider the extent to which the following points relate to your past and present experiences. Then ask yourself this: What are my prevailing thoughts, attitudes, beliefs and assumptions regarding what's possible in my life? How much of this stems from past conditioning?

The vital information rarely taught early in school

Education does not mean teaching people what they do not know. It means teaching them to behave as they do not behave.

John Ruskin

Let's examine the context in which you began your educational journey, long before you were aware of the work-life jungle; these were the primary/elementary school years (ages five to eleven). Consider your school days:

» *During this time, to what extent did you feel frustrated or overburdened by being forced to complete futile statutory assessments or fretting over your rank positioning relative to your peers within exam league tables?*

» *Were there aspects of your curriculum or lesson content that, to this day, you still find perplexing or irrelevant compared to what's actually required to navigate the jungle of work life successfully?*

» *Did some of your curriculum topics feel outdated at that time or unrelated to what interested you most?*

» *Was much of your experience of school simply a case of learning how to comply and become a good little learner, obediently following the rules, knuckling down and reciting the answers required by the marking scheme in your yearly exams?*

» *Were you allowed time to immerse yourself in solo or team-led activities that ignited a sense of wonder, bold imagination and opportunity to innovate freely or create solutions to problems that really mattered to you?*

Did you tick all the boxes at school?

Think back to your early school days and the impact they had on your current levels of intelligence, confidence, self-awareness, fulfilment and meaning within your work life. On a scale of 0–5 (where 0 = not at all and 5 = totally), score how adequately the education system equipped you to truly thrive in the following areas:

Knowledge, skill or ability	Score 0–5
Gaining a thorough awareness of your talents or creative abilities and learning style, following frequent opportunities to develop and share them throughout your school years.	
Being fully self-aware, happy with who you are, and embracing all personal qualities and imperfections as well as understanding the difference between happiness and fulfilment.	

Knowledge, skill or ability	Score 0–5
Having the ability to express yourself, including speaking confidently and transparently to an audience, using the power of story to develop engagement to share ideas and establish connection.	
Having an open mindset rather than a closed one and having an appreciation of the role divergent thinking has in solving problems, following plenty of opportunities to explore creative thinking at an early age when you're naturally accustomed to originating fresh ideas.	
Possessing high levels of resilience and mental agility to navigate change or combat demoralisation, failure or despondency, and accepting no one owes you anything.	
Having the ability to utilise the full range of critical skills required to thrive in the twenty-first-century world of work, including the ability to apply the skills of vulnerability, humility, empathy and authenticity to engage and share ideas with other people across a range of situations.	
Having a deep sense of meaning, self-control and the ability to practise simple mindfulness techniques to help bring balance or calmness of mind to help navigate a path through periods of adversity or challenge.	
Having the ability to appreciate and demonstrate in everyday life the behavioural skills of inclusion, diversity, allyship and belonging awareness.	

Knowledge, skill or ability	Score 0–5
Having a basic understanding of the power the mind has over your habits and emotions, and then practising techniques that help create empowered, focused thinking.	
Understanding the negative health issues associated with sustained withdrawal, immersion within virtual worlds or social media, and the glamorisation of idols, which can blur the line between fact and fiction.	
Being aware that you can grow your mind's capacity (neuroplasticity) and increase all the various intelligences, not just logical or linear thinking, and that all have value.	
Possessing a range of collaborative team-building skills that prevent you having a micro perspective that only focuses on yourself.	
Total score	

What was your total score (out of 60)? Perhaps you scored reasonably well in some of the boxes, or did this exercise leave you feeling somewhat let down or short-changed by the education system? This exercise highlights some fundamental gaps within the culture, curriculum and learning environments of many educational systems.

The three fundamental problems with the established education system

Three fundamental problems within the established education system require attention, which are summarised under the following headings:

1. New world

2. New approach

3. New intelligence

1. New world

The world of work has changed radically from the world our parents operated in. The notion of simply keeping your head down and working diligently through the hierarchical structure of mainstream education to attain the key to opening the doors to a steady career for thirty years, culminating in a utopic retirement at sixty-five, has crumbled. Change is the name of the game, and it's affecting all our lives – whether we like it or not. Welcome to the new world!

The exceptional pace of global change is unlikely to diminish; it's the driving force that's demanding we all keep up to speed – to adapt constantly and to pivot in order to stay ahead of the competition. To compound this pressure, many people have to navigate an unpredictable future in which technology, AI, and robots will change the dynamics of certain job roles (for example, there will be fewer manual-labouring jobs), certain qualifications no longer stand the test of time, and adopting multiple work roles throughout your working life is now the norm.

Do you find it difficult to stay the course, combat stress, think big and sustain a vision, all while juggling the challenges of education and earning a living? Other factors that can contribute toward stress, distraction and demoralisation include the long-term burden of paying off debt or university fees, getting a foot on the property ladder, and successfully monitoring your personal mental health and well-being issues. Many young people are now prioritising preventative mental health measures over a focus on physical fitness alone. The pace of change and complexity of psychological demands being inflicted on all of us must be counterbalanced by allowing people to understand their limits, seek perspective and develop more self-care.

In order for humanity to overcome the extreme environmental and societal challenges ahead, it's essential that education plays a full part in preparing and equipping young people with the psychological tools, resourcefulness and bold imagination needed to overcome challenging circumstances; combat demoralisation; formulate fresh, creative solutions; and look beyond the obvious.

2. New approach

Curriculum content within many educational establishments has remained largely unchanged for the last seventy-five years. The same is true for many school learning environments. You only need to compare nineteenth-century and twenty-first-century photographs of a typical classroom layout to realise just how stuck education is in doing things the old way (for example, children sitting in rows, often organised into ability sets, facing the teacher who's delivering content from the front of the classroom). The current system doesn't adequately equip young people with the mindset skills to thrive in the modern world. A new approach is required.

Many young people, however, can see past the façade of what traditional education has to offer, and they're searching for new ways to consume content, ideas and solutions, which will enable them to become their best selves and flourish confidently in this new world of change.

As a means of alleviating the pressure imposed on young people, studies in mindfulness, resilience and growth mindset are now common place in many school curricula, but are these enough? They certainly aren't subjects, but are they too often delivered in this same way? Are these topics fully understood or exemplified? Were you provided with plentiful opportunities to explore comprehensively, value and embed these empowering thought processes into your daily life outside the classroom so they matured and served you in later life?

You may be asking, 'Are these topics just too complex and time-consuming to wedge into an already overcrowded curriculum?'

Of course, the reply that would truly advance meeting the needs of young people isn't a straightforward yes or no, but rather it's that we're asking the wrong question! Simply supplementing an already overcrowded curriculum with new content isn't the answer. It's time to simplify radically and overhaul an outdated curriculum load and replace it with a fresh approach that truly serves the needs of young people. This also involves designing a curriculum that listens to the concerns expressed by those it serves, while also synergising curriculum content with the needs of the new world as a whole. Unfortunately, although there are many talented and forward-thinking educationalists working very hard to create the change that's required, the intent is often missing where it matters most: at the core of the established system in which the governing powers monopolise the content of state education. Presently, it's a case of those at the edge of the system slowly informing those at the centre about new ideas or initiatives.

3. New intelligence

> *An educated man is not, necessarily, one who has an abundance of general or specialised knowledge. An educated man is one who has so developed the faculties of his mind that he may acquire anything he wants, or its equivalent, without violating the rights of others.*
>
> Napoleon Hill (2009, p.117)

The most common fault lines in every avenue of education are the lack of educating young people on the exact meaning of the term 'intelligence' and the lack of providing opportunities to practise intelligent thinking. The word 'intelligence' creates an instant reaction within many people's minds, as it can portray a variety of different things or have false connotations that can even turn people off, but within the context of this guidebook intelligence is defined as follows: *the ability to think openly and critically.*

It encompasses the following:

- Processing information independently, rather than simply reacting or going along with the crowd or whatever those in higher positions of authority say.

- Pausing and evaluating before making an assumption.

- Maintaining a high level of integrity and self-respect while not being afraid to ask questions even if it leads to embarrassment, ridicule or ostracisation.

- Recognising patterns in behaviours to help inform or make a judgement.

- Behaving purposefully, through acts of love and humility, in pursuit of the truth or in generating original ideas or solutions.

- Looking beyond the obvious or mass consensus before making a decision.

- Basing personal values and goals on integrity, rather than simply chasing money or status alone.

In contrast to the ideas just given, the established school system teaches young people obedience and reward for utilising memory and supplying the 'correct' answers required by an exam's marking scheme.

There remains a consensus in society that those who climb the education ladder successfully and achieve the highest grades or who accumulate a vast array of qualifications, attend the most prestigious universities, and go on to achieve a doctorate or hold a position of authority (scholar, politician, professor, magistrate, etc.) are intelligent, and by default, 'successful'. Some people do indeed attain a degree of intelligence this way; however, it's naïve to assume that intelligence is acquired by simply possessing the ability to memorise facts, pass the bar, and regurgitate information based on the opinions of those who hold higher positions of expertise or authority.

The eight new curriculum foundations

There follows eight curriculum foundations that could be embedded at the heart of education, which would, as a result, help equip young people with the psychological skills and attitudes to thrive in the modern world of work. If you're thinking, *This is all very good, but what about my current circumstances having now left education? Where can I go now to help myself understand and develop these skills further in my daily work life?* then this is why this guidebook found you. It's not impossible for you to attain these skills right now – all will be revealed later as you progress along your journey.

Foundation One: Learning and applying the critical skills that are so in demand

Note that these critical skills are often called 'soft skills'. However, they're anything but soft as they represent a core set of personal attributes that enable a person to communicate and interact effectively with other people across all professions. You'll find more detail on these skills later in your guidebook (in Route Guidance Eight).

Unlike at any other time in the history, young people are feeling the pressure of being constantly reminded by employers of the importance of acquiring certain critical skills to be ready for work.

The traditional qualifications and academic credentials found on a CV now form only part of what employers are looking for. Character qualities – such as initiative, authenticity, team collaboration, communication, humility and creativity – are now equally, if not more, important.

The problem is that many of the most sought-after critical skills employees desire are hard to pin down and can't simply be acquired: they're forged over time through a sustained journey of self-awareness and honest self-review. With this in mind, would it not make sense to begin actively developing the foundations of these skills considerably earlier in a young person's path through education and to make this the centre of the curriculum?

Foundation Two: Understanding and demonstrating the value of authenticity and vulnerability

Authenticity

Authentic behaviour primarily centres on being true to yourself while acting with transparency and honesty. Do you know or work alongside anyone who's genuinely open, honest, self-accepting, reliable, trustworthy and respectful toward others?

Even when there are high levels of economic confidence and opportunity within the workplace, many young people can still feel disconnected and unable to internalise effectively or communicate authentically. As a result, they can find it increasingly difficult to develop meaningful job satisfaction or fulfilment. The pressures of getting by in the modern world, making a difference, climbing the promotion ladder and navigating a highly competitive career market force many to withdraw or hide behind a false persona.

This problem is compounded when we consider the barrage of mind-numbing distractions and instant gratifications readily available and promoted by modern society (alcohol, drugs, fast foods lacking nutrition, social media, online gaming, etc.).

By numbing themselves as a means of escape, many young people subsequently find it harder in the long term to develop critical mindsets and perspectives to foster resilience and level-headedness during times of stress or challenge. Withdrawal, low confidence and isolation can also create a lifestyle that makes young people more susceptible to mild depression, a lack of ambition or feelings of low self-worth later in life.

Vulnerability

Without realising it, many young people are numb to another key behaviour that's essential in developing effective communication and relationships: vulnerability (not to be confused with the notion of weakness or oversensitivity). It includes the ability to choose the appropriate opportunity to share with others an honest self-review or imperfection, which may include admitting mistakes or describing periods of struggle. Obviously, it's important to understand when it's appropriate to share such behaviour within work life, but the following summary provides some useful insights:

- Hiding vulnerability numbs our ability to connect fully with others and develop honesty, empathy and trust.

- It takes twice the energy to fake it and hide than it does to be transparent about your experiences.

- Young children are wired for adaptability, openness and struggle, yet some parents overly protect their children from experiencing imperfection, fear, failure and/or disappointment. When parents strive to create a seamless early-life-journey experience for their children, they run the risk of their children developing problems later on. Overly protecting young children from these experiences can contribute to withdrawal behaviour in their later teenage years, such as a preoccupation with counting the number of 'likes' on social media platforms or following a celebrity-style 'perfect me' social media post (that is, hiding behind a mask).

- When we fail to embrace vulnerability, we're striving to make the uncertain certain, which can contribute toward us finding unhealthy satisfaction in proving to others 'I'm right, and you're wrong!'

- Effective leaders have a strong sense of empathy. They understand the power of sharing a measured and appropriate level of vulnerability as a means of connecting with the people they lead. They understand the value of respect and empathy. Inspiring leaders very often communicate a unique narrative of challenge or adventure, underpinned by humility and transparency.

- A lack of vulnerability inhibits the development of empathy. When we hide behind a perfect mask and numb our vulnerability, it makes it harder for us to consider whether a message we're sending via email, for example, is effective in conveying the appropriate impact, urgency or quality. Furthermore, are we considering the implications if the message isn't carefully crafted?

These critical aspects of behaviour, which have such a huge bearing on the art of successful communication and connectivity within the world of work, must be explored far earlier as an essential component of the school curriculum.

Foundation Three: Thinking big while remaining economically independent

Education is not the filling of a pail, but the lighting of a fire.
Plutarch (though often attributed to William Butler Yeats)

Young people are driven to be the change and the promise of the future, and they're increasingly attracted to new career roles in organisations that mirror the spirit of entrepreneurism while offering opportunities to contribute fresh ideas. A sense of belonging, autonomy, trust and teamwork while working toward a meaningful venture supported by a range of well-being initiatives is also an important experience that young people might look for when applying for jobs. Traditional companies that fail to engage with these emerging trends and fail to provide opportunities for young people to exercise this spirit of adventure fully can find it increasingly difficult to recruit fresh talent.

A trend emerging within the world of work is the rise in popularity of the solopreneur (a person who develops a new business on their own), but also those who actively seek a career they feel passionate about while operating a parallel solo venture or new start-up remotely or from home.

Being a solopreneur is an attractive proposition for many young people as it offers adventure, the opportunity to think big, independence, and the spirit of self-determination in creating solutions that have a sustainable or sociological global impact.

Young people also deserve regular opportunities to access the very best guidance and advice from successful business owners concerning the management of money and access to fresh ideas on delivering social or environmental impact and responsibility. Successful entrepreneurs and new-start-up leaders have a huge amount of wisdom and experience to share because they understand the challenges associated with managing personal resources, as well as sustaining personal resilience and a growth mindset.

Foundation Four: Developing a failure-resilient attitude of mind

The hidden guide lets no one enjoy great achievement without passing the persistence test. Those who can't take it, simply do not make the grade.
Napoleon Hill (2009, p.233)

The concept of 'thinking big' is a wonderful message to share with young people, but they also need to understand the highs and lows that accompany any brilliant success story. They need to learn what it feels like to face disappointment and how this experience is often labelled as 'failure' – something to regret or push to one side.

The word 'failure' has so many negative connotations, but the experience of failing provides an invaluable learning opportunity to pivot, re-evaluate our options, and build character and resolve. Many success stories are engrained with long periods of perseverance and trial. On reflection, failure can encourage us to make slight adjustments to our plans or approaches, seek out fresh information, and set a new course toward success. With this level of understanding, vital mental energy – which can be lost in mulling over disappointment – is channelled and redirected so it serves the development and enlightenment of an individual, rather than inhibiting growth.

Young people should learn to understand that, when misfortune presents itself, they always have the choice to press on and assume that more could likely follow. What matters most is harbouring the resilience to resist negative self-prophecy, remaining open to an infinite range of new possibilities, learning and pressing on. This approach involves thinking in a certain way (more on this later in Route Guidance Ten).

Foundation Five: Developing personal meaning and fulfilment

Tell me, I'll forget. Show me, I'll remember. Involve me, I'll understand.
Chinese proverb (believed to be Xun Kuang, in the *Xunzi*, but often incorrectly attributed to Benjamin Franklin)

It's also important to realise that fulfilment comes through developing what you already have: the spirit of life! Or to put it another way, meaning occurs as a result of discovering a project that's highly important to you, so you continue to honour the call and press on over a long period of time. During this process, an individual can grow to appreciate that acknowledgement or approval from others isn't necessary. Being absorbed in deep, satisfying acts of concentration that sustain your attention can also carry you through periods of hardship or combat distraction.

Ultimately, fulfilment isn't something you find out there in the world, but it's something you experience within yourself. You first have to accept and grant yourself permission to feel worthy of feeling fulfilled before embarking on an activity.

Did you ever experience periods of low confidence or repeatedly affirm you were no good at something and simply give up when you were at school? Education has a responsibility to provide young people with the opportunity to learn from role models who avoid this trap and to demonstrate this focused mindset to think beyond circumstances.

One of the best ways to develop self-confidence, meaning and fulfilment in children is to allow them more time to share and develop a purposeful activity they care about most and to provide them with the support and encouragement needed to deepen and specialise this pursuit.

Foundation Six: Working alongside fabulous inspirational mentors and leaders who demonstrate an agile mindset

People will forget what you said, people will forget what you did, but people will never forget how you made them feel.
Maya Angelou

Being aware that we have the power to select and redirect our thoughts toward more-empowering choices or decisions when faced with failure or disappointment is very different, of course, from actually putting this idea into action. For this reason, it's important to facilitate regular opportunities for children to work alongside mentors from the world of business or sport (entrepreneurs, athletes, new-start-up leaders or leaders of large organisations with agile mindsets, disrupters for positive change, etc.) who demonstrate peace of mind, self-respect, focus and humility. Furthermore, it's critical to share the specific attitudes – such as resolve, endurance and self-discipline approaches – that these individuals apply to avoid the temptation to give up after missing the mark or encountering unfortunate circumstances.

Young people recognise integrity intuitively, so it's also important to demonstrate how success can incorporate social conscience and a willingness to serve and make a difference in the world. The most inspiring entrepreneurs don't seek self-gratification, but they build a fascination with the tasks contained within the present moment, delivering benefits to others, relishing their journey of unfoldment and tackling each day with the spirit of discovery.

Young people should learn from visionaries who exude a calmness of mind, put others at ease and inspire their followers to act in more-empowering ways. By demonstrating trust and integrity, they can inspire their followers to continue their legacy and become the future orchestrators of change.

Foundation Seven: Accessing inspiring literature centred on intelligent thinking

Many people go all the way through the school system without ever being introduced to the key messages contained in timeless classic books that share some of the most inspiring and pioneering ideas on critical thinking, growth mindset and creative thinking. Many of these books grace the private libraries of the most successful visionaries. These books aren't always mainstream in terms of subject matter; nevertheless, they encourage you to access different areas of learning, open the mind and challenge assumptions. This can also include learning from the context of the past to inform the future by examining some of the classic authors' experiences of human potential or the power of the mind (Viktor E. Frankl, Napoleon Hill, Wallace D. Wattles, Genevieve Behrend, Thomas Troward, James Allen, Thomas Edison, Neville Goddard, Earl Nightingale, Dale Carnegie, etc.).

A common theme runs throughout these books:

- The author has invested considerable time in researching or interviewing those who have succeeded in achieving extraordinary results. They use examples borrowed from real success stories to inspire and enlighten their readers. Napoleon Hill (*Think and Grow Rich*) spent a lifetime questioning and researching the secrets of some of the most financially successful people in the world.

- They approach their topic from a deeper level of understanding or a radically different way of viewing life that sits outside the norm to explain the inner workings of the mind.

- They share wisdom and insight attained through a deep, authentic engagement with the process of life, including huge challenges, endurance or setbacks.

- Following the accomplishment of their life goals, they made it their life's purpose to share with the world the richness of what they'd learnt regarding certain success principles or the power of the mind.

- Their message often contains universal appeal, resonates with people and stands the test of time.

- They develop a deep affinity and connection with their readers, as if they were speaking the readers' language.

Foundation Eight: Valuing, through practical experience, the role we can all play within communities

Young people need to appreciate the value of belonging and contributing to a community at all levels (for example, family, work teams, business ecosystem, collaborative environments, neighbourhood, local area, region and the world). There are huge personal benefits from sharing fellowship, cooperating and contributing toward community projects:

- It helps counterbalance feelings of loneliness, detachment or self-doubt.

- It creates a sense of satisfaction, purpose and fulfilment from being involved in group projects that share a common good.

- It develops socialisation skills and teaches the art of cooperation and trust.

- It improves decision-making.
- It develops the ability to connect with, learn from or ask for support from other people outside close family.
- It develops empathy, open-mindedness, compassion, and an appreciation of the hardships or misfortune experienced by others.
- It helps prevent insular behaviour, which stifles creativity.
- It allows access to new skills not taught or experienced in school or the home.
- It increases a sense of pride or accomplishment.
- It improves overall mental health and well-being.

More young people are making the effort to travel longer distances to socialise, network, unwind, share in meaningful conversation, and work alongside new start-ups within an atmosphere of entrepreneurism, synergising fresh ideas and change. The recent trend springing up in all manner of environments is the emergence of physical, innovative 'free work spaces' (coffee shops, pop-up innovation lounges, co-working hubs, etc.). Young people are also spending more money on physical, collaborative, experience-based products and services, sharing trust and mutual support that's experienced within a safe and meaningful environment. Spending time with friends sharing a holistic activity is becoming increasingly popular. These collective, playful and recreational activities unite young people in sharing memorable, novel and, sometimes, nostalgic experiences. In recent years, there have been enormous strides made within many higher education establishments toward developing more enriching learning environments that mirror these trends. Did you experience similar learning environments in school? If not, would your engagement and focus at school have been improved if these experiences had been incorporated into the course of your daily learning?

The curriculum foundation that eclipses all others: Know thyself

Challenging the status quo

Throughout time, humanity has demonstrated a habit of procrastinating when it comes to embracing radically new ideas that challenge the status quo – unless, of course, the circumstances in the outside world force an awakening. The philosopher Arthur Schopenhauer put it so eloquently:

Every truth passes through three stages before it is recognised.
First, it is ridiculed.
Second, it is opposed.
Third, it is regarded as self-evolved.

Humanity is currently experiencing a momentous reckoning, brought on by the impact of the climate change crisis, pandemics, environmental devastation, economic instability and the technological impact on jobs. These wake-up calls are having a dramatic effect on the focus of mass consciousness on a better awareness and prioritisation of humanity's more nurturing qualities, such as empathy, tolerance, holistic well-being, connection, compassion, inclusion and global responsibility. However, while considering this positive shift in consciousness, it's important to still be alert to some of the more recent darker sides of humanity, such as the growth of nationalism, patriotism, protectionism, fear and division.

Obviously, we haven't quite reached the critical tipping point that will initiate a complete positive transformation or global awakening. At present, humanity is somewhat stuck between the second and third transitional stages of Schopenhauer's 'mass awakening of truth' and is still grappling to come to terms with the enormity of the challenge that awaits us all in putting things right.

It's going to take a dramatic global effort and commitment to fix the problem.

In much the same way, nothing short of a miracle is required to kick-start the transformation that education so urgently requires. As Sir Ken Robinson so articulately summarised at the beginning of this route guidance, the shift education demands is truly a matter of revolution rather than evolution.

We could, however, take the first steps in initiating the change required in education by introducing a radical idea right at the heart of the curriculum, which is the overarching missing piece from the education puzzle that has the potential to revolutionise anyone's stage of life: helping young people acquire the confidence and curiosity to not just know the world but also, more importantly, to *know themselves.*

What's meant by the phrase 'know thyself'?

Ironically, the term 'know thyself' has been around for centuries. In fact, the ancient Greeks considered the phrase to be of such importance that they carved it in rock at the entrance of the pronaos of the Temple of Apollo at Delphi.

The phrase 'know thyself' could also be associated with a relatively more recent (sixteenth century) phrase: 'peace of mind'. The term 'peace of mind' relates to an individual's ability to feel at ease, self-aware, content or fulfilled, despite the upheaval that may be taking place in the outside world. Discussing the core principle of peace of mind is guaranteed to disrupt and unsettle many of us, as it requires an awkward and uncomfortable honest self-review of the ego and asking key questions such as these: *Am I truly happy with my life? Have I allowed my potential to spread its wings fully? Can I tolerate my own company? Ultimately, am I at peace?*

It became profoundly evident in the 2020–2022 Covid-19 pandemic – during which, for the first time, millions of people were forced to pause and take stock of their lives – that a dichotomy emerged between those who remained calm, exercising relative peace of mind by reframing their circumstances positively, and those who suffered inexorably, feeling frustrated, lost and cut off from the world that normally provided opportunities to become preoccupied with activities designed to facilitate temporarily forgetting ones problems or responsibilities.

Not discounting people who were helpless in reframing the situation and suffered inexorably (the very old, physically unwell, immobile, isolated or cut off), for those who were able to exercise peace of mind, the pause imposed on the pace of life did create opportunities for people to explore deeper meaning and gain perspective or clarity on what really mattered (for example, being present, reconnecting with nature, discovering new hobbies, and spending more intimate time with family or loved ones).

For those who lacked this quality, time simply couldn't move fast enough until things returned to normal. Suddenly, life felt intolerable without the opportunity to withdraw into the outside world's distractive hustle and bustle of consumerism and entertainment, or the approval gained by continually being around other people.

Relating to this idea of dramatic splits in the ways in which people adapt to circumstances, a similar dichotomy remains among the attitudes and behaviours of millions of young people regarding their perception of their self-worth, confidence and place in the world. Although many young people do indeed succeed in finding meaning, fulfilment and purpose in their lives, there's an equal number that miss out and never experience these qualities.

The common human qualities, attitudes and mindset that all teachers and parents desire most in their young children often centre on resilience, confidence, self-belief, focus, self-control and vision. However, these qualities can only grow outward when a child feels fully comfortable and engaged, learning more about themselves and pursuing the joy achieved through curiosity, creativity and developing meaningful activities to be proud of. A child who first understands a little about who and what they are and the potential they hold within are far more likely to remain receptive to the idea of self-determination and faith or belief in them tackling new things.

What do you need to do to get to know thyself?

Let's begin addressing this question by reviewing an idea from one of the most inspirational writers of the early twentieth century: Wallace D Wattles. He shared an idea that challenges the assumption that riches are accumulated by doing certain things, replacing it with this:

> *... getting rich is the result of doing things in a certain way!*
> **Wallace D. Wattles (2007, p.8)**

You may ask, 'What's the relationship between attaining certain riches and knowing thyself?' The answer lies at the end of Wattles' quote – 'a certain way'. You could rephrase the line as this: getting to know thyself is the result of doing things in a certain way. Note how Wattles avoids the idea of attaining certain things or acquiring specific information, but he instead stresses the importance of how you go about doing things (that is, the manner, spirit or style surrounding your thoughts or actions). This includes the following:

- The certain way you define yourself as a human being regarding your limits or potential.
- The certain way you manage and direct your moment-to-moment thoughts.

Why shouldn't these ideas apply to the primary approach education takes in helping young people equip themselves with the skills required to developing greater confidence and self-worth?

The certain way young people should be encouraged to forge a positive self-concept and imagine grander possibilities

We have to understand fully who we are before we can flourish and develop a new vision of the future. Neglecting this responsibility while expecting a full unfoldment of our potential is like asking somebody with no basic IT knowledge to navigate successfully and utilise the various files and full range of applications within a laptop.

There's only one reason why a young person in school will say they're bored, useless or have no ideas, and that's because they haven't been introduced to the enormity of their potential and the unlimited power of the imagination.

In short, it's essential that young people learn very early in life how to foster self-respect. They deserve to experience the awe and wonder associated with being a spiritual human being. They deserve more opportunities to explore who they are (soul, being and individualised spirit) and the magnitude of power and potential they were granted at birth. They deserve to be taught how to use correctly the faculties of their minds, which if skilfully directed, can allow for a lifetime appreciation of unlimited possibilities.

The certain way young people should be encouraged to direct their thoughts

When faced with the topic of thinking, many people respond with a generalised remark: 'Well, we all think... so what?' But there's a difference between the automatic, subservient thinking habits (such as simple decision-making and idle thoughts) and those of fully independent, constructive, originating and creative thought.

Growing aware of this choice and endeavouring to select the thoughts that empower and serve you is a good example of thinking in a certain way, and the most fulfilled and successful people make a habit of living this way. At the heart of this phrase lies the unsettling truth that, ultimately, every child becomes what they think about the most.

Young people should be educated about the choices they have to tackle a problem by selecting a convergent (closed and linear) or divergent (open and creative) thinking approach to find a solution, and they should experience regular opportunities to put these thinking approaches into action.

My dad always says I'm daydreaming,
but that's not the right word.
I'm making mental images and connecting them together.
'I'm not daydreaming,' I tell him, 'I'm thinking!'

Corey (ex-pupil)

Shifting the focus back to you – your new curriculum

... research shows that the single biggest cause of work burnout is
not work overload, but working too long without experiencing your
own personal development.

Robert Kegan and Lisa Lahey (2016, p.2)

Welcome to the introduction to your new LEAD curriculum, which firmly places you at the centre of a consciousness revolution!

In order to get the most out of your guidebook, and sticking with the theme of 'know thyself', begin your journey by remaining open to bold ideas and try thinking *in a certain way*. You'll need to take command, so begin this process by forming the habit of regularly reciting the following three key ideas, which firmly position you as the master and your mind as the servant:

1. I am a spiritual entity dwelling within a physical shell.

2. I am gifted with the greatest power in the universe: imagination.

3. I ultimately become what I think about (consciously or subconsciously).

Despite the more obvious finite physical limitations that exist in your life (that is, your physical body or things in the outside world), how often do you stop and affirm your true spiritual origin and, subsequently, your unlimited, infinite potential that's channelled through an intellect and imagination? How often do you assert this power as a means of protecting yourself from the allure of self-doubt or defeatism?

You're here to create new possibilities and to go where no one has gone before. You're now going to think from the inside out – not the outside in.

The power of imagination

Imagination is the greatest power in the universe. Imagination is the beginning of everything. Imagination is the means by which we can create something from nothing. It's where all your habits, attitudes, self-belief and vision of what's possible are forged.

You're using your imagination right now to read this book. The text on these pages (represented by words, which come from symbols, which originate from the images held in the author's mind) is fixed, but how you interpret the information and assimilate it within your current situation is your choice. You may perceive information as being out there, but you actually experience the world from the inside out. You give your life meaning. Taking this idea a stage further, you create your reality.

The amazing visionaries channelled their spiritual force through imagination to look beyond their circumstances and visualise a future untethered by lack or limitation. When President Kennedy asked Wernher von Braun (the leading German rocket scientist in the 1960s) what it would take to put a man on the moon, he received a straightforward reply: 'The will to do it.'

When you imagine, spirit moves! Inspiration comes from the Latin word *inspiratus*, which means 'to breathe into'. The union between the visions of spirit and the focus of willpower on thought images held within the imagination creates an unstoppable chain reaction.

How to monitor your thoughts in a certain way

All spiritual, theological and philosophical literature since the beginning of time shares one common message: you become what you think about. Think about the ongoing dialogue you rehearse about *how* your life is, *how far* your thoughts can take you and *how* things are in the world. How do you feel about the idea that your thoughts and feelings affect everything that comes into your life?

Imagine standing on the edge of a tall cliff, looking out to sea. You're buffeted by a strong wind blowing around you. You look down beside you and notice a feather pinned firmly to the ground by a heavy rock. You crouch down and free the feather from the weight of the rock. Next, you stand up and, with your fist clenched tightly around the feather, you hold your arm out straight over the edge of the cliff. The slightest loosening of your grip and you can guarantee the wind will swipe the feather away from you with immutable force and send it hurtling out to sea. In much the same way, you may assume your ultimate power grip centres on the exertion of your willpower alone in manipulating changes to certain things in the outside world. The truth of the matter is that the largest force of change begins as you apply your will to correctly hold a vision or image tight within the storehouse of the mind – your imagination. Any thought, if grasped long enough within the imagination, will eventually be released into the outside world and be swept away by a power far bigger than any wind. It then initiates a chain of incidences that will feel like life's prime movers (good, bad or indifferent) entering your consciousness.

Which thought choices do you hold on to the most: the haste and fear of confusion or the peace and serenity of the certainty of spirit?

Two vital decisions that precede personal transformation

All transformation begins with an intense,
burning desire to be transformed.

Neville Goddard (2010, p.9)

Dael and Lead decided to meet one evening at the Firefly Coffee House at the jungle's centre. Dael had been looking forward to seeing Lead all day at work. It was obvious to Dael that Lead was no ordinary chameleon. She radiated so much infectious energy and a zest for life. Her joy of learning and study had inspired Dael to start collecting a range of inspirational books in which he underlined or annotated (much to the disapproval of his friends) specific lines or passages that resonated with his current situation or perfectly answered some of his deepest questions. As the two lizards sipped their coffee and shared more about themselves, a special bond grew. Dael plucked up the courage to share more about his dissatisfaction with his life and work, how stuck and unfulfilled he felt, and how much he wished for all this to change. Lead listened intently.

After Dael's outpouring, a long pause followed before Lead asked a rather random question: 'Now tell me, Dael, what did you do to learn how to catch fireflies when you were younger; I mean before you even started work?'

Dael thought for a moment and replied, 'Well, I went to see the wise Goliath frog (the largest of the species), who showed me what to do.'

'And?' asked Lead.

Dael thought harder. 'Umm... well, I can remember being amazed that she didn't have vocal sacs, unlike most frogs, and whistled instead.'

'Yes, but apart from that?' insisted Lead.

'Well, after that first meeting – which took a whole day, I think – I went away to practise what she had taught me.'

'Good, but how did the Goliath frog spend that first half of the day with you?' There was a persistent tone to Lead's question, as if she were digging deeper.

Again, Dael thought for a while, then he suddenly replied, 'Ah... she spent that whole morning telling me all about the full range of fly-catching techniques I have at my disposal and lots of other information about us lizards that I never knew. I certainly came away feeling completely different about myself and somewhat enlightened. I didn't know I had that kind of potential.'

'And what agreement did you have to arrange with the Goliath frog before any further lessons could commence?'

'Well, she said that, before we could progress, I had to agree to engage with critical information and prove that I was willing to practise her fly-catching programme.'

Lead smiled enthusiastically. 'And so before I can help you practically too, just like the wisdom the Goliath frog shared, you must first agree to engage with special information about yourself and how this information relates to what you're experiencing in your world, and then make a commitment to change. More importantly, you have to accept the programme wholeheartedly and get going with it. Don't worry, this will take a little time, but I promise to share this information in a fun and novel manner. I don't wish to be bossy; I also need to know I'm not wasting our time.'

Dael nodded enthusiastically, intently following everything Lead was saying.

Lead continued, 'Now, engaging with something new wasn't really a problem for you back then because you understood that, if you didn't do the things she taught you, you'd at least become very hungry and at the very worst... you'd starve to death. I know you're older now, and accepting change or radically new ideas isn't always as easy, but will you join me in reigniting the same inquisitive attitude you had back then to improve your current situation?'

Dael gazed up into the night sky, as if searching for inspiration, before muttering to himself, 'Accept new information in a novel way and wanting to apply... umm.' He then lowered his gaze, looked squarely at Lead and announced boldly, 'Yes, I do.'

'Excellent,' said Lead. 'This is your pathway to liberation: ahead of our journey, you'll be unlocking vital information all about you, your relationship with the world and what you're truly capable of. Your decision to act courageously on this question is your secret weapon to combat confusion, procrastination and fear.'

It was at this point that Lead produced a diagram etched on a banana leaf for Dael to peruse:

What was the beginning of your route of learning, or where it all started?	What, where and whom did you gain this from?	What did you practise or engage with emotionally?	What did you achieve or acquire, and what did this look like?	Where are you currently?	What's your level of desire and how may you share it?
1. You were exposed to certain information 2. You chose to get involved	Teacher School College Parents' kitchen Role models	Certain food-preparation skills Enjoying entertaining	Competency across a range of food-preparation skills	How are your cookery skills?	Chef Banquet cook Caterer Food decorator Baker
1. You were exposed to certain information 2. You chose to get involved	Inspirational literature College courses and mentors	Fresh ideas Self-development Application to everyday life Knowledge of the mind	Experience Resilience Focus Faith in yourself Knowledge of psychology	How is your growth mindset and sense of fulfilment in work life?	Motivator Coach Positive role model Leader
L		**E**	**A**		**D**
Liberate		Emotions	Achieve		Desires

Lead continued her lesson. 'Study the diagram carefully, Dael. Let's say I asked you "How are your cookery skills (highlighted in the fifth column)?" You could provide any number of responses, but let's imagine your reply was "Amazing!" Reading across to the right, your desire, within that particular area could subsequently lead to your proficiency as a chef, for example.

'Now let's move back through time and examine the titles of the preceding columns that connect the dots to where you find yourself right now. The stage before has a title: "What did you achieve or acquire, and what did this look like?" In this example, your response could be something like "Competency across a range of food-preparation skills."

'Take another step back in time (to the left) and examine the question "What did you practise or engage emotionally with?" In this example, it would involve certain food-preparation skills and enjoyment entertaining your friends with dining invitations.

'Take another step back in time and examine the question "What, where and whom did you gain this from?" In this example, this could be a teacher, school, college, parents' kitchen, role model, etc.

'Finally, take a further step back in time and examine the two vital starting points that you had to have in place before any of the subsequent stages could have developed. The two vital starting points are, of course, these:

'1.   You were exposed to certain information.

'2.   You chose to get involved or engage with a process of learning.

'It may appear rather obvious, but without establishing this critical starting point first, the subsequent steps and the end result are impossible to achieve. Put simply, this first state leads the way. For meaningful, positive change to occur in your work and life, everything begins with information and engagement.

'Now work through the chart again in the same manner I've just described, but this time, examine this question: "How is your growth mindset and sense of fulfilment in work and life?" As you examine your answer and trace your journey back in time, you'll discover that *you ultimately arrive at the same critical starting point that preceded everything else: information and engagement. If you currently lack this quality, then somewhere back in time you also failed to engage fully with certain information. Do you now see why I stressed the importance of commitment when it comes to embarking on a path to liberation?'*

Study – your gateway to freedom

As human beings we're set up to protect ourselves – but it is just as true that we're set up to grow psychologically, to evolve, to develop.

Robert Kegan and Lisa Lahey (2016, p.2)

All high achievers, visionaries and spiritual masters have one thing in common: they all understand the importance of study, self-analysis and lifelong learning. Many people succumb to entertaining thoughts such as, *I'm too old to study new things,* or, *I don't have the time* or *concentration skills required.* You're never too old to study or develop new skills, and you're certainly not limited. Those who achieve the most continue to study, even during periods of challenge or upheaval.

In times of change, learners inherit the earth, while the learned find themselves beautifully equipped to deal with a world that no longer exists!

Eric Hoffer

Sustained study on topics of critical thinking will do the following:

- ✓ Help you feel less isolated by transforming a book into the perfect ally

- ✓ Improve your standing during a job interview, as many employers value enrolling new employees who demonstrate a commitment to learning or personal development

- ✓ Develop your authority, empathy or leadership qualities
- ✓ Improve your self-confidence and sense of fulfilment
- ✓ Improve your language and conversation skills
- ✓ Improve your memory and sharpen your mind
- ✓ Increase your analytical skills
- ✓ Increase your concentration
- ✓ Inspire and motivate you
- ✓ Combat boredom or lack of direction
- ✓ Increase your connection with your family and peers
- ✓ Maintain and stimulate a healthy mind that's designed to access new information
- ✓ Give more opportunities for focus, quiet contemplation and mindfulness
- ✓ Improve your sleep quality

Keeping a journal and recording quotes that inspire you presents a great starting point for internalising or organising new insights. A journal can grow into a highly personal oracle and it creates a perfect backdrop in which to track your journey of self-discovery. Try allocating a short period of time daily to studying inspirational texts, and you'll soon reap the benefits. You can't move forward by remaining chained to old ideas or thought habits. You could try beginning each day by listening to or reading short passages of information that uplift and direct your thoughts toward new ideas about what's possible in life.

When it comes to searching out the right uplifting book, information source or mentor who could help release your true potential, remain alert. You'll discover that, very often, the perfect situation will present itself just at the right time – when the student is ready. This is because when you subconsciously carry a desire or question around in your head, it doesn't simply remain stuck there, but it flows out mysteriously into the world and, subsequently, attracts all the necessary circumstances to deliver the perfect source of information that matches your silent request. Remaining in this state can cause books to quite literally jump off the bookshelves to find you! New and exciting people may enter your life within quite ordinary situations. Before long, you may even find yourself establishing a home library. Joining study groups or book clubs will further strengthen your knowledge, as well as resulting in making new friends. Consider for a moment how you came across this particular guidebook and if a sense of perfect timing played its part.

***Liberate** your perception of self
and unlock the control of your emotions,
and then you'll achieve your desires.*

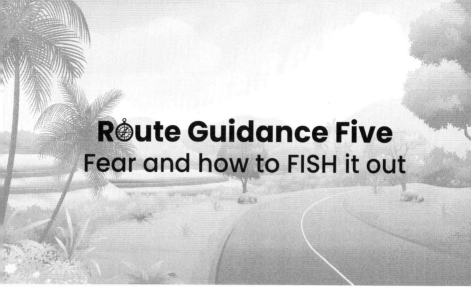

Route Guidance Five
Fear and how to FISH it out

*Unless you try to do something beyond
what you have already mastered,
you will never grow.*

Ronald E. Osborn

Like the deep ocean currents that sway the fish in the sea, there's a host of equally disruptive forces that can distract and interfere with your plans to think and act with greater self-confidence or acuity. These disruptive currents generally emanate from three sources.

The three sources of disruptive currents

1. Neighbouring currents

2. Inner currents

3. Global currents

Let's take a look at these in more detail.

Disruptive Current One: Neighbouring currents

Perhaps the most subversive distraction is the opinionated noise and commotion emanating from your immediate environment. Resisting the temptation to succumb to such noise is a major challenge.

How many of these can you recognise?

- Twenty-four-hour media news broadcasts delivered across a profusion of electronic devices, and tabloids fixated on despondency, drama, scandal, fault-finding, disharmony, alarm, fear and conflict. News headlines on TV are very often relayed by grim-faced presenters and accompanied by shocking imagery with the sole intention of monopolising your attention. Have you ever had the experience of settling down to open your smart device or watch TV feeling content or upbeat, only to drop to levels of despair and gloom minutes after being hit with the news headlines?

- Invasive advertising is a central feature of most entertainment and media channels. This relentless form of indoctrination only serves to reinforce the feeling of dissatisfaction, feeding you the message there's something lacking in your life and you need substantially more things to feel complete.

- Glamorised reality TV shows, soap opera dramas and social media channels, all fixated on materialism, seduction, disharmony, sexual scandal, crisis, chaos, shock and violence. All of this noise can give you the impression that serenity, harmony, stability, contentment and peace are somehow abnormal states that only a few lucky people discover.

- Socially toxic work environments (including pressure to engage with office gossip, politics, taking sides, fault-finding, judging or blaming others, and complaining) that, ultimately, force many to take the path of least resistance and simply follow the herd and conform to fit in or gain approval.

- Scepticism, distrust or ridicule from family or friends when you step out of the norm and exercise your freedom to think and act independently; for example, adopting a new spiritual practice such as meditation, starting your own business, attending study courses on holistic personal development or changing to a vegan diet. This is especially true if the activity sits outside mainstream thinking (including acts of faith, vision boarding and prayer) and can't easily be measured or validated. If people don't fully understand the choices you're making as a means of honouring your true self, they can even resent you. If you continue to ignore people and hold fast to these new values and beliefs, you can fall victim to narcissistic behaviour, which can result in you re-evaluating your decisions as being selfish or self-centred, despite the fact that you're doing no harm to others (for example, spending time alone for mindfulness, spiritual connections, clarity or self-preservation).

- Pressure from family, peers or friendship groups to get emotionally drawn into other people's problems, disputes or feuds that centre on disharmony or dysfunctionality. This can prove immensely draining and sap your energy or divert your focus from other things.

- Pressure to comply with society's limiting generalisations about what's possible, such as these: 'Life's a bitch, and then you die'; nothing has validity unless it can be seen or proven; there's not enough to go round; and we should all know our place.

When we comply automatically with any of these negative assumptions that are fed to us from our neighbouring environment, we're not thinking. This is a mental state of suffocation. The alternative is to pause, scan the horizon, exercise more awareness, listen to your intuition and respond calmly, rather than simply reacting with bias or subconscious compliance. By behaving in such a manner, you're exercising a higher level of consciousness.

When disharmony from the outside world invades your space, you can stop and ask yourself these things:

- » *Do I really have to adhere to that point of view or negative energy?*

- » *What thought choice could I replace it with that operates from a higher perspective that's centred on truth, peace or love?*

- » *Is my best decision right now not to say anything?*

- » *How can I listen to another's point of view in a calm and respectful manner without feeling angry or righteous?*

- » *Are there questions or alternative viewpoints I could explore right now that originate from an elevated point of consciousness rather than simply adhering to somebody else's opinions that, ultimately, don't serve me?*

Remember that your greatest power is choice, and you have the choice to challenge any of the examples provided earlier about *how* things supposedly *are*, and you can step back to view the horizon from a neutral or more-objective perspective.

Here are some examples:

- It's not all bad news! An infinitude of amazing, wonderful events occur every second, often right under your nose. You have the power to choose the headline that kick-starts your day! It's worth thinking critically about the information the mainstream media presents to you, who's controlling the headlines, and whether a complete, balanced and transparent story is indeed being told concerning world affairs.

- Regardless of circumstances, you always have the choice to step away from all the noise and distraction and to appreciate fully life's gifts that are immediately in front of you. Fostering a moment-to-moment state of gratitude is the best endeavour you can master in allowing further ease and flow in your life.

- Practise applying your imagination constructively by building images that reflect your heartfelt visions, free of constraints or limitations, rather than labouring on thoughts that pull you down. Remain faithful to your vision, dream big and never forget that nothing can prevent you choosing how you wish to think. The thoughts you select create your state of being, and your state of being determines your actions. Endeavour to forge an inner world infused with possibility, vision, hope and nobility, which will stand taller and broader than the narrow or restrictive outside world views.

- Try occasionally switching off the TV, mobile phone or social media channel, and then notice how these distractions swallow up your time, clear-headedness and energy, as well as rob your appreciation of clarity in the present moment.

- Personal growth toward self-empowerment seldom takes place without some form of challenge or upheaval within, but the noise in the outside world can compound this conflict, continually broadcasting the message that it's all a waste of time, it's taking too long or you don't have what it takes. However, have no doubt that, if it feels a little scary embarking on something new, you're probably heading in the right direction when it comes to forging a more meaningful and adventurous life. When we stop stretching beyond our comfort zone and place limits on how far we can raise our awareness or challenge our limiting beliefs, we deny ourselves the experience of personal alchemy.

- Reality isn't finite – you live in a quantum, holographic universe comprising infinite potentialities and opportunities (more on this concept later in Route Guidance Fifteen). The extent to which you can at least speculate on this idea is vitally important when it comes to examining your level of open-mindedness. What's more important to you: An open or closed mindset? Possibility or opportunity? Freedom or entrapment? Faith or despair?

Moving outward from these neighbouring distractions, what about the wider currents that can tug at our long-term efforts to swim against the tide? Make no mistake, setting your compass toward uncharted territory will inevitably unsettle the masses and cause them to shout, 'What are you doing that for? Why are you sailing straight into a storm? Are you mad?'

Outnumbered – a fish out of water

Never underestimate your greatest power: the right to think freely and independently while retaining humility and self-respect. It's worth considering that, long before political and ideological structures created the notion of a democratic society encompassing liberty and fraternity, humans were already ordained to thrive freely on an earth set up to provide the ideal playground in which to grow and learn. Choosing *how* you wish to think and *how* to live your life is your timeless human birthright.

It's important to open this paragraph by stressing that what's being referred to as 'personal freedom' or an 'act of self-determination' doesn't imply any wrongdoing or malicious intent toward other people or the wider world. Personal freedom carries a huge responsibility. It's probably the most important of the human rights, but it's important to consider that, when our acts of freedom infringe or affect someone else, there can only ever be one of two results: compromise or conflict.

Many of us, at some stage or another, have experienced acting in opposition to the path taken by our peers (refusing to be drawn into an argument, for example). Often, the catalyst for our abstinence in such matters is simply the notion that something doesn't feel right to us. However, what about some of the big, life-changing decisions we make, the ones that cause people's heads to turn in alarm as they scrutinise our every move? Although we never intended to disrupt or upset those around us, these acts of self-determination to move in new directions can cause severe ripples among the people closest to us. This is especially true when we attempt to initiate dramatic lifestyle changes based on gut feelings or a hunch that feels perfectly natural and beneficial to us, but to others is rather foolhardy or even naïve. This judgemental lens through which others may scrutinise our actions can cause us to check our motives, feel guilty and perhaps re-evaluate our decision.

Moving up the scale, we come to 'gaslighting', which is a covert attempt to pressure an individual to conform by making them question their sanity or perception of reality. At a group level, this subversive and manipulative pressure may be imposed by large groups of people upon a minority who are choosing to think and act in opposition to the prevailing narrative. This can include coercion in the form of urging individuals to reconsider their motives and 'do what's right' or 'not let others down'. Ultimately, this kind of pressure can cloud our ability to think critically or behave purposefully. Choosing to think outside the common narrative, which risks isolation or scrutiny from the masses, doesn't automatically grant anyone the permission to ostracise or ridicule that decision.

Sometimes, the masses justify their distrust and contempt for those who refuse to swallow the prevailing narrative by citing evidence that, at that time, appears immutable in supporting their views. However, the direction in which the masses sway isn't necessarily a reliable barometer from which to gauge what's true or false. Before the 2020–2022 Covid-19 pandemic, being seen to work entirely from home would have been regarded by the masses as rather an odd decision to make. Jump ahead to the present and working from home is regarded as quite self-evident and normal. When old habits or assumptions control our behaviours, we're often blind to the alternatives. Millions of workers never questioned the long and expensive commute to the office or imagined an alternative work ethic prior to the pandemic.

Conformity is the jailer of freedom
and the enemy of growth.
John F. Kennedy

To complicate matters, the outside pressures to conform have allies that, ironically, reside even closer to home and are disguised as self-doubt, fear or worry – which leads nicely on to the next distraction.

Disruptive Current Two: Inner currents

Low vibrational thoughts – such as negative self-talk, worry, anxiety, doubt and imagining the worst – only serve to hijack personal growth. Left unguarded over time, these emotions can transform into a state of hopelessness or even despair. If you find it hard to reorganise these thoughts, try disregarding them as perpetual requests for what you don't want. These impulses often appear to have your best interests at heart. However, they're neither noble nor courageous, and they serve only to contract your experience of a fuller life. Remind yourself continually that your natural birthright is to shine brightly, not to cower and extinguish your flame.

You may ask where to start to adopt this counterbalance attitude. As always, you begin by raising your awareness. These powerful, subversive emotions that attempt to keep us frozen in the familiar and safe comfort zones are called 'paradigms'. A paradigm is simply a fixed set of internal or external beliefs or assumptions, thought loops, theories or consensus that paints a false picture of what's possible in your life and holds you back from real growth and adventure. The personal paradigms we harbour are made up of a multitude of habits formed in the basal ganglia part of the brain. Every time you give in to a certain activity – for example, lying in bed late every morning – the brain releases the hormone dopamine. Once this behaviour has been rehearsed over time, a strong connection is formed between the basal ganglia and the reward centres within the brain. Subsequently, the habit becomes hardwired.

Finally, other inner obstacles that can hinder personal growth are the fixed mindsets and blind spots we abide by concerning other people's beliefs, culture, backgrounds and experiences. Commonly referred to as 'prejudices', these mindsets explain why two people can view the same topic in completely different ways. Unconscious bias, however, inhibits compassion, cooperation, emotional intelligence (or emotional quotient [EQ]) and spiritual growth. This is why so many spiritual disciplines encourage much empathy and tolerance. Operating in such a manner allows an individual to act with greater compassion, pausing and collecting data that builds a more accurate picture of reality that's free of prejudice or bias, even if this challenging of existing assumptions proves uncomfortable. This enlightened review of the people and circumstances in your life is thinking freely without the shackles of ignorance. Thinking and acting in this way allows a person to admit unashamedly they were wrong about something, to stand back and learn more, and to act less defensively – thus allowing deeper connectivity and better communication with wider groups or communities.

Disruptive Current Three: Global currents

The third distraction, and probably the most challenging one to navigate, is the collapse of global certainty affecting humanity. The financial crisis of 2007–2008, the Covid-19 pandemic of 2020–2022, food shortages, rising fuel prices, job insecurity and continual global conflict are all recent reminders of unimaginable global change that can strike without warning. For many people, these dramatic global circumstances serve only to solidify the notion that it's pointless to keep an optimistic outlook on life when far larger negative global issues loom, imposing disharmony and fear.

There are no quick fixes to prevent or avoid this kind of uncertainty. How we react and rise above the challenge is, however, a matter of choice. Huge upheaval will no doubt continue to affect the human race until a spiritual transformation occurs, during which humanity takes full responsibility for addressing the imbalance within, while at the same time healing and reconnecting with love and compassion toward each other and the earth. With this in mind, until that time arrives, your only focus during these hard times right now is to remain true to who you are, be kind to yourself, be the best you can, and serve others through love and understanding.

Catch your fear and net your inner FISH

Fish rarely leave the ocean and reach for the sky above unless they're flying fish, and even for them, their excursions are brief. You can use this analogy to help you appreciate and remember that stepping out of the norm is rare, and everything around you will reinforce the risks and pitfalls associated with such a move, but this doesn't mean you should simply give up and never stretch your wings. The only way to combat this perspective is by raising your awareness and understanding some of the subconscious limiting emotions and behaviours that will inevitably rise up as a consequence. Sticking with the nautical theme and the topic of fear – let's fish it out!

FISH

Fish stands for the following:

FISH = Fear, Is it worth it?, Suspicion, Hard work

Fear

But what is fear?
Nothing neither more nor less than the negative use of faith...
Ernest Holmes (1998, p.156)

The emotion of fear is produced by the amygdala, which is positioned at the base of the brain and is responsible for releasing adrenalin.

Fear can be broadly categorised under these types:

A. **Phobias or fear of the unexplained** – fear of spiders, flying (it's estimated that between 33 and 40 per cent of people have a general fear of flying [Deane, 2022]), snakes, the dentist, death, events out of your control, ghosts, etc.

B. **Growth, challenge or change** – risk, ridicule, the unknown, uncertainty or failure.

Before we examine fear further, it's essential to ponder a significant truth: fear hijacks your freedom and autonomy. Playing it safe is no life, and abiding by fear equals ignorance.

Babies are natural risk-takers – we're not born afraid, yet all the way through childhood, many adults and teachers instil in young children the idea that fear *may* be encountered or, at most, avoided. Instead, children should learn to embrace the idea that there's no *may* about it: fear will be encountered, and building resilience around fear is an essential life skill. It's estimated that the average two-year-old child hears 432 negative statements per day compared with thirty-two positive statements each day (Lenoir, 2016). Much of our psychology, including beliefs around fear and risk, is a by-product of someone else's programming.

Children should have opportunities to explore the idea that, although some fears are based on very real experiences, many fears are falsely generated and contain no substance, but they're perceived to be real. If left unattended, they develop into beliefs, which in turn translate into debilitating emotional behaviour. Once the sensation of fear is assimilated and learnt, the body is put on heightened alert. It doesn't matter whether the fear is imagined, the body still responds by displaying automatic reactions; for example, waking up in a sweat following a nightmare involving your biggest phobias. Even when you try not to think about certain hardwired fears, they still pop up in your head.

When we operate from the familiar, doing what we've always done and playing it safe, there's no reason for fear to surface, because in this state, risk and challenge have been minimised. The problem is that we can never truly grow from this risk-aversive state of consciousness.

Challenging the status quo, embracing risk, stepping out of the norm, or embarking on paths of self-discovery or entrepreneurism trigger a single emotional response: all hell breaks loose internally! Upsetting this equilibrium and positioning ourselves into vulnerable or unfamiliar circumstances also unsettles the ego's hold, throwing us into a state of victimisation or self-pity.

Personal growth, however, requires us to stretch, admit we don't have all the answers and face uncomfortable learning challenges occasionally. Any successful entrepreneur will tell you that fears have to be overcome in order to advance an idea or product with the world.

Both faith and fear cause you to believe in something you can't always see, but fear lacks the nobility and wisdom of faith. When faced with psychological fear, most take a safe step back into the known as the flight or fight approach kicks in. The brave and courageous, however, adopt a different approach – they recognise the signs, assume the risk is worth taking, sacrifice security or the comfort of the known for a nobler cause, take a deep breath, and then move right on.

For many, this type of decisive action is often left far too late in life, triggered by sudden personal crises, a serious medical diagnosis or trauma. This is the point at which we finally throw the towel in and say, '*That's it, I'm doing it... I'm simply not going to be that person any more – it's change or perish!*'

Nothing great is achieved until our natural resistance to facing fear is tempered. This may involve tackling issues very close to home (for example, bad habits, procrastination, or even fear of what our peers, family or loved ones might say). When we face fear head on, we're initially cloaked in feelings of isolation and detachment, but when we eventually pass through the curtain of fear, we shed limiting beliefs, redefine who we are and rise to new heights of self-respect. We can then step out into the world, set an example and inspire others to follow in our footsteps.

One of the most powerful ways in which skilful orators connect and empathise with their fellow human beings is through sharing personal stories demonstrating how fear and struggle were overcome. It's for this reason that the most successful and engaging business pitches often begin with a narrative comprising three essential ingredients:

1. The hero is trapped or facing fearful danger.

2. The hero walks an unfamiliar path accompanied or supported by an ally.

3. The hero overcomes adversity, attracts followers and triumphs, releasing a higher calling and personal transformation.

Although it may not appear immediately obvious, deep within you there lies a similar narrative if you look hard enough. While this experience can feel incredibly at odds with what everybody else is doing, this venture will in due course reveal the hero within you, allowing you to share more of whom you truly are with the world. At the opposite end of the spectrum, yielding to fear and compromise will ultimately equate to losing an enthusiasm for life. This is why entrepreneurs, great visionaries and ambassadors for change never compromise their attitude concerning fear, instead affirming this: *fear, bring it on!*

One big truth of life is that fulfilment emerges as a by-product of this adventure, not through acts of complacency, neglect or procrastination. Fear is simply interference and living a fearless life is a lie.

When fear strikes, go to speak with those who excel at achieving amazing things or walk exciting and less-familiar paths. Ask them to rank which of the following qualities deliver the largest sense of meaning or buzz in life: happiness, fulfilment or adventure. Examine how they accomplish personal satisfaction in life. Study the trials and tribulations of the great visionaries, explorers, inventors and pioneers, many of whom stood alone or unsupported during their lowest points. When you do, you'll discover that fear isn't a thing or entity to slay, but it's a false perception that diminishes its hold with each courageous and persistent step forward.

My wise aunt once said this: 'Fear, pain and discomfort have one thing in common with jubilation, joy and ecstasy: they're seldom permanent and shall pass!'

Suggestions for overcoming type-A fears

- ✓ Recognise your habitual thought routes when confronted with fear, and then experiment by replacing them with alternative empowering messages.

- ✓ Reframe your situation and experiment by telling a different story (for example, face the fear and do it anyway, knowing courage, self-respect, strength and more freedom will emerge as a by-product).

- ✓ Study the law of polarity (what may appear to be bad has to have an opposite good contained within it).

- ✓ Exercise the power of choice by distracting your mind away from catastrophising or change your inner dialogue. This can be done by practising steady breathing exercises, counting slowly to ten, or calming and centring your emotions by pinching your finger as a means of reminding yourself to trigger alternative feel-good thoughts or emotions.

- ✓ Remind yourself of your spiritual origin and that you have the ability to choose to look beyond the obvious; practise letting go, remaining present, visualising a perfect resolution, or asking for divine strength or guidance.

Suggestions for overcoming type-B fears

- ✓ Learn to embrace, affirm and visualise the fact that you can do anything you set your mind to.

✓ Reverse the word 'can't' by affirming, 'My mind is a centre of divine operation' (Thomas Troward), or simply say, 'I can – just watch me.'

✓ Embrace the idea that no growth is possible without some form of failure – you'll never grow in a comfort zone. At the very least, you'll learn something new about yourself following your experience.

✓ Study the exploits of some of history's great pioneers or visionaries (Emmeline Pankhurst, the Wright brothers, Nelson Mandela or Rosa Louise McCauley Parks), and find out how they overcame fear.

✓ Combat fear by developing an understanding that belief is all that matters.

✓ Remind yourself continually that any previous success in your life came about through overcoming some form of fear or challenge and taking small steps through the highs and lows.

✓ Begin small and scale-up fast. Remember big trees emerge from small shoots.

✓ Keep going, do it anyway and think of the rewards (courage, strength, liberty and freedom). Challenging and growing yourself isn't the same as gambling or acting irresponsibly. Bet instead on the best thing going – yourself!

✓ Imagine jumping ahead in time to when you're older. Will you look back on life with regret that you didn't face your fear to do the things you really wanted to? Do you wish to develop a life in which you're proud of your accomplishments or simply play it safe?

Is it worth it?

Fear harbours an ally – the repetitive inner voice of procrastination, which will try to pull you back to the known. It's disguised in four simple words: 'Is it worth it?' This seemingly simple phrase is highly invasive because it reminds you continually that risk carries uncertainty. There are no guarantees on the journey of life, but you can guarantee a lifetime of regret if you fail to act on the one thing that matters most to your soul: growth. For this reason, be on guard against one of the most disruptive comments that certain people will throw at you, which merely serves to reinforce the message 'Is it worth it?' This is often disguised as, 'Oh, I tried that, but it didn't work for me!'

Suspicion

If we successfully navigate the first gatekeeper of fear ('Is it worth it?'), we inevitably encounter the next fear distraction – suspicion!

Suspicion can include disempowering self-talk such as the following:

- *Oh, you just want to have your cake and eat it!*
- *You're never satisfied!*
- *Be careful dabbling with things you don't fully understand or that haven't been quantified by science.*
- *What could you lose?*
- *You're being swallowed up by some else's warped opinion.*
- *Are you sure you have it in you?*
- *Why make changes at this point? Don't you have enough going on?*
- *Why would you give up so much for something you can't guarantee?*
- *How long is this going to take you? You've been at it for ages.*

It's at this stage that you'll have to employ all your focus and resolve to seek out the support and guidance from the mentors or allies you value the most, who'll provide wisdom and guidance during difficult times. These are the people who truly understand the message you're trying to share with the world and go out of their way to inspire and motivate you consistently.

Whatever you do, avoid asking the opinion of those who never step out of their comfort zone or frequently play it safe. These people could indeed be your best friends, partner or family.

These are some other examples of disempowering assumptions based on suspicion:

- *I can't endorse solutions to my problems that I can't see or prove. I'll do it if someone can guarantee a result.*

- *My negative situation is all someone else's fault.*

- *It's bound to go wrong.* (predicting the worst outcome)

- *It's alright for them.* (making negative comparisons)

- *That's just how it is!* (accepting lack and limitation)

Hard work

Finally, the last gatekeeper deployed during your adventure into the unknown is the fear of hard work. It may sound obvious, and no one can escape the fact that choosing a bold path of personal growth and transformation is just that – hard work. Personal growth requires concentration, resilience, patience, persistence, focus and determination. At the very instant you contemplate creating a dramatic change in your life, a barrage of easily accessible and enticing habits will inevitably raise their heads (for example, waking too late, losing yourself watching TV and putting off things that feel uncomfortable), and like a tug-of-war opponent, they'll assiduously bellow, *'Give in; come my way. You know it's too hard!'*

The good news is that this opponent (another paradigm) is the voice in your own head, and because it's close to home, it's easy to corner. Once isolated, its hold can be softened by reminding yourself continually of what you'll lose in terms of self-respect and fulfilment if you give in and stay grounded in your comfort zone. Couple this approach with revisiting inspiring books that uplift and reinvigorate your resolve. Make yourself accountable by investing in the support of someone you respect, who will monitor your progress. Diligence and resolve are vital, and it may feel like a marathon at times, but the best marathon runners are those who pay close attention to the rhythm of each of their strides while also remaining alert to what's unfolding around them.

These are other examples of disempowering self-talk that can arise when you consider executing sustained periods of hard work:

- *The information is too complex, and it will take too long.*

- *I don't have what it takes. Good fortune doesn't happen to people like me.*

- *There's too much going on in my outside world; other people need my attention.*

- *Why bother with all the fuss? Life doesn't work like that!*

- *I haven't got enough time, and there's too much to do.*

- *It will take too much effort to get out of the rut of making negative assumptions.*

- *I'm too ahead of my time. Do I really want to disrupt the norm and thus make it harder for myself? Is this approach really worth it?*

- *I bet other people don't spend as long as I do on getting this done.*

- *What if no one wants what I've been working on for so long? Where do I go from there?*

- *No one else I know makes life this complicated and arduous.*

There may be no heroic connotation to the word 'persistence', but the quality is to the character of man what carbon is to steel.
Napoleon Hill (2009, p.229)

Liberate your perception of self
and unlock the control of your emotions,
and then you'll achieve your desires.

Route Guidance Six
How to grow more fearless

Nothing in life is to be feared. It is only to be understood.

Marie Curie

One morning, Dael discovered an unusual note posted through his letter box. To Dael's surprise it was a page ripped out from Lead's diary:

Dear Dael,

I just had to share this story, considering your stage on the journey of self-discovery. Last night, I took myself out for a late-night walk, looking for inspiration on the subject of fear. Fear can rule your life, but it's a low rate of vibration. Fear attacks your confidence, immunity levels, energy and clear-headedness.

Something happened yesterday that made me feel doubtful and scared. Getting outdoors was my only solace. Then I looked up and noticed a beautiful full moon. It was shining brightly and bold against the darkness, but, of course, the light it emitted originated from an entirely different source — the sun.

That got me thinking. In the same way that a dark and desolate rock in space can be transformed into a bright beacon, just by being bathed in the light from the sun, millions of miles away, so too can the apparent immutability and darkness of fear be transformed by being doused in the light of hope and faith.

You see, you can't remove or destroy fear through willpower alone.

But you can shed light on it and reveal it for what it is: rather like the moon, it's a desolate and lifeless collection of rocks and dust!

When you do, you release your birthright to imagine a future in which you shine and act out your vision unbounded and courageous.

Best wishes, Lead

The seven perspectives for a fearless mindset

The following are seven perspectives to consider when forging a more fearless mindset. The most effective way to internalise these fresh attitudes is to make a habit of reading this chapter carefully every morning before you step out into the world.

1. Limitless potential

Begin by endorsing the idea that you have limitless potential.

Timeless mystical teachings and ancient sacred texts written with the sole aim of liberating the mind and advancing human consciousness toward greater acts of love and tolerance all agree on the following premises:

- ✓ You have infinite potential.

- ✓ You become what you think about!

- ✓ A shift in inner awareness is reflected in what you experience or attract in your outside world.

- ✓ When you change the way *you* look at the outside world, the outside world changes accordingly.

- ✓ Your biggest gift in determining the direction of your life (if used in the right manner) is taking your focus away from the finite thoughts of limitation delivered by your senses and choosing instead to grow more aware of the limitless creative power of your imagination.

This power begins with developing a mindset for real momentum.
The first mark of such a mindset is
believing that reality is bendable to our will.
Those who lack this belief never advance with great
power and constancy.
Brendon Burchard (2014, p.138)

What's the most powerful creative force in the universe? The answer (drumroll) is *you*!

Start by considering your amazing physical body and the invisible forces that sustain the life within you. Without having to spare a thought, the organs in your body perform incredibly complex operations, such as cleaning out toxins, repairing and growing new cells, chasing off infection, and transforming food into energy and growth. These facts, however, pale into insignificance compared to the creative mental forces contained within imagination.

You're one of a kind and have access to the unique, spiritually driven, infinite supercomputer called your mind. Your mind ignites the spark of divinity every time you birth a new creative thought or imagine vast possibilities. This is what's meant by the term 'mind power', but a more accurate definition of 'mind' is 'thought in movement'. This is where the phrases 'you are what you think' and 'thoughts become things' are derived from. No one has ever seen the mind or calibrated its limitless depths of potential, but this shouldn't stop you from exploring and pursuing that deep sense of knowing within yourself that there's far more to you than meets the eye. There's only one way to expedite this process – and hopefully, you're fully familiar with the term by now – yes, you've guessed it: raising your awareness.

2. Identifying your spiritual I-ness above and beyond fear and limitation

*The real voyage of discovery consists not
in seeking new landscapes,
but in having new eyes.*

Marcel Proust

Presumably, when you selected this guidebook, you had the thought, *There's information here that might help my ability to find more fulfilment in my world of work.*

Let's begin by examining the terms 'my' and 'me'. You're you – an entity – and a pretty amazing one at that:

*I gaze through eyes,
but perceive within mind.
My touch without fingers
is a different kind.*

*I set free with a voice
the echo inside.
A truth heard without ears
is for me to decide.*

*I recognise a fragrance,
although not through my nose.
I am that I am –
God's presence that grows.*

(Dedicated to my wonderful mentor Alex Naylor, 23rd January 2023)

When you began life, you were already a miracle as a result of having overcome all the odds to get here in the first place.

As you grew up, your individuality and sense of self were predominately reinforced by the ego, but there are many layers to you. It's a bit like the layers of an onion: when we peel back our behavioural façades and mental chatter, we eventually arrive at a place of silence: our spiritual heart or true self, pure consciousness or self-awareness – the I am that I am. This is the perspective that stands outside the ego – the authentic core of your being infused with spiritual energy. Energy can't be created or destroyed: it's infinite and everlasting. Think of this as a bit like the (life) 'force' that was so well articulated in the *Star Wars* films.

You're an individualised aspect of the universal spirit, transcending time and space. Spirit is omnipresent, which means it's in all places at the same time. There are no boundaries to the infinitude within you. The essence of your soul is peace, acceptance and love. Your soul will never look outward to blame everything on others or events. Your soul delivers a sense of security and harmony, and it knows you already have all you'll ever need. No question is unanswerable and no vision is impossible. This is worth remembering when you find yourself succumbing to the distractive inner voice explored earlier, such as thinking, *Oh, I'm useless!* or *I don't have it in me!*

You can't achieve anything until you believe you can have it, so it might be a good idea to review your current beliefs:

>> *How comfortable are you with the idea that you're a channel or conduit for infinite abundance in a universe geared up for expansion?*

>> *Can you imagine that, as your awareness grows, so too does the evolution of the universe?*

>> *Do you argue for your limitation or envision a wonderful future of embracing your limitless potential that can open up endless possibilities?*

» *Do you accept the idea that any aspect of your life (financial, health, relationships or career situation) could change with a shift in consciousness?*

» *How open are you to the idea that you have the ability and birthright to allow greater ease and serendipity in your life? Are your work and lifestyle activities centred on exhaustive acts of force or a gentler process of allowance or flow?*

» *How open are you to the idea that you have access to infinite guidance and wisdom channelled through your imagination as you calm your mind and body through the act of meditation?*

» *Do you think first before uttering the words 'I am...' followed by a list of adjectives ('I am sick of...' or 'I am terrible at...')? Do you understand the immense power contained in such acts of self-declaration?*

3. Keep the ego in check

You may be asking what the ego has to do with becoming more fearless. The ego is fragile, highly reactive and thrives on fear and defensiveness. Only the ego seeks advice from your fears. It searches out threats everywhere and proceeds to pull you back to the familiar, rather than have you repeat an experience that went horribly wrong in the past.

The ego is the part of your personality that creates the sensation of self, separateness or identity, along with owning or acquiring certain things of value. Your ego takes everything personally and is continually dissatisfied. Its purpose is to provide a sense of identification by comparing or contrasting itself to others. This can involve standing out, jumping ahead of the line, disregarding others' opinions, acting overly judgemental, making comparisons and achieving satisfaction through an accomplishment that helps reinforce the feeling of superiority. The ego hates criticism, but it encourages self-pity, pride, emotional neediness, inferiority, drama, resentment, rightfulness or detachment immersed in self-importance.

The notion of replacing this fixation with a state of allowance and an embracement of uncertainty, flow or contentment in the present moment makes no sense to the ego. At best, the ego serves to help us remain self-assured, focused or assertive in order to get things done. At worst, the ego is rooted in suffering – in complete contrast to the spiritual identification involving thoughts and actions centred on love, peace, harmony, surrender and contentment in the present moment. When operating at this higher level of consciousness, an individual is far more likely to achieve fulfilment as a natural by-product of how they're doing something, rather than obsessing over how long it takes or where it might potentially get them to. Whenever you're faced with a fearful situation, try to stop, be still and listen to your soul.

4. The importance of being yourself

A key author and orator of the new thought movement at the turn of the twentieth century was Thomas Troward. He possessed a deep understanding of certain spiritual qualities that lie within all of us. Troward wrote extensively on the invisible mind power we have at our disposal to transcend limitation and fear, and he also wrote in-depth about the importance of being yourself and developing what you already have.

Some of his most eloquent teachings include these:

- Spirit is pure life and expresses itself by flowing into form. We don't need to go any further to find this life-giving energy. All we have to do is allow it to rise to the surface like the water in an artesian well – continuous and inexhaustible. This force doesn't need to grow, it just requires our recognition of it! You're already a light in the darkness; your job isn't to strike the match but to burn brighter, degree by degree!

- So many are trying to be somebody else or trying to go one better, which results in endless strain and struggle. Live naturally with yourself, otherwise you'll attract unnecessary weariness and labour! Release negative thoughts about yourself. Instead, focus on the power within you and the positive things you can do.

- It's perfectly noble to have aspirations and challenging goals that stretch us, and we can do this by simply following an ideal that's always a stage ahead of us. The attainment of these goals is a matter of growth! This growth must be the expansion of something that's already in us. So, where we are and what we are to begin with must be the logical starting point.

- We should feel confident and relaxed in employing a force much larger than we believe ourselves to be. It is, after all, part of us.

- There's no need to travel huge distances to find the right spiritual teacher or to labour over theology to attain this spiritual connection, because the connection is already in us. Many fantasise about the idea of jumping to some idealised future, but we can only reach it by continuing steadily from where we are.

- Neither force nor strain are required. What's more important is to stop trying to be something you're not. Just do what you're able to do today, as this subsequently opens another tomorrow. This is a lot easier than trying to compel things. It's not, however, about sitting around being lazy and waiting for things to happen; it's a matter of fully applying your mental faculties to the task in hand. Use your will power wisely by focusing your assumptions on beautiful and empowering things. Allow events to evolve naturally from this premise. By doing these things, you'll learn to appreciate that we have all that's necessary for our unlimited development for a bright and abundant future!

- Rather than making things happen, it's about expressing what and who we are. We realise the treasures that are already ours and celebrate all that we are now!

- When we embody all of the aforementioned points, we'll astonish ourselves with the possibilities that arise.

5. Abundance is your birthright

You can't fear lack and limitation or dwell continually on worst-case scenarios if you truly believe abundance is your birthright. You may ask, 'If abundance is my birthright, why does it appear so difficult to access?' The answer lies in most people's definition and relationship with the term 'abundance', which, of course, normally centres on the accumulation of money. You're already naturally wealthy, simply by being alive and because like attracts like, so it's important to start with your own beliefs about the experience of abundance. If you begin by developing the habit of fully appreciating the natural abundance that surrounds you and then remain in that vibration, you're far more likely to experience some form of financial equivalence further on.

The most valuable form of abundance is actually peace of mind, but few people achieve this, because they begin looking for answers to life in the wrong places.

Simply stepping outdoors into green spaces will allow you to connect with the essence of abundance flowing through nature. You can use this opportunity to give thanks in sacred moments of mindfulness. When you allow for more opportunities for peace and harmony in the ordinary, everyday events of your life, you'll naturally attract similar experiences in your outer world and innately become more self-assured. This includes the people you'll attract into your life and the wisdom they'll share. Simply saying thank you for the things that so many take for granted (for example, health, natural wonders, friendships, family and freedom) can be a fantastic starting point.

Finding your purpose, doing more of what you love and serving others will also contribute to your experience of abundance. When you discover this form of prosperity, ideas flow with greater ease, and you'll have more energy to focus on the things that matter most to you. The timeless saying, 'the answers lie within', becomes even more relevant when we embody an attitude of appreciation, not just for things in our outside world but also for the natural abundance we harbour within.

6. Self-awareness first

IT IS only by a change of consciousness, by actually changing your concept of yourself, that you can 'build more stately mansions' – the manifestations of higher and higher concepts.
Neville Goddard (2010, p.5)

Beliefs centred on fear are very often stored subconsciously. This often creates a problem when people focus on a single desire, assuming they're generating the appropriate thoughts to aid in its accomplishment, but they instead unwittingly trigger a set of opposite beliefs. Your guidebook will examine this process in more detail later (in Route Guidance Thirteen). The only solution to tackling this problem is growing more self-aware and studying how your mind works.

The whole premise of the LEAD concept – for supporting your growth and development – is that you need to know who and what you are (this includes your mind) first before you can move forward with your dreams and goals. Even the satellite navigation device in your car has to identify where you are first before it can direct you to where you want to go.

7. You're not alone

Finally, remind yourself you're not alone on this journey of self-discovery. The global expansion of the internet has had a fundamental effect on allowing millions to access information that was previously cloaked in mystery and secrecy.

The self-development movement, popularised throughout the 1960s, has grown exponentially in recent years, and there's a plethora of social media channels and blogs continually reinventing new ways to communicate and entertain their viewers with empowering information. The global shift in interest in this *uncommon knowledge* relating to our potential is extraordinary.

For the first time in human history, the quest to refine personal meaning, purposefulness and connection is now top priority. For millions of people, this endeavour to discover more about themselves isn't simply a matter of acting inquisitively, but is acting out of necessity.

Furthermore, scientists are continually discovering new facts about the brain and the power of intention. This has ignited a wider interest in neuroplasticity (the ability of the brain, throughout its lifespan, to be shaped, moulded, or altered in response to thought or intention, and then adapt or change over time by creating new neurons and building new neuro networks). If the brain is such a responsive organ, this has huge implications when we re-examine our ability to change certain negative patterns of thinking and develop more-empowering mindsets or abilities.

So why should all this information matter to you right now? Put simply, you couldn't be living at a better time in history to gather up a myriad of resources to support your quest to unlock your potential, and this includes acting more fearlessly, as millions are now walking the same path as the one you're on.

How fearless do you think you can be?

Here's an affirmation for you:

'When my fear situation becomes intolerable, regardless of all the noise, I always retain the right and power to choose the way I'm thinking. This begins by regularly reviewing the information in the first route guidance in my guidebook.'

Tough times never last, but tough people do!

Dr Robert H. Schuller

Liberate your perception of self
and unlock the control of your emotions,
and then you'll achieve your desires.

Route Guidance Seven
The five colours of health, vitality and balance

The first wealth is health.

Ralph Waldo Emerson

One day, Dael asked Lead how she defined 'well-being' and what practical steps she undertook to maintain optimum health and balance.

Lead replied in her usual engaging manner by asking Dael a direct question. 'What are you, Dael?'

'Well... I'm a lizard, of course!' replied Dael.

'Yes, you most certainly are, and the letters contained in the word "lizard" will provide us with the perfect starting point to help you remember the holistic aspects associated with good health and well-being.'

True to fashion, with the tip of her tail, Lead carefully sketched another message in the sandy jungle earth:

Liberation = ingest, zest, abundance, relationships, discipline

The first letter of each word spelt out the word 'LIZARD'.

Below this definition, Lead sketched a further breakdown relating five of the words to a colour:

Lizard = liberation, ingest, zest, abundance, relationships, discipline

Ingest (green) – monitoring the nutrition you put into your body as well as the particular information or messages you're placing in your mind from the outside world

Zest (yellow) – energy, movement, agility and exercise

Abundance (orange) – an evolving spiritual connection to self and the universe

Relationships (blue) – healthy emotional intelligence (or emotional quotient [EQ]) and communication with community, colleagues, family and friends

Discipline (red) – growth mindset, focus, concentration, willpower and personal leadership

'Well, when you put it like that, that's easy to remember!' exclaimed Dael.

'Yeah, I thought you'd like it! To be a completely fulfilled, full of life, zesty LIZARD, you'll need all five well-being colours embedded. Have you noticed that – unlike most chameleons, who show a single skin colour – I emanate these five distinct colours all at the same time?'

Dael chuckled. 'Yes, I was wondering about that.'

'It's pretty comprehensive, but can you see how each colour stands for a different aspect of health? The trick is keeping all five in good nick, because if one is lacking, it ultimately affects all the others and thus your overall sense of holistic well-being. However, the most important aspect of well-being, which is both a product and input, is the ability to feel **liberated**. When you're liberated emotionally and intellectually, you're better prepared to take responsibility for all of the other five well-being qualities. Personal leadership requires self-awareness and self-discipline. The state of liberation is a bit like being fully informed, responsible or awake!

'When you take an honest review of these LIZARD colours, you paint a clearer picture of where your strengths or shortfalls may occur relative to your overall health.'

Dael hastily reviewed the colour chart sketched into the sand.

Lead continued, 'For example, I know a friend who has recently reviewed their colours and discovered they weren't keeping themselves adequately hydrated throughout the day (the colour green). They also realised that most of their food intake was based around dry, salty and processed meals. They addressed this imbalance by drinking more water and beginning alternate days by consuming a nutritious, organic, green smoothie. They also kept a simple food diary in which they recorded the basic overall nutritional content of each meal (fibre, carbohydrates, proteins, vitamins, minerals and unsaturated fats) and checked these were balanced.

'When it came to the colour yellow, they made a commitment to take a brisk walk through the jungle occasionally rather than simply hopping on the back of the leopard express to get home from work. They also began attending an evening meditation class once a week and keeping a daily gratitude journal. These activities, of course, are represented by the colour orange.

'They gave their blue colour some much needed attention by making a concerted effort to practise greater acts of empathy and compassion toward the creatures they worked alongside. This wasn't overly complicated, and it just meant they made an effort to ask people occasionally how they were or offer a helping hand without being asked. They soon became known as the uplifting character at work who brought a smile to everyone's faces simply by sharing a little unconditional warmth or humility.

'Finally, my friend developed the red aspect of well-being by studying, over breakfast each morning, a paragraph from a book centred on inspiration or true wisdom.

'Thriving lizards look after all five well-being colours because they understand it's essential for supporting their holistic roadmap to optimum growth and fulfilment. As you know, we chameleons never stop growing.

'My colour blue on the well-being spectrum is fulfilled by regularly inspiring and guiding others toward enlightenment. That's why I asked so many questions that first day we met. I care about you and I wanted to find out as much as possible. You see, I feel energised, purposeful and connected when I inspire other jungle animals.'

Dael looked puzzled and asked, 'Can you explain a little more about the colour green? I mean why there are two aspects to ingestion?'

'Ingestion basically refers to elements that you absorb into your body and mind,' Lead explained. 'There are two specific aspects that relate to the term "ingestion": 1. food and how you're fuelling your body, and 2. your mental or psychological information intake.

'Taking the first example, are the foods you're consuming energising and fuelling your body? Are you considering the impact various foods have on your body, mood and performance, once they've been ingested? For example, swapping processed, sugar-based breakfast cereals for organic porridge or oatmeal will provide you with a healthier, longer-lasting energy boost throughout your day.

'The second aspect refers to psychological ingestion. For example, what are you studying and who are you listening to regularly? How do you protect your mind from harbouring despondency? Do you have strategies to combat worry, doubt and insecurity?'

Planning: The key to greater health, vitality and balance

Dael thought for a moment and then asked a further question: 'Don't you think time is the issue here? Most of my lizard friends say they never have enough time to do everything you've highlighted.'

Lead replied, 'There's a common misconception that preparing healthy meals or adding exercise routines into your day requires too much effort or time. Many creatures simply feel overwhelmed. Begin by writing out a list of objectives. What do you want to achieve? Is your aim to lose weight, detoxify, look better, nourish your bodily organs, release energy or feel more confident in the clothes you wear? Simply clarifying your 'why' will help focus your commitment and create a sense of purpose.

'Next, begin to plan. Planning and focus are key. If you want to improve your diet, for example, begin by listing carefully the weekly foods you intend to purchase before you visit the jungle supermarket. Randomly preparing meals is one key factor that creates unhealthy dietary habits. When it comes to preparing meals, the secret is keeping to simple things that slot into your daily lifestyle. It sounds obvious, but creating healthy food solutions that you actually enjoy is vital. Could you bulk cook and freeze healthy meals to use at later times? This is an excellent way to save time and effort. What do you have planned for the week ahead and where will you be? Do you have outdoor space to grow your own vegetables and fruits? Other small dietary changes such as reducing sugar or salt intake in your food don't actually impact on time.

'Drinking a glass of water in the morning with a hint of lemon juice, rather than two cups of strong black coffee, is another change you can easily make that will cleanse your body. Other examples include replacing high-sugar cereals with a green smoothie for breakfast, eating nuts or fruit rather than processed snacks between meals, adding a handful of blueberries to porridge rather than sugar, and eating an orange at lunch rather than a cereal bar. Of course, hydration is important.

'Remember that your body is sixty-five per cent water. Your biological system operates more effectively when it's sufficiently hydrated. Fluid is required to transport nutrients around your body and renew your biological systems. Also don't forget that, at the microscopic level, your body's cells are water based. Regarding the quantity of water you should drink daily, I always drink a sensible amount: say, one and a half litres.

'Without overdoing the process, just be aware, check yourself throughout the day and ask, "Am I taking care of the hydration requirements of my body?" Note the changes in your mood when you're adequately hydrated. You'll feel more alert, energised and positively focused. Remember that leafy, green food sources plucked fresh the same day will contain water and are easily absorbed by the stomach, so nutrients can be released quickly and efficiently around the body. Furthermore, don't forget the brain requires adequate hydration to perform well, especially when its engaged in solving problems or studying.

'You could try applying the ZEN principle, which was created by the author and fitness coach Mike Hendricks, as a key strategy for supporting a healthy lifestyle. The Z stands for "Zero refined foods" (foods close to source and as nature intended). The E stands for "foods that are Energy rich". The N stands for "foods that will Nourish, repair and aid the healthy function of the body".'

'I'm always snacking on the wrong sorts of meals, which I'm sure aren't ideal for me, such as fast food, and salty and dry snacks, but it's so appealing. It's really hard to break the cycle. Why is that?' he enquired.

'That's partly due to the habits we've inherited from our ancient ancestors, who had to eat whenever food was available,' Lead answered. 'This primal food-craving habit remains within us. When our stomach detects it's empty, it releases a hormone called "ghrelin" from the stomach walls, which results in the craving to snack that you referred to.

'The problem is that we tend to make the mistake of reaching for the foods that will provide us with a quick fix by delivering satisfying sugars throughout the body. Within minutes, these sugars are used up and we crave more. This is compounded as the brain releases the chemical dopamine, which serves the addiction even further, driving us toward consuming more salty or sugary snacks. Instead, try to consume foods and drinks that release energy slowly over a longer period of time, such as fruit (because of the fructose), 100 per cent wholegrain foods, milk (because of the lactose), non-starchy vegetables, avocado and nuts.'

Dael drilled down further on these issues: 'The problem is that it's hard to maintain this level of commitment. Do you have any suggestions on how we can help ourselves stay on track?'

She thought for a moment. 'Excellent question, my friend. I think there are several key points. First, be clear on your vision – create a weekly or monthly plan. Celebrate the moment-to-moment accomplishments and break your grand goal into manageable, small steps. There's no need to have everything done in one go, and remember to take time out occasionally. Next, understand it's perfectly normal to feel some form of unease. Remember, when you step out of your comfort zone and start something challenging or new, knowing it will stretch your capabilities, it can feel rather unsettling. However, hold firm because this is a sign that you're inviting positive or worthy changes into your life. Finally, try to inject as much fun or play into your goals as possible. Reward yourself when a milestone is achieved.'

Five points of balance to energise your work

Lead (always full of surprises) startled Dael by jumping up suddenly onto a termite hill and holding a pose in which she balanced her entire weight on one front leg and the tip of her tail. For a moment, she held her position with extreme grace and dexterity before beaming at him, her mouth ajar and her eyebrows raised in an expression that was obviously intended to throw both lizards into fits of hysterical laughter. Her plan worked, as the two friends collapsed on the forest floor, laughing uncontrollably and rolling around like juvenile lizards, gasping for breath between fits of giggles.

'What was all that about?' he panted.

'Ah, the final secret I wish to share, my friend, when it comes to remaining energised is maintaining the appropriate balance of activities in your week – hence the rather dramatic pose,' Lead explained. 'Normally, we lizards retain balance by resting all four feet on the jungle floor, but when we're fooling around on tree branches, we deploy our tail as an extra grasping aid, of course, just in case we accidentally swing upside down, for example.'

'Yes – just like the monkeys.'

'Indeed, but this brings me to the point. How many points of contact do we have when it comes to maintaining a state of maximum balance and composure?'

'Well... five, I suppose.'

'Yes – five indeed. Now look.'

Lead etched out a further five letters on the side of the sandy termite hill, much to the disgust of an army of ants, who hastily scurried around trying to minimise the damage. She then completed the acronym:

POISE = Productivity, Outdoors, Inactivity, Socialise, Eat

*'When you think of your week ahead,' she suggested, 'try to plot how and where you might deploy these **five points of balance**. It's very important not to skip any of the points if you want to reap the full benefit. Obviously, each activity doesn't require the same amount of time to complete. It's*

more a case of visiting each and creating a collective set of habits. When you've completed all five, you can start at the beginning again. The order of each activity is unimportant. Let me go through each letter in POISE.

'P stands for "productivity". Put simply, this relates to your work. To feel productive, you must ensure that you complete some of your work tasks or at least cross things off your job list. We all need to feel productive from time to time.

'O stands for "outdoors". It's important to walk, stretch and exercise moderately in nature. This could include a long walk through a dense forest or a jog around the prairies. It could include working in the garden or tending to a vegetable plot. The essential thing is just to get outside and breathe fresh air while absorbing nature's green therapy.

'I stands for "inactivity". Ensure you spend some time resting or connecting with your spiritual centre (through meditation, prayer or yoga). This may simply involve sleep or relaxing at the Firefly Coffee House, watching the pelicans fly past or losing yourself in a good book.

'S stands for "socialise". Going a whole week without spending some time with someone outside of the needs of your immediate family isn't healthy. Time spent merely chatting, playing and relaxing with a friend provides a vital contribution to your sense of connection and meaning.

'Finally, the letter E stands for "eat". To reaffirm the points made earlier regarding maintaining a balanced diet, try beginning the week by consuming a breakfast that's rich in lush, leafy greens and fruits packed with antioxidants, such as spinach leaves or blueberries, respectively. These food sources must enrich, cleanse and provide your bodily organs with the sustenance, fibre and vitamins they require to function correctly. You know what happens to the poorly fish in Green Pond when their gills get blocked: they lose the ability to filter oxygen from the water and die. Many of your organs, such as the liver and kidneys, apply a filtering effect on the liquids flowing around your body. If these organs can't operate correctly, then your overall health and vitality will be affected. Consuming a green smoothie helps hydrate and restore these organs. If you begin the week in this manner, you'll find it easier to compare how the other foods you're consuming throughout the rest of the week stand up against this standard. You'll begin to consider if the food you're about to munch on is going to repair or rejuvenate you, as opposed to simply providing a blast of pleasure via your taste buds. Some foods provide energy and fibre, and this is fine as long as your intake is balanced. For example, you may consume a green smoothie on a Monday morning, but the next day, you have muesli or cereal.

'I'm sure you can imagine the idea of spinning plates on poles. If you take your attention off one plate for too long while attending to another, it will fall, and it's the same with this POISE idea in creating balance. If you continue with this approach, I promise you'll soon reap the benefits, and you'll notice this first in your productivity and energy levels. The secret lies in taking small steps, acknowledging your progress and celebrating your win by sharing the good news with others. Try gathering allies for your cause from your family or friends. As well as making you more accountable, this can bolster your commitment to press on during the times when your enthusiasm may waver.'

After all this talk of food, Dael was tempted to suggest they both went foraging for jungle truffles or bananas, but time had run out. Instead, the lizards set a new meeting date to continue their tutorials.

Liberate your perception of self
and unlock the control of your emotions,
and then you'll achieve your desires.

Route Guidance Eight
The critical competences needed to flourish in the jungle of work life

It is well within our power to build a world in which the vast majority of us wake up every single morning inspired, feel safe at work and return home fulfilled at the end of the day.

Simon Sinek (2018, p.xiii)

The following pages provide a useful smart guide to help you grasp an overview of the critical competences required for navigating the jungle of modern work life effectively. They're broken down under bite-sized headings and packed full of examples that will help you retrieve information quickly if you ever need to refer back to them at a later date.

Critical competences can be defined as a range of personal skills, attributes and perspectives that are developed continually over time, aiding in the development of your sense of emotional stability, fulfilment and ability to connect harmoniously with others while striving confidently and resiliently through the challenges of modern work life.

Remember, it's never too late to start developing some of these qualities. Familiarising yourself with them will also place you in a stronger position when answering questions in job interviews, improving the content of your CV, or simply helping you to build confidence or a deeper connection with the people you serve or work alongside.

What will I gain from developing these qualities? Happiness and fulfilment

A profound incentive we all share as human beings is the drive to establish ever-increasing states of happiness, success, fulfilment or strength of character, but these states don't just fully materialise without us first developing a range of foundational behavioural disciplines or competences that enable us to interact successfully with other people and the wider world. Before we explore these critical competences, let's first examine the terms 'happiness' and 'fulfilment'.

Happiness vs fulfilment

The sensation of happiness is associated with a more short-term, temporary release of the chemical neurotransmitters dopamine and serotonin from within the brain when engaged in pleasurable experiences.

Fulfilment, however, includes a more sustained, deeper state of satisfaction, which is acquired through either completing or advancing steadily on a project that feels meaningful or purposeful. This type of endeavour isn't always driven by the allure of gaining more money, possessions or personal gain. Instead, through acts of fulfilment, a person can find themselves deeply absorbed in the present moment, valuing the insight and learning that occurs en route toward a specific goal.

This can include a greater self-awareness of the evolution of certain qualities – such as perseverance, resourcefulness and self-respect – which can develop after enduring the long periods of challenge or hard work inherent in completing a project of significant value or worth. In this sense, a greater depth, perspective or appreciation of life emerges as a by-product of completing such endeavours. For example, you may hear someone express, 'It's been so fulfilling absorbing myself in writing my first book. It's taken me four years and, at times, has tested my reserves of patience and commitment to breaking point. However, the process also helped me appreciate deeper levels of creativity and unearth writing abilities I never thought I had.'

Fulfilment is gained by doing what you love, and it can release the following:

- ✓ A deeper connection with yourself, other people and the world (compassion, humility, generosity, or a desire to inspire or motivate others), plus better senses of personal well-being, purpose, meaning and autonomy

- ✓ A higher resilience, more responsibility, and a fuller awareness of your strengths and weaknesses

- ✓ The development of certain values, learnt experiences or skills that can be drawn upon later (for example, optimism, intention, concentration, resourcefulness and higher personal standards)

- ✓ A more comprehensive understanding that being yourself is good enough, without requiring the approval of others (self-acceptance)

- ✓ An improved transparency in behaviour and the ability to be trusted by others

- ✓ A fuller appreciation of the unfoldment of new experiences along the path toward a goal; for example, making new connections with people or learning new things

The critical competences

By continually developing and incorporating the following critical competences into your work life, you'll be far more likely to move closer to achieving the states of happiness and fulfilment described earlier.

Character

Character defines the mental and moral qualities of an individual. It describes the manner in which we show up in the world, the qualities we bring to the table and the energy we share. We're all aware of those individuals who demonstrate a strong sense of character (a cheerful disposition; high levels of humility, authenticity or integrity; etc.)

How often do you formulate a clear picture of how you intend to 'be' consistently around other people? Have you ever considered how your colleagues might describe your character? Have you considered what personal character traits you have that are worth developing further?

Parents and teachers, in particular, have the privilege of watching how their children develop over time and will quickly identify the emergence of certain negative character traits (greed, selfishness, detachment, etc.) and celebrate the more positive ones (creativity, calm or optimistic attitude, industriousness, resourcefulness, etc.).

Strength of character can incorporate the following:

- Maintaining focus and positivity during periods of challenge or crisis, which can result in other people turning to you as a reliable and dependable presence

- Having the ability to maintain a growth mindset (remaining calm and resolute when others give in and being willing to learn new things, free of resentment or negativity)

- Consistently exemplifying integrity and humility

- Exercising grit and determination in completing a project, while avoiding acts of desperation or neediness

- Having the ability to reframe failure as an essential learning experience that informs and redirects your focus

- Having the ability to behave congruently with your values and beliefs, remaining true to whom you are, refraining from sharing a false persona and continually undertaking honest self-review

- Being motivated and focused, applying daily actions toward a goal, and all while remaining calm working around others

- Demonstrating advanced social-interaction skills (the ability to connect, empathise and share ideas), plus the ability to captivate, set the scene, engage or light up a room through having a command of language, charm, energy, warmth, hand gestures, novelty, intrigue and a compelling narrative

Once an individual has met their basic physiological needs (strong self-esteem, and feeling comfortable, satisfied, confident, peaceful, curious, joyful, loved, safe and relaxed), they're able to progress and develop more-complex cognitive and aesthetic qualities. It's only when these stages of human development are satisfied that an individual can aspire toward the mastery of their full potential or a self-actualised state.

Growth stages

There's a general consensus within the field of psychology that Abraham Maslow's hierarchy of needs provides a good starting point for outlining the key stages of emotional, physical and psychological growth required to reach a state of self-actualisation (that is, the state in which an individual reaches their full healthy and fulfilling life).

These growth stages include having the following abilities:

- Remain responsible and resilient while carrying out the work required to see a vision or task through to the end, without necessarily having support or acknowledgement from your peers

- Develop courage when embarking on the new or challenging paths necessary to fulfil a goal, and appreciating the broader learning that can accompany these challenges, even through a change of plan or failure

- Think independently, listen to your own feelings, and calmly evaluate experiences instead of immediately adhering to the voice of tradition, authority or the majority

- Have the courage and wisdom to let go of defences
- Choose honesty over pretence, including having a deep understanding that success isn't about trying to be someone else or be somewhere else, but is about remaining authentic and applying your best abilities to what's directly in front of you
- Develop integrity and a deeper sense of meaning by endeavouring to study higher planes of reality through spiritual practices, holistic connection or the appreciation of nature
- Understand your talents or skills and consider how this may add value or service to others

Empathy

The term 'empathy' (not to be confused with sympathy) is the ability to show interest in another person's situation and to attempt to understand it by clarifying their feelings while refraining from getting overly immersed or drawn in emotionally to the extent that your own performance is compromised. This perspective allows for a more-objective response when providing the appropriate support or guidance necessary. Good leaders know where and when to draw this line, ensuring a balance between knowing when to intervene and when to stand back. The ability to understand and display empathy in the workplace is one of the key critical competences desired by employers during the recruitment process.

Growth in empathy can incorporate these:

- Developing high levels of emotional intelligence (or emotional quotient [EQ]); sharing warmth, interest and curiosity; and/or initiating a conversation with a stranger
- Having the ability to attempt to view the world from another's standpoint (in terms of culture, background, life experiences, beliefs, etc.) and appreciate a situation from multiple perspectives

- Social tolerance, which is the ability to embrace individuality and challenge prejudices

- Considering the feelings of others and gaining clarity by listening carefully, articulating their situation, and communicating this information back clearly and succinctly

- Switching your role as a leader and physically putting yourself temporarily in the place of an employee to gain an understanding, insight or perspective of what's involved and to help inform or make the right balanced decisions

Humility

The word 'humility' is derived from the Latin word *humilis*, which means 'low'. In this sense, we're given the impression that it involves a display of non-aggressive behaviour, bowing down, having a measured and honest opinion of yourself, or moving out of the way of others. In fact, humility within the context of critical-competency development involves reaching an understanding that you're no greater or lesser than your work colleagues, and therefore treating them equally.

Humility involves accepting your own self-worth, the assets you value and the limitations you may be working on. Also important is accepting the fact that you don't have all the answers and therefore you embrace new learning continually, sometimes over long periods, to make improvements to your life (evolving new levels of awareness, taking more responsibility for your thoughts and actions, developing higher integrity, etc.).

Within the field of leadership, humility can be identified when leaders continue to encourage others to develop their competences even though they may risk being outranked in their own position of authority. In this sense, they embrace the idea that, even though someone may be doing something better than them, rather than reacting with feelings of jealously or envy, they encourage that person's development. This may also involve having the ability to admit you don't have all the answers and can listen and take on board the advice of others, which may involve challenging or stretching your current safe and familiar position of authority. Behaving in such a manner can keep you grounded and help you to avoid falling into the trap of thinking you're better than others – and are worthy of greater respect or admiration.

Humility can incorporate the following:

- Embracing fully the skills and talents others bring to the table, while temporarily shifting your position of authority to one side, which allows the opportunity to listen actively and find out as much as possible about the contributions others can make and how they operate

- Having a calm and reflective approach to evaluating personal achievements, which doesn't rely on boastful or self-absorbed behaviour or validation

- Demonstrating patience and diligence in the long haul toward the achievement of a personal goal

- Abstaining from displays of frustration or jealously when others receive praise or acknowledgement, and having the ability to celebrate and encourage the success of all the people you work alongside

- Having an open and reflective attitude toward the situations or events in life that don't go according to plan, and then transforming them into opportunities to foster resilience, new learning, insight or self-belief

- Sustaining the pursuit of lifelong learning and open-mindedness, in which continual constructive feedback and self-appraisal are welcomed – even when things go wrong

- Being content with your own company and having an appreciation for what's already been accomplished

Mindfulness

A mind too active is no mind at all.

Theodore Roethke

Taking time out to observe the natural view out of your office window, listening to a babbling brook in a forest and counting the clouds in the summer sky are all simple examples of mindfulness. The act of mindfulness essentially involves creating opportunities to cut out background noise or distraction and lose yourself in a moment of serenity. Creating this experience within your daily life can allow you to let go of some of the frantic or obsessive thoughts that can monopolise your day and, instead, to surrender to a more peaceful singularity of focus or observation. Practising regular acts of mindfulness has tremendous holistic health benefits and can help support the immune system, stabilise emotions, improve memory capacity, improve concentration, lower blood pressure and help ease anxiety. This sacred act also allows our mind and body to reset and allows space for fresh ideas, altered states or perceptions to emerge.

Acts of mindfulness can involve any of the these:

- **Meditation** – This can be simply closing your eyes, resting in silence and stilling your mind, and it can allow other less frantic modes of thought to seep into your consciousness, such as intuition, self-forgiveness, inspiration, creativity and flashes of enlightenment.

- **Body scan** – The simple act of taking time out from the hustle and bustle of life to be still and fully present while reviewing which parts of your body feel physically tense, and then relaxing gradually; this process can be accompanied by paying attention to the subtle visual or auditory stimuli within your immediate environment (the hum of a refrigerator, birds singing, the creaks in the timber of a house as it cools at night, etc.).

- **Realigning attention** – The act of just slowing down, removing yourself from a stressful environment, and realigning your thought energy away from the energies of tension and haste into a submission of ease, flow and acceptance. Completing an act of mindfulness provides the perfect breathing space in which to come up for air and calmly and objectively assess or gauge our current state of being. We can then compare or contrast how we currently feel alongside previous states in which we experienced joy, flow or appreciation in life. We can then go on to adjust our current thoughts accordingly to pull us back on track emotionally.

- **Sensory walk** – Walking outdoors, breathing in fresh air and enjoying the serenity of nature; this space can help you feel less self-absorbed and ease depression.

- **Distant viewing** – Pausing and focusing on distant objects within nature can expand your sense of clarity and perspective; the simple act of watching clouds moving gently by or morphing against the backdrop of a blue sky nourishes our sense of freedom, serenity and possibility. Observing clouds also helps release us from our own sense of self-importance.

- **Gardening activities** – These can help soothe the perfectionist inside and quench our human need to connect with nature (biophilia).

Emotional intelligence (or emotional quotient [EQ])

Emotions trigger certain feelings, which in turn determine our actions. EQ is the ability to understand, monitor, manage and select appropriate emotions in a manner that positively affects your ability to communicate and interact with other people. If you can identify somebody within your world of work who's approachable, centred, calm, respected and trustworthy, it's highly likely they possess some degree of EQ. EQ develops from an early age and varies considerably from person to person. This doesn't imply, however, that certain EQ competences are fixed during early adulthood and can't be developed later in life.

EQ can incorporate the following:

- The ability to step out of a situation, observe your behaviour from an objective standpoint, and take responsibility for managing or articulating your emotional cycles and how your thoughts translate into feelings and subsequent actions.

- Taking responsible ownership for your decisions, being aware your thoughts and actions have implications, and considering how this impacts other people; looking for opportunities to gain feedback regarding your behaviour or actions from those you spend time with; and avoiding rash decisions.

- Conducting an honest self-review to identify your strengths and weaknesses; articulating your feelings and noticing certain behavioural cycles or trigger points, including asking yourself searching questions such as these: *How does my behaviour impact others? How do I manage criticism and can I identify the ego voice within?* And at the end of each day, asking yourself questions such as these: *Did I take the time today to put aside my own concerns or agenda and ask anyone how they were feeling? Did I actually listen attentively to their response? How often today did I fall into the habit of taking myself too seriously? What did I do today that was totally different from the day before? What did I learn today that was challenging enough that it's worth sharing? What has triggered my mood swing today? Have I been judgemental today? What natural or spontaneous qualities such as curiosity, imagination, play, awe and wonder did I foster today?*

- Controlling negative self-talk and opting to choose more-empowering affirmations that encourage a growth mindset when faced with anxiety, worry and doubt. When embroiled in such situations, an emotionally intelligent person may pause and ask themself this: *Is this thought serving me?*

- Implementing certain physical choices to help combat negative emotions and gain perspective (meditation, taking time out, exercise, etc.).

- Being approachable and displaying acts of empathy and respect toward others' views so they feel seen and heard.

- Having the ability to build strong relationships and support others through challenging situations.

- Having the ability to behave and cooperate accordingly during group or team-building situations. This may involve standing back, putting your own views or prejudices to one side, and listening non-judgementally and attentively to others; sharing honestly; conveying emotions or feelings succinctly; avoiding compulsive behaviour; and helping resolve a stalemate situation to aid in steering a team in a more constructive direction.

- Continually developing more self-respect, understanding of others, resilience, ethical values, purpose, lifelong learning and belief in yourself, interest in life and sharing a passion (while learning to calmly navigate each success and failure), appreciating the journey from a varied or holistic perspective, and forging ahead purposefully and optimistically.

Motivational intelligence (or motivational quotient [MQ])

MQ is a more recent term that's used to describe a person's ability to deal with challenging situations and to remain focused, adaptable or upbeat while moving through change. A person possessing this quality is far more likely to lead successfully or inspire others.

The following are other aspects of MQ:

- It's one of the three quotients (which are often referred to as 'intelligences') – intellectual intelligence (or intelligence quotient [IQ]), EQ and MQ.

- Although all three intelligences play an important part in determining the skills required to operate confidently in the modern world, MQ is very much the bedrock quotient as it unlocks and supports all the others. MQ governs your ability to make decisions and consider particular situations as opportunities to grow and learn new things, rather than being pitfalls to avoid that threaten stability (fight or flight mode).

- Our past experiences can hugely influence our current level of MQ. Young children are born with high levels of natural curiosity, but as we grow older, we tend to become more risk averse. It's important to consider that humanity is naturally geared to survive and evolve. Many of the biggest accomplishments achieved by humans can be attributed to their ability to adapt and thrive through extreme challenge or crisis.

- MQ can be developed once a person identifies the underlying habits that might be holding them back from deploying more proactive or positive behaviour patterns.

- People with a low level of MQ will avoid taking risks, make excuses or provide reasons why it's more sensible not to try new things. This is known as having a 'fixed mindset'.

- People with high levels of MQ lead by trying new things and persist even after experiencing failure. They develop the ability to see the big win or learning opportunity within situations or experiences that others may run away from.

- Individuals who see the hidden opportunities inherent within periods of challenge, transition, crisis or deviation from the norm are more likely to succeed.

- MQ is one of the key skills many organisations currently identify as lacking most in their teams, hindering their ability to work more effectively and confidently during a period of significant global change.

Resilience

Beyond the more obvious definition of 'resilience' (which is to recover then grow from a setback or challenge, remaining steadfast and focused), there exists a variety of other – sometimes, less celebrated – qualities including these:

- Remaining self-aware, as your own best friend, even during the difficult periods of adversity or solitude; maintaining high levels of self-encouragement, composure, acts of mindfulness and calm focus

- Applying the ability to reframe, step out of or observe a challenging situation objectively during the pursuit of a goal

- Reframing your inner thoughts from negativity or doubtful self-talk, and replacing this with more-empowering affirmations

- Chipping away diligently at a goal without continually seeking approval, validation or praise; understanding that no one owes you anything!

- Highlighting negative patterns in your behaviour that may impact your performance and taking steps to fix them (for example, poor time management, lack of well-being, poor diet, procrastination, lack of sleep, burnout and adhering to negatively charged conversations)

- Being prepared to seek out and learn from expert advice, mentorship or support, including the ability to accept constructive criticism and to use this as a basis to learn and refine ideas

- Doing the things that need doing over long periods of time (including the mundane) while avoiding burnout

- Pressing on following a setback or disappoint *(that which tries to defeat us – only serves to release us!)*; redefining failure as a learning opportunity and creating the necessary marker points that create the slight redirection in course necessary in the pursuit of a goal; and converting experiences that test and stretch our capabilities into opportunities to develop wisdom, courage or strength of character

- Applying will, imagination and visualisation to help maintain focus and direction despite a setback; holding a clear image of what it would look and feel like to come out the other end successfully

- Pressing forward with an upbeat optimism, meaning and purpose that serves to inspire or encourage others

- Appreciating that the quality of resilience is an attribute that improves with practice and experience

- Finding meaning, gratitude and joy in the ordinary, and not taking yourself too seriously

Authenticity

Authentic behaviour primarily centres on being true to yourself while acting with transparency and honesty. It's the opposite of being manipulative or adopting a fake persona. Work culture and peer pressure can force some people to adopt a false persona in order to fit in or belong. Remaining true to yourself and acting authentically takes courage and resolve. Authentic people find it easier to nurture and share their skills or talents.

The following are some of the characteristics and implications of authentic behaviour:

- Authentic individuals review their weaknesses and admit their mistakes or inadequacies

- They act without the need for secrecy

- They share personal experiences, ask questions, and listen carefully to the views or ideas shared by other people;

they use these attentive-listening skills to foster positive relationships – which is a crucial quality of leadership

- There's evidence to prove that greater displays of authenticity within the workplace can contribute positively toward the level of employee well-being, work ethos, productivity, retention and performance

- Authentic individuals refrain from people-pleasing behaviour and are more successful at finding fulfilment or meaningful job satisfaction

- Leaders who inspire their teams with authenticity are better able to build trust and collaboration

Twenty-first-century work skills

> *Companies across industries are facing massive gaps for vital future skills, and they will need to re-skill or upskill massive sections of their workforce to get ready for the 4th industrial revolution.*
>
> Bernard Marr (2022)

One of the biggest challenges facing education or apprenticeship training is equipping young people with the necessary experiences and life skills to help them reach their full potential within the complex and ever-changing twenty-first-century world of work.

The following are some of the skills required:

The art of learning and thinking expertly and creatively

- Being able to engage with others confidently and resourcefully; solving complex problems and offering solutions, including critical thinking, applying imagination, innovative suggestions and flexibility in putting these ideas into action

- Communicating effectively, empathically and collaboratively as a team player regarding a common purpose or joint project

- Pulling many aspects together in complex systems and having the ability to ask the right questions to further develop innovation

- Having the ability to make effective judgements or decisions

- Engaging others by displaying warmth, empathy, novelty, narrative and intrigue across a range of communicating channels, so as to get a point across or to share an idea, message or vision

- Embracing creativity and enhancing opportunities continually through lifelong learning, so as to challenge yourself and broaden your horizons, including developing greater empathy and tolerance, and understanding the beliefs and cultures of other people from a global perspective

Effective and imaginative digital technology skills

- Selecting and implementing effective digital technology skills in a range of circumstances, coupled with imagination; for example, using digital technology to elaborate on a message and engage (a product launch or pitch, application, slide show, blog, proposal, data report, etc.).

- Being proficient in finding different ways to retrieve information and knowing how and where to use the appropriate research statistics responsibly

- Remaining ethically responsible using social media, video, data, surveys and social networks

- Selecting and adapting digital technology skills to improve the effectiveness of sharing information with participants globally (this may include overcoming language or cultural barriers)

- Synergising a range of technological applications that serve to enhance unique creative human qualities (imagination, art, music, communication, etc.)

The critical (soft) skills for the world of work

- Continually developing both personal leadership skills and the ability to focus, organise and prioritise

- Having the abilities to negotiate and to manage or coordinate people effectively

- Acting responsibly and authentically, with morality and empathy toward others

- Remaining adaptable, resilient and flexible through periods of great change or uncertainty

- Remaining enthusiastic and open to developing a growth mindset through lifelong learning that provides an avenue through which to inspire or support others

- Developing the qualities/skills of self-reliance, proactivity and excellent time management to achieve peak performance while avoiding burnout

- Maintaining high levels of EQ, adaptability and resilience, and then using these skills to engage with others and create lasting relationships

- Developing both global cultural and inclusion awareness and an empathetic and tolerant understanding of how best to communicate with a range of people with different needs or backgrounds

- Identifying global needs or opportunities that make a difference to people's lives; articulating your own unique 'why' and providing solutions that solve current needs (related to the environment, social inclusion, equal opportunities, health, poverty, technology, etc.).

Diversity awareness

One recurring theme continually impacting the workplace is that change is constant. This is coupled with the increasing necessity for all of us to lead ourselves, know who we are, become our best selves and remain aware of what's going on in the world while appreciating our unique place within it.

The development of diversity awareness is a critical necessity for anyone endeavouring to become an effective and responsible leader. Diversity awareness goes beyond simply acknowledging and respecting the visible differences you see in other people (ethnicity [there are approximately 650 different ethnic groups in our world], appearance, race, skin colour, age, body shape or size, physical abilities, etc.) and also includes taking into consideration less-evident factors that affect the way people work and the priorities they have (living with a neuro disorder, caring for an elderly relative, taking a disabled child to school in the morning, etc.).

To broaden and appreciate the meaning of 'diversity', it's important to consider the following points:

- Diversity doesn't describe a person; it describes an awareness of a range of people within a particular environment, workplace, team, ecosystem, etc. This includes recognising people's beliefs, ideology, socio-economic/ cultural background, political beliefs, sexual orientation, philosophical views, lifestyle and interests. The gender landscape is changing with transgender, non-binary, transsexual, polyamorous, pansexual, homosexual and heterosexual issues being discussed more openly.

- 'Neurodiversity' is a term used to describe the range of different ways in which people think, learn or exhibit certain behavioural traits, depending on their individual brain function or condition (social anxiety, autism, Tourette's syndrome, attention deficit hyperactivity disorder [ADHD], dyslexia, dyspraxia, etc.).

- A civilised and inclusive society strives to value all people and support their right to develop a sense of purpose and contribution within a safe and caring culture.

- Humanity thrives best when ecosystems, societies or civilisations function with harmony between cultures while simultaneously avoiding classing one culture as fundamentally superior to another. Societies that embrace diversity also contribute toward individuals and groups experiencing greater success, better cooperation, more innovation and thriving communities.

- Leaders have a responsibility to endeavour to create an empathetic and respectful working environment in which all people are valued and accepted, irrespective of age, marital status, religion, political perspective, race, gender, income, or socio-economic, educational or geographical background. Excellent leaders back up their understanding of diversity awareness with specific actions and behaviours.

- In the same way as we may value our right to articulate or share our own opinions, experiences or uniqueness, it's important to understand that so too do other people.

- People with high levels of diversity awareness appreciate the fact that they may not be able to understand comprehensively or share everyone's experiences, but they still make space to listen, respect, tolerate, appreciate and celebrate the value that can be gained from sharing time working or living alongside other people who share a range of experiences.

Inclusion awareness

Inclusive environments emerge intentionally, not by accident, and allow every person – regardless of their rank or position – to feel valued and accepted. Facilitating individuals being able to operate with autonomy and confidence is vital, but equally important is for leaders to ensure every individual is genuinely treated equally when it comes to expressing their talents.

Here are some points to consider:

- Diverse human ecosystems can exist anywhere, but a purposefully driven inclusive culture may not always be evident.

- An inclusive environment can't develop completely unless the people who work within that space are fully consulted, valued and actively involved. There's no room for token gestures.

- An inclusive culture allows every person, regardless of their rank or position, to feel they belong within a safe and supported environment in which they can achieve their full potential. Every member is allowed space to be their authentic self and feel comfortable expressing their voice.

- In order to develop an inclusive culture, it's critical to first address any subconscious bias that certain team members may harbour (automatically making assumptions, labelling or placing people in boxes, etc.).

- For some leaders who strive to advance their understanding of inclusion awareness, the process can prove rather challenging or uncomfortable, as it requires a thorough and honest examination of personal blind spots or unearned privileges. Opening up and sharing this learning curve with colleagues or teams is a good indicator of effective leadership, and it's critical before an inclusion action plan can be formulated. This isn't easy, which explains why poor leaders instead choose to pay lip service to the development of inclusion initiatives within the work environment.

- Inclusive leaders develop a cultural intelligence, accepting individuals for whom they are, while remaining open, fair and respectful toward the people or things they don't understand. They invest time in studying and understanding more about the needs or backgrounds of those they lead, and they pass the baton on, encouraging others to get involved in developing further inclusion initiatives. Individuals who feel included are more likely to contribute, participate, and consider elements of safety, health and integrity at work.

Leadership qualities

Now, more than ever, we need leaders who are not afraid to show compassion, who consciously role model healthy working practices and foster an environment where people feel safe to speak about health issues and seek help.

Rachel Suff, Senior Policy Advisor, Employment Relations (Chartered Institute of Personnel and Development [CIPD], 2022, p.2)

If you were asked to pinpoint one or two inspiring global company leaders, do any names immediately come to mind? The organisations these individuals lead are very often the ones that spring to mind when you overhear someone say something like, 'Oh, you're so lucky to be working for x; it's such a great company and always forward-thinking. I hear such great things. I'd do anything to work there!'

The traditional leadership stereotype is often portrayed as being overly commanding and possessing certain masculine traits (assertiveness, strength, courage, independence, aggressiveness, competitiveness, confidence, etc.). Within the evolving workplace, however, great leadership actually relies on a set of far broader skills and abilities.

Although there's no single definition or model of leadership, as every leader operates in their own unique manner, there are **four core principles** that underpin effective leadership.

The four core principles of effective leadership

1. Having a mastery of positive character traits and EQ skills working alongside others

2. Managing day-to-day affairs effectively

3. Actively developing others

4. Deploying self-awareness to gain clarity and perspective in taking on new positions of leadership

1. Having a mastery of positive character traits and EQ skills working alongside others

- Monitoring and managing personal emotions, feelings and reactions effectively through difficult or uncomfortable periods (employee dispute, changes in pay or working conditions, etc.)

- Understanding that complexity, unpredictability, uncertainty and disruption are normal parts of the business world, but what matters is learning how to react and adjust behaviour accordingly

- Being clear and consistent in choosing how to behave fairly toward others

- Remaining transparent and honest when sharing their strengths, weaknesses, faults, blind spots or limitations, and focusing on what can be changed; giving themselves permission to share their vulnerabilities or pain with their teams, even admitting that they don't have it all figured out; remaining secure in themselves despite their faults, as they go about leading others; and understanding, working through and utilising this knowledge to help build trust and connection with the people they lead

- Understanding that humans are social creatures designed to support each other through trust and a deep sense of belonging
- Acting authentically and avoiding manipulating others
- Pursuing opportunities to develop high levels of EQ
- Engaging in continual study and curiosity on the subject of personal development, human performance and/or success principles
- Engaging in mentorship, keeping abreast of technological advances, conducting research or data analysis related to their field of specialism, and following trends or changes within the market place
- Maintaining a growth mindset and not being afraid to fail
- Understanding different learning styles when considering the best way to communicate with others and appreciating the unique qualities each person brings to the table
- Developing the ability to share compassion and foster trust among those they serve
- Acknowledging and thanking others for their contributions toward a shared goal
- Taking an honest and regular review of their current role, performance, stress management or work-life balance, and then making appropriate changes if certain conditions aren't aligned with their core values or are inhibiting their ability to flourish
- Prioritising purpose and passion in what they do and not being driven by monetary targets alone

2. Managing day-to-day affairs effectively

- Refraining from micromanagement, which can drain morale and increase anxiety, suspicion, stress and lack of trust among teams

- Promoting a safe work culture and environment that values trust and cooperation *(we're all in this together; we can do so much more through collaboration)*

- Exercising situational awareness, standing up and taking responsibility, flexing leadership style during a crisis, and delivering instructions in a clear and respectful manner (leading a fire evacuation from a building, making tough decisions or strong judgements during challenging times, etc.)

- Being able to clearly rank and prioritise the tasks required at any given moment, so as to help enable an organisation or project to run smoothly

- Articulating clearly the objectives of the organisation while balancing this drive with experiences that are meaningful to people

- Having an awareness that being sensitive and understanding is vital, but so too is developing the ability to motivate, energise and galvanise a team of people to work on priorities that drive the business forward, especially through challenging times

- Refraining from simply standing back or withdrawing from a difficult or complex situation (stalemate, volatile situation, etc.), but instead, managing people effectively while assessing if a response or strategy applied to deal with the situation is effective and making appropriate adjustments if necessary

- Endeavouring to remain visible and approachable as a means of supporting teams solving particular problems

- Actively supporting and leading the development of people's full potential alongside accomplishing a common goal

- Supporting people by helping them understand that personal growth develops when we challenge ourselves

- Sharing specific skills, talents and authenticity to encourage others to fulfil their roles to their full capacity (for example, transparency, honesty, having the ability to admit you don't have all the answers or remaining open to learning from your colleagues)

- By communicating clear objectives, allowing people to function as naturally, freely and autonomously as possible

- Managing the problem not the person, and providing both formal and informal forums to facilitate feedback

- Creating a two-way dialogue, and being open to giving and receiving information

- Refraining from favouritism, and understanding that the holistic well-being of every human relies on them developing a sense of value, purpose and the opportunity to be acknowledged

3. Actively developing others

- Inspiring others to aspire to fulfil a leadership role by drawing the best out of people and helping them develop their own creative skills, talents, sense of meaning, uniqueness and authenticity

- Providing thoughtful and constructive feedback continually in an appropriate and timely manner (avoiding leaving it too late after an incident to address a competency issue with a work colleague)

- Being committed to developing people during challenging times

- Leading by example and rising to the challenge of pursuing a just cause (a new start-up for change, a global movement or vision, etc.)

- Inspiring and serving others with acts of courage and engagement that, ultimately, encourage them to join you in the pursuit of your vision

- Developing the ability to empathise and show compassion for the people that follow you in your vision

- Maintaining a genuine interest in other people, both personally and intellectually, and getting to know more about them, including their family life, hobbies and interests

- Refraining from promoting a position of leadership by reminding others of your authority, privilege or power; instead, working on asking yourself how best to serve and connect with others by sharing specialist knowledge in your field of expertise that could have a positive impact on other people's lives (writing books, articles or blogs; speaking engagements; etc.)

4. Deploying self-awareness to gain clarity and perspective when taking on new positions of leadership

- Familiarising yourself with the culture, systems and running of a new organisation

- Fostering openness in collecting feedback, asking questions and engaging in dialogue with employees across a range of roles to gain clarity, insight and understanding about day-to-day life

- Listening attentively and asking direct questions to gain an understanding of any shortcomings or obstacles that may affect the smooth operation or performance of an organisation; for example, asking this: 'Are you getting what you need to operate successfully? Where exactly are the problems? What do you and your colleagues say about where you work? Do you feel supported?'

- Consulting with people before imposing new ideas, systems or procedures that may affect their working environment

- Remaining aware of and responsive to the diverse nature of social and cultural differences that may exist within teams and appreciating the benefits and qualities these bring to the workplace; communicating and celebrating this awareness across the width and breath of an organisation and continually taking steps to improve the workplace's inclusive culture

Now you've become familiar with some of the definitions of the critical competences required to thrive within the world of work, consider what aspect of human behaviour (highlighted as skills, attributes and perspective in the following chart) each might fall under. Although there's some interchangeability between these headings, skills can generally be practised, developed and specialised in over time, whereas attributes are the more-personal or natural qualities we forge throughout life that can help us communicate or engage with others. Perspective is often acquired through practising prolonged acts of open-mindedness, immersion in rich and diverse life experiences, and the pursuit of wisdom over complacency.

Skills	Attributes	Perspective	
Twenty-first-century skills Emotional intelligence (EQ) Motivational intelligence (MQ)	Humility Character Authenticity	Empathy Diversity awareness Inclusion awareness	
	Mindfulness Effective leadership	Resilience Entrepreneurship	

*Liberate your perception of self
and unlock the control of your emotions,
and then you'll achieve your desires.*

Route Guidance Nine
What about entrepreneurism?

Success is the progressive realisation of a worthy ideal.

Earl Nightingale

An entrepreneur is someone who sets up their own business or enterprise, offering fresh ideas or delivering products or services with the aim of making a profit, scaling the business and making a difference in the world. They also step up to the challenges facing them and accept the inherent risks or obstacles arising from embarking on such a venture (failure, rejection, the challenge of securing a successful investment pitch, working in isolation, commitment, hard work through periods of challenge or adversity, etc.). It's possible an entrepreneur may already be employed in a job for an organisation, but they still continue developing the spirit of entrepreneurism behind the scenes from home, with a vision of stepping out eventually and launching a start-up business of their own.

Ideas are the currency of the twenty-first century

Carmine Gallo (2014, p.1)

The eight arms of entrepreneurism

One morning, the two friends found themselves engrossed in a debate to decide which essential attributes lie at the heart of launching a successful entrepreneurial venture. Dael found it difficult to formulate a simple list of qualities that might be required.

Lead asked her friend a question: 'Dael, have you ever travelled north to the far reaches of the jungle where the great salt waters meet the land?'

Dael thought for a moment, recalling the odd occasion in the past when his father had shared tales of such mysterious locations. 'I've heard of such wonders, but I was never allowed to venture too far from home when I was a young lizard, so I've always regarded such places as somewhat mythical – a good bedtime yarn to tell. Please do tell me more.'

Lead continued, 'Well, I had the good fortune of hitching a ride on the back of a parrot that needed to travel north to deliver an important message to one of its relatives, warning them of an impending storm. This was many years ago, and I was a lot younger then, of course, but I remember the trip well. After hours of breath-taking flight, scaling immeasurable heights, I saw with my own eyes the legendary location where palm trees give way to long stretches of dazzling white sand that gradually sink beneath a vast expanse of turquoise salt water that's even bigger than Green Pond!

'During my short time exploring the huge rock pools that stretched across the sands, I learnt of a peculiar creature that lives in holes among the rocks and corals just below the surface of the water. This creature shares a similar smooth, hairless skin to you and me, but it has the most bizarre body shape from which eight long, bendable legs protrude outwards in all directions. These legs can twist and wrap around objects with far greater dexterity than any lizard's tail or tongue. I've later come to learn that the correct name of this creature is an "octopus", but at that time, my parrot friend kept referring to them as "amazing entrepreneurs".

'I learnt that one definition of an "entrepreneur" is a highly motivated and focused individual who identifies a problem or need in the world and seizes the opportunity to develop a vision into a product or service that provides a solution to that problem. This may include setting up a profit-

based business venture, but it can involve simply making a difference to the world. Either way, they fully accept the risks and challenges associated with initiating such a bold venture.

'The parrot explained that these entrepreneurs (octopuses) possess eight unique attributes that allow them to adapt and survive. He shared eight examples of octopus behaviour that mirror the skill sets necessary to become a successful entrepreneur.

'Still to this day, I find this quirky comparison between an octopus and an entrepreneur really useful in helping me engage and introduce the topic of entrepreneurism with my students for the first time.'

Lead picked up a stick with her tail and etched into the jungle floor an image of the creature she had just described. She then went on to describe the eight key entrepreneurial qualities that can apply equally to employability competences: 'You must be a proactive creator, a resilient problem-solver, adaptable, and willing to collaborate, communicate and lead.' (In case you're wondering, both of those first two points count as two things each.)

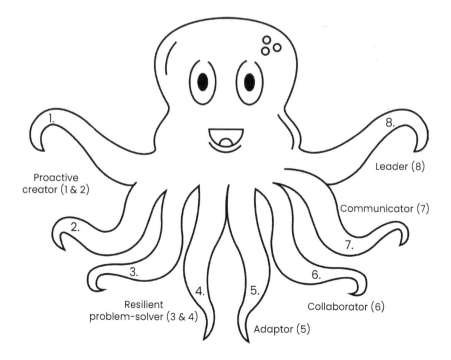

True to form, she elaborated by adding further detail to her drawing and then went on to inscribe a table on the sandy floor:

Entrepreneurs	Octopuses
Proactive creator (1 & 2)	
Successful entrepreneurs are proactive and curious. They're stimulated by finding opportunities to create new products or services that solve a problem or add value to people or the wider world.	Octopuses are naturally curious and need stimulation. They proactively make use of tools (natural resources within their immediate environment) to create dens.
Resilient problem–solver (3&4)	
Resilience is a critical attribute for every entrepreneur to develop as there are plenty of risks or obstacles inherent in such ventures (failure, rejection, working alone, running out of resources, etc.). Each entrepreneur's journey relies on persistence, the continual revaluation of ideas and steadfast determination in solving problems.	Octopuses' brain–to–body ratio is the largest of any invertebrate, which makes them very clever creatures and great problem–solvers. They can open clam shells and even work out how to remove lids from jam jars! When challenged in manoeuvring through a complex maze or tight spot, they succeed by exercising great acts of resilience and adaptability.
Adaptor	
Successful entrepreneurs must be willing to exercise critical thinking, learn from experience, and possess the ability to pivot and adapt ideas based on fresh information fed from continuing research or feedback from the people they intend to serve.	Octopuses learn from experience and possess superb camouflage capabilities, allowing them to adapt quickly and blend in with their surroundings. If they lose an arm, they can adapt by growing a new one in its place.

Entrepreneurs	Octopuses
Collaborator	
To advance an idea, successful entrepreneurs understand the advantages of collaboration as a means of pooling ideas, knowledge and/or skills.	Although octopuses display complex social behaviours, there's some evidence that they collaborate and work well together, living in small communities.
Communicator	
Effective communication is a vital skill that any successful entrepreneur must develop to enable them to communicate their ideas (sales pitches, applying for investment, or promoting a product or service).	Octopuses communicate by changing their bodies' colour patterns. Their skin contains cells that can produce colour (chromophore) as well as light reflectors. They can rapidly change colour to attract mates, warn of danger and distract their prey.
Leader	
Effective entrepreneurs must exercise high levels of personal leadership, vision and self-discipline to coordinate and implement a range of complex tasks efficiently.	Each of the octopus's arms has a mini brain, allowing it to complete a range of tasks efficiently, but it's led by a centralised brain that tells each arm what to do, not how to do it.

__Liberate__ your perception of self and unlock the control of your emotions, and then you'll achieve your desires.

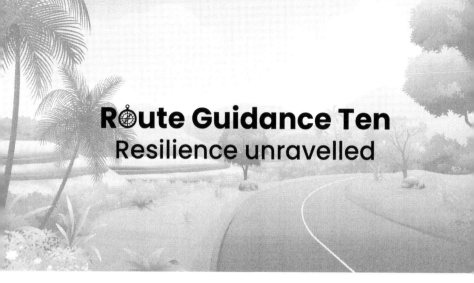

Route Guidance Ten
Resilience unravelled

When you get into a tight place and everything goes against you, till it seems as though you could not hold on a minute longer, never give up then, for that is just the place and time that the tide will turn.

Harriet Beecher Stowe

RESILIENCE = **R**eacting **e**motionally **s**table **i**n **l**ife's **i**ntriguing **e**xperiences; **n**ever-**ce**asing **e**ndurance

The resilience poem

Resilience is stepping wholeheartedly into the unknown,
Burning all bridges, embracing courage with resolve.

Resilience is avoiding self-pity, standing tall
Despite being told you have no credibility.

Resilience is entering a room full of strangers,
Shaking hands and sharing your story with no strings attached.

Resilience is steadfastness when alone in the dark
With the ghosts of fear, doubt or failure stalking.

Resilience is walking that lonely journey home
With your head still held high after losing the pitch.

Resilience is showing up smiling,
Even if the big boys are breathing down your neck.

Resilience is shining light into hope,
Grateful for what is, rather than worrying what's missing.

Resilience is the patience to allow, to let go,
To ask, to listen and to learn.

Resilience is being your own best friend.
Going within for the truth, direction and focus.

Resilience is being at peace for the long haul,
Still proud just to be you!

The silent resolve of resilience

Dael found the meetings with Lead so refreshing. At last, somebody was taking the time to show some real empathy and understanding toward the things that troubled him most. With every meeting, the information he gathered from his new mentor grew ever more intriguing.

Over time, Lead's encouraging support helped Dael to slowly grow more confident and to feel less of a victim and more of an architect of his circumstances.

Dael had heard Lead mention the term 'resilience' quite a few times during their conversations, and one day asked her to clarify it more.

True to form, Lead addressed the question by relying on the signs and metaphors that surrounded her in the jungle. She drew Dael's attention to a beautiful butterfly (an emerald swallowtail) that was resting on a nearby flower, its delicate wings quivering in the breeze and displaying every shade of green.

The two friends sat silently for a moment, watching the butterfly flutter between flowers. Dael was so engrossed that he was unaware Lead had withdrawn her attention from the antics of the butterfly and was frantically inscribing a set of letters into the surface of a palm leaf using a sharp stick.

Eventually, she leant in closer to Dael and handed him the palm leaf. On its surface was inscribed the word 'resilience'.

Lead whispered, 'Look at this and note how the word "silence" makes up practically the last two-thirds of the word "resilience". When I think of the quality of resilience, I always picture the butterfly going freely about its business, collecting nectar from flowers. But I also picture an earlier period of its life: a necessary and vital stage of its growth fraught with fragility and silent resolve.'

Dael looked puzzled, but before he could interject, Lead continued, 'When we see a beautiful butterfly displaying its magnificently coloured wings, seldom do we ponder all the patience and toil that little creature employed during the pupal stage of its development, metamorphosing discreetly from caterpillar to butterfly. But here's the point: it did all this with silent resolve. Similarly, the act of resilience is often a very private, unglamorous endeavour and one in which you seldom attract recognition or support from those around you. Fundamentally, the act of resilience is about diligently chipping away at your goal without the need to continually seek approval or praise from others! With practice, it's a quality you can certainly develop and strengthen.'

Honouring the time of resilience

At that point, the two friends found their conversation interrupted as their attention was drawn toward a sudden flash that lit up the sky. This was followed, after a few seconds of silence, by a distant thunderclap that reverberated far above the mountains.

Lead immediately took the opportunity to embellish her teaching by sharing a fact she'd learnt many years ago from her father. 'When I count the time it takes in seconds between the flash of lightning and the rumble of thunder, I get a rough estimate of how far away the storm is, with each second roughly corresponding to a mile in distance from the source of the storm to where I stand.

'The birth of your vision or goal within your imagination is your lightning moment. It's the spark of creation! Remember that there's often a period of silence between a flash of lightning and the sound of the thunder, but they're actually happening simultaneously. And in the same way, there'll always exist a period of time – perhaps days, months or even years – between the spark of your idea and the experience of *actually witnessing its fruition as a physical manifestation, but the two are actually interwoven. For this reason, it's important to honour this period of time and the daily actions and perseverance required to reach your goal. Just because you're experiencing silence, it doesn't mean the thunder isn't coming! Every day you honour your vision, trust your instinct and carry out all the steps required to reach your goal, you'll grow not only in wisdom but also in fortitude. This endurance is never meaningless. In fact, you could say that a vision sustained with passion and self-belief is already a done deal or an assured success waiting to birth itself within the outside world, and with this realisation emerges a deeper level of awareness!'*

As the storm grew closer, the rumble of thunder transformed into a more aggressive crack, which reverberated above the two lizards' heads, causing the trees and ground to shake violently. The two friends brushed off a multitude of tiny insects that had fallen on their heads and shoulders, having been shaken from the tree branches high above them.

Honouring the diligence of resilience

Lead again drew Dael's attention to the sky above as she noticed the commotion had caused a flock of parrots to abandon their hideouts in the trees and swoop low over the two friends' heads, squawking and screeching in fear.

She stated, 'It's funny, but that reminds me, on the topic of resilience, you can learn a lot about persistence by observing the feathered creatures of the sky – specifically, the manner in which they build their nests.

'I can remember one particular spring when I was watching a group of these creatures building their nests high up in the trees while battling through a particularly aggressive storm. They encountered numerous failures as the gusts of wind snatched the sticks from their beaks and tossed them mercilessly to the ground. Nevertheless, they continued. They persisted!

'To my amazement, when the storm finally ended, I noticed that many of the sticks they'd dropped had been collected from a willow tree and were all of a similar size and thickness. There are obviously clear ground

rules for building nests, with each stick having been selected carefully. Here's the point: they were driven by a vision – a precise roadmap, if you like – for nest building, and they never gave up. Furthermore, despite the risks involved, they ventured forward with utmost diligence and courage.'

Dael interjected, 'And sometimes these repetitive steps can appear rather tedious or boring to the average onlooker, rather like small drops in the ocean, yes?'

'Indeed,' remarked Lead. 'Resilience often requires us to complete the less glamorous or mundane things (such as filling out applications, completing a business plan, writing to-do lists, tidying up the diary or office, perfecting a design, planning, gathering information, study, and networking). Nevertheless, these less celebrated and rather dull activities form the backbone of success. They're essential stepping stones, and without them, you wouldn't be adequately equipped and prepared to endure the long haul. It's also important, however, to understand that you don't have to be everywhere and do all things. Focus on the twenty per cent of the tasks that really matter and the rest will normally follow on or take care of themselves.

Honouring the patience of resilience

'Finally, here's another sometimes-forgotten character quality associated with resilient behaviour: patience. Try as much as you can to remain patient in transforming your vision into a tangible reality, because mastering this quality will allow you to experience several benefits:

'When you retain a patient attitude toward the accomplishment of your goal, you free up energy that could otherwise be wasted on worry, overspeculation, or undue force and haste.

'Patience creates space in the mind for creative ideas to emerge.

'Patience makes you an attractive person to be around!

'Patience strengthens your focus, allowing you to tend calmly to the important things that need doing right now.

'Patience creates space for you to notice the serendipity and synchronicity (good fortune and meaningful coincidence) that may cross your path and embellish your journey.

'And patience improves your health (stress control, general well-being and heart rate).'

How to reframe failure

Dael felt compelled to ask what seemed like an unavoidable question: 'What about the times when all doesn't go according to plan and we undoubtedly experience the dreaded word 'failure'?'

'To answer your question, let's begin by studying the following quotes delivered by two of the human species. The writer Napoleon Hill put it so beautifully: "Every failure brings with it the seed of equivalent success." And I'm sure you're aware of this famous Alexander Graham Bell quote: "When one door closes, another door opens!"

'It's important to remember that success is often made up of a multitude of failures. The secret is to pivot at each of the crossroads of failure, asking yourself, What have I learnt? and then keep going while holding the vision, because behind every failure lies a rebirth.'

Dael replied, 'Yes, of course, but it's sometimes hard to accept this advice when you're right in the midst of experiencing a painful rejection or huge disappointment.'

Lead thought for a moment, searching for the right reply. 'Indeed, my friend, but after multiple failures, you'll learn to understand and appreciate why certain things happen. Sometimes, they happen for a reason, and when you look back on these misfortunate events later, they'll take on new meaning. This perspective on life can only really be discovered through experience.'

Dael pressed further with his questions. 'I felt like a failure the other day when I was left out of a work team meeting in which management were gathering new ideas to help solve a sales problem. I thought the organisers might require my skills, but they simply didn't run anything past me. I was thinking, Aren't I good enough? Did I do something wrong? Have I offended someone in the past? I'm still struggling to get over it. Can you offer any advice?'

Immediately, Lead stood up, tall and commanding, and replied, 'Notice how the second half of the word "failure" contains the word "lure", and that's precisely why so many lizards find it hard to recover. Long after actually experiencing the moment of failure, the sensation can still continue to lure you into far lower depths of despair, such as throwing you off focus or sapping your energy. Although the experience of failure can slow you down, the "lure" trap can quite literally paralyse you!

'When you encounter failure, the immediate sensation of disappointment can often feel impossible to shake off, but in time, you'll inevitably get over it! Meanwhile, it's important to go and do something entirely different over the next twenty-four hours or lose yourself in doing something you enjoy. This isn't about running away from your responsibilities, but it's simply taking time out to stabilise your mood gradually. When you've calmed down and come back to reflect, you can try repeating the phrase: "Every failure moves me closer to my goal and always contains the seed of success!"

'Any noble, significant or worthy endeavour that leaves a lasting legacy relies on persistence, and persistence inevitably involves failure because every failure clears a new pathway ahead. Combat the hold that the sensation of failure may have over you by unearthing the learning or wisdom gained from your experience – that is, the light at the end of the tunnel – or replay the experience by explaining to others how it made you stronger or gain further insight about a particular aspect or theme of your life.

'Amazing, inspiring leaders understand the impact of sharing personal stories of failure or setback, as it's a means of connecting and engaging with the people they serve. They revisit these stories to demonstrate what they learnt and how they reframed an unfortunate experience (which for many would undoubtedly knock them off track) into a more-empowering or constructive self-assessment. A great story is worthless without a beginning (the hero's quest or a problem encountered), middle (a challenge or suspense) and end (the resolution). It sounds so clichéd, but new doors will always swing open following failure. Looking back on your life and reframing your journey of resilience as an adventure, rather than something to regret, liberates you from the lure of failure!'

'Over time, as you embrace each failure, several things may happen:

'You'll appreciate the bigger story.

'The next time disappointment raises its head, you'll be better prepared to let go and move on.

'You'll join the ranks of all the great visionaries and inventors – all of whom have endured the same test.

'You'll grow to appreciate the saying "That which doesn't destroy you only makes you stronger."

'It's all about the journey, and success isn't defined simply by a prize that awaits you in the distant future; it's with you now, every step of the way as you venture forward.

'Failure and disappointment will help you develop the three crucial "R" skills: **re-evaluation, reset** and **resilience!**

'Another recovery technique I apply when I encounter disappointment – such as a failed pitch or job interview, or my best laid plans crashing to the floor – is to think of cats! Oh, and by the way, I rarely see any of the big cats in the jungle behaving particularly stressed. They're always lounging around, purring, under the sun!'

'Cats!' spluttered Dael. 'You do make me laugh.'

'There's method in my madness,' Lead said with a chuckle. '"CAT" stands for three states of mind that are essential to resisting the lure of failure: **calm, attention** and **trust.**

'Let's examine the first letter, C, which represents the word "calm". Any successful entrepreneur, inventor or business owner will tell you that pursuing a worthy or challenging ideal is never plain sailing, in just the same way that a life full of fulfilment and adventure is never accomplished without some form of risk.

'It's simply a fact that the pursuit of any worthy ideal is a dynamic process, and by law, it often incorporates sudden misfortune or unexpected shifts in direction. How on earth could you move forward in achieving anything of great worth or substance without first encountering life's ups and downs? That's not how life works, I'm afraid. A successful product or idea often goes through multiple rejections or setbacks before it's finally accepted and released into the world, but remember that this isn't about you; it's not a personal thing. You have to separate yourself from the product, idea or thing you're trying to grow. In this way, you'll remain more present by focusing your attention on the necessary improvements or tasks at hand.

'The key point is to accept this fact and focus instead on endeavouring to develop a calm level-headedness when it comes to navigating setbacks or failure, rather than getting overly worked up and wasting valuable energy at a time when your focus should be on re-evaluating the lessons learnt from the experience.

'Calmness of mind also helps you think more objectively, which promotes effective problem-solving.

'Next, the letter A stands for "attention". When you're faced with disappointment when things don't go according to plan, pay careful attention to the sorts of habitual thoughts that bubble up within you and the type of language you use to describe your situation. Are you musing over every detail, labouring over what could have been, repeating the dreaded "if only I had..." type of thoughts and wishing you could rewrite the entire scene?

'The important point to remember in a situation like this is that where attention goes, energy flows! With this in mind, you always have the choice to reframe your situation or stand back and observe it from a slightly different perspective. By paying attention and reviewing your circumstances more objectively, you can return to formulating the sorts of positive feelings and emotions associated with what's actually working or going right in your life. It's from this positive state of being that you ideally want to springboard on to greater things, rather than being held back by the shackles of despair or disappointment.

'Finally, the last letter in cat is the letter T, which stands for "trust". The quicker you can trust the learning process that inevitably emerges from any failure, the easier you'll find it to regroup and plan ahead. Put simply, let it go and move on!

'More importantly, learn to trust yourself! Your break will come, but meanwhile, honour your intuition or gut feeling when pursuing your goals.

'When you learn to control your emotions calmly and trust yourself, you're sending a powerful message out into the world that you're prepared to endure the long haul and step up to the mark even without the recognition or adulation of others. In effect, you're practising humility, and the world will love you for that!'

Dael was still puzzled. 'But how do you go about developing that level of trust in yourself?'

'Well, my friend, there's only one way,' she explained. 'You simply have to learn from the lessons delivered through the experience of failure, maybe multiple times, before you learn to relax and get out of your own way. The development of self-trust only comes through years of experience.

'When you think of it like that, it seems to make more sense. I think I need to repeat that message to myself more often.

'So the next time disappointment or failure raises its head, build that feline picture in your imagination, use the elements of the acronym CAT in an affirmation, and remind yourself of the appropriate attitudes to focus on when forging a resilient attitude of mind.

'It's worth noting this powerful affirmation in your journal, Dael: "That which tries to defeat us only serves to release us!"'

'But what exactly does this mean?' asked Dael.

How resilience builds character

Lead answered, 'I want you to think about a recent personal challenge, crisis, instance of adversity, worry or fear. You came out the other end, yes? Stronger maybe? This is because the experience – however awful it appeared at the time – served to strengthen a certain quality within that you didn't know you had, and that released a deeper perspective or appreciation of life.

'Consider these important truths: when you're cornered, scared and alone, sharpen your resolve and self-belief, because before too long, new horizons will appear and the things you imagine are constraining your growth will slowly release their grip upon you. Remember that just outside your comfort zone resides the space for personal growth, and conquering your fears is one way to shift yourself into this void. Success will always depend on your mental agility and willingness to reach fearlessly into your stretch zone.

'Another point to mention is that you're only as good as your weakest point, and it sometimes requires somebody else to reveal this to you! With this in mind, in order to develop your resilience, you must continually learn from those in positions of expertise within the field you're trying to develop in. To seek help in this manner requires a degree of humility and openness. You want to seek out advice from those who don't beat about the bush but say it as it is! This may require you to face up to certain uncomfortable home truths, such as taking greater responsibility or modifying certain attitudes or behaviours that are holding you back. Great mentors very often see doors inside us that were shut; we just needed to open them!'

Affirmations to strengthen resilience

'I know we've briefly covered the role self-talk has in building resilience, but do you have any more ideas about the sorts of things we should repeat to ourselves when faced with adversity?' Dael queried.

Lead smiled. 'When things get bad, I always create an affirmation with one or two of the following phrases or ask myself one or two of these questions ...' She again began to write in the sand:

1. Is that thought serving me?
2. I know my true power.
3. Which inspirational source can I study right now that will bolster my self-belief? (You could try the chapter on persistence in *Think and Grow Rich* by Napoleon Hill.)
4. Exercise would probably help right now.
5. What's the worst that can happen?
6. There's always a solution – everything works out for me.
7. Where are my negative thoughts coming from? What's the cost of allowing these thoughts to prevail?

8. What evidence can I find around me right now that prove I'm perfectly placed to accomplish my goal?

9. Am I willing to tolerate the fact that quite ordinary people, just like me, achieve great things, and am I really exempt from joining their ranks?

10. I can and I will – watch me!

11. The people or opportunity weren't the right match for me right now. The right opportunity will come along.

12. What am I learning and how will I turn this experience into a wonderful narrative to share with others that will inspire and motivate them?

13. Let go and let God!

Lead chuckled to herself. 'Connected with the theme of self-talk, I believe we'd reinforce the resilient mindset of many a young lizard if all the truths I've mentioned so far were used as affirmations, like a mantra, in school at the beginning of each day.'

Forging resilience through the power of choice

This led Dael to his next question: 'I'm beginning to understand what you're sharing about pursuing certain goals, overcoming fear and remaining positive, but what about those split-second moments when everything you've planned implodes and goes horribly wrong? I find it really difficult to manage that sudden shock, especially when people are watching and things turn ugly.'

'Let me tell you a quick story,' suggested Lead. 'The other evening, I planned a jog to the far end of the jungle and back, but before I got even a quarter of the way around my route, a huge thunderstorm erupted out of nowhere, and I got absolutely soaked by rain and hail. Brilliant, I thought, that's typical!

'Now I could have stopped and sheltered under a palm tree or scurried back home immediately, defeated and with my head bowed, but instead, I pressed on with my planned running route. You should have seen me...

water was running down my face, and my feet squelched on the jungle floor! I got thinking that resilience isn't always glamorous; it sometimes involves acts of raw resolve – simply pressing on despite setbacks. But as I ran, I became aware of another act of resilience: reframing misfortune by exercising my greatest power – choice! Choice allows you to redefine the meaning you associate with a certain event.'

Dael looked even more puzzled.

'I know it's hard to visualise, but here's the key point, Dael: I chose to stand back and view the situation I found myself in objectively. I applied my greatest power of choice by imagining myself hovering outside my body and looking in on the event, as if I were a separate observer – I carried on running despite the rain.

'Once I took this decision, I actually began to run with greater vigour. I then chose to embellish the event by picturing myself as a fearless adventurer or movie hero, filled with grit and charisma, running through the rain to rescue the damsel in distress and saving the day.

'A negative situation birthed a positive outcome as I stretched my stamina and fitness to new heights while imagining my mind and body building stronger levels of immunity and vitality.

'By pressing on, I celebrated the adversity and reframed the situation as a character-building opportunity.

'Here was an opportunity to grow stronger out of a situation that could initially have been viewed as unfavourable! I found myself thinking, I ain't letting this rain stop me! You see, resilience sometimes involves examining our interpretations of events that challenge and stretch us. This is why choice is one of our greatest powers. It's not always easy, but by applying our imagination correctly, we have the ability to replace specific negative assumptions with more-empowering emotions. You see, that running experience in the rain contained the opportunity for me to exercise a variety of interpretations, but in this case, I chose to regard it as a rich opportunity for personal growth rather than a setback. When we learn to navigate our setbacks in such a manner, we gain emotional control, which in turn helps propel us forward toward greater achievements. We've removed the interference! This is a useful equation

to remember, which was coined by Timothy Gallwey ...' She scribbled in the sand once more:

$$performance = potential - interference$$

'Very often, our greatest enemy is the negative or doubtful voice within. Let me share my "flip it" tool for building self-control and resilience.'

'Hold on,' blurted Dael, 'say that again. I'm trying to write all this down in my journal.'

Lead was happy to oblige. 'Let's imagine you find yourself stuck emotionally – paralysed in a state of fear fuelled by an inner dialogue rumbling around in your head. It might go something like this: "What if I lose my job next year?"

'You have the ideal opportunity to flip this statement over. For example: "I'm fortunate I have an income now that allows me the freedom to save so I can plan for bigger and better things in the future – don't waste this opportunity!"

'Another example: picture an entrepreneur's predicament (although a necessary component of their adventure) having to endure considerable patience and long periods of time working from home, diligently developing a prototype or world-beating idea that could potentially solve an urgent global problem as they affirm this: "I'm fed up with being chained to my home office with time on my hands!"

'Flip it to "I must make the best of this precious time because I bet, in years to come when I'm successful and busy touring the world, promoting and selling my product, I'll wish I'd had more free time and space to relax or be creative on my home turf."

'Does this make sense?'

'I think so,' Dael confirmed.

'OK, now imagine yourself within the following situation: "I've taken a temporary break from working from nine to five to pursue my real passion, but what if my money runs out?"

'How could you flip this example?' she questioned.

Dael scratched his head and thought for a moment. 'I could start by saying out loud, "Is that thought serving me?" and then flip to, "I've earnt and saved the money I have in my bank right now, and I can do it again! I'm never going to become penniless or abandoned in the desert if I'm sensible and willing to think creatively. Where there's a will, there's a way!"'

With a twinkle in her eye, Lead sat back, crossed her arms and proclaimed, 'Now you're gaining mastery, my friend... bien joué!¹ So tell me, what have you learnt about resilience now?'

Dael had been put on the spot, but he gave it his best shot. 'Resilience is having the ability to step in and out of challenging situations and observe objectively what's happening around you. It's all about staying true to your vision, with composure and humility, while redirecting negative or doubtful self-talk. By behaving in such a manner, you'll steadily achieve the things that need doing, sometimes over long periods of time, and ultimately, you'll avoid burnout. Resilience involves remaining calm and focused, even during stressful times, and being prepared to seek expert advice or support when appropriate, rather than leaning unnecessarily on others.'

'Yes, indeed,' replied Lead, 'and I like your point about being open to ask for help or advice. Establishing the appropriate connections, mentors and allies along your journey is critical.'

Dael continued, 'I see that now. You gracefully accept that learning arises through challenge, continually refining ideas, taking inspired daily action, and converting this into inner strength and courage.'

There followed a moment of silence as both friends took a slow, deep breath as if coming up for air – appreciating the enormity of information that had been shared.

Lead concluded the session: 'The act of resilience incorporates colourful grit, optimism, and a wonderful opportunity to encourage or inspire others. You learn not to take yourself too seriously and to create time to take care of yourself. And when you eventually emerge from your pupal-like state of resilience, after growing and working so diligently toward

---

¹ "Well done!"

your goal, you'll finally break free and soar to new heights, radiant and beautiful as you share your colours for all to share – just like our little butterfly friend.

'Think about how many times the newly hatched birds of prey fail before they soar through the sky after leaving the nest. Observe the leaping trout swimming upward against the relentless force of a waterfall. Think about how many times a newborn deer collapses awkwardly before mastering the skill of balance and the ability to walk. Think about your own goals and dreams, and take courage from those that have succeeded by exercising continual resolve following huge adversity or challenges. Nothing of great value, nobility or respect can spring forth unless it passes the resilience test.

'Finally, and I'm not sure if you've already come across it, but I want to share with you some facts about the resilience tree.'

'What's that?' he asked.

She explained, 'If you walk south through the jungle as far as you can, you'll eventually arrive at a sparse and barren landscape. Growing alone at the edge of a desert, with very little water or sustenance, is the gnarled and weathered resilience tree! It deserves this name because of the severity of its location. It's very distinctive as it only has five gnarled branches. This stubborn little tree always reminds me of five less-obvious qualities associated with resilience, and I imagine them as statements etched into the bark of its branches.

'On tree branch one, I imagine the engraved phrase: "Stick at it." Now this may seem rather an obvious or unglamorous aspect of developing a resilient state of mind, but don't be fooled by its apparent simplicity. We all know many give up just before the finish line, so it pays to lend this attitude of mind a degree of respect. Staying on track and persisting with your goal or vision also allows the universe to linger, observing your personal evolution as well as joining in with you when you celebrate your inevitable success!

'On tree branch two is inscribed "Know thyself." It's vital to continually invest time in studying and developing your mental faculties (that is, willpower, imagination, intuition, memory, reason and perception) to aid in the accomplishment of your goals.

'Tree branch three contains the statement "No one owes you anything." Now this sounds rather harsh, but when you understand and accept this great truth, you'll refrain from blaming other people for every misfortune, and you'll avoid falling into a state of self-pity or wasting time manipulating others into propping you up when a crisis occurs. Remember that you have infinite potential. This means you not only have the gift of creation within you but you also have all the resources at your disposal to make it happen. Hard work and long periods of concentration may be required; nevertheless, you'll get there, even if you have to do it alone!

'On tree branch four are the words "It's all down to you." A useful affirmation to repeat often is this: "If not you, then who?" It's rather ridiculous when you think about it, but some people expect some outside channel to make things happen for them. No newly hatched bird can leave the nest in flight unless it stretches and flaps its own wings!

'Tree branch five is inscribed with just two words: "The mundane." Learn to make peace with the idea of having to carry out the boring, everyday and sometimes less significant tasks that accompany the route toward your goal. Every moment in your journey is an opportunity to learn.

'Finally, in just the same way as the law of gravity and the change of seasons are immutable laws, there's also an abiding law of resilience that I like to think represents the roots of the resilience tree, anchoring and feeding this attitude with the correct sustenance. This law states that if you keep going, you'll eventually succeed. It sounds so simple and straightforward that it's often brushed aside, as you assume there must be more-complex processes at play to ensure a safe passage to success.'

As the two lizards departed and said their goodbyes, Lead turned to Dael and repeated, 'Remember: knowledge is power!'

Liberate *your perception of self and unlock the control of your emotions, and then you'll achieve your desires.*

Route Guidance Eleven
Recalling our ancient origins to understand stress

A sad soul can kill you quicker, far quicker, than a germ.

John Steinbeck

Developing higher states of awareness, much like climbing the steps of a ladder, allows us to continually appreciate a slightly broader or more elevated perception of the world.

This includes developing a deeper consideration of our cultural and historical roots, how our ancestors worked and survived, and the part our heritage has played in shaping the discord we may feel today when trying frantically to compete within the modern hustle and bustle of the twenty-first-century world.

Our ancient origins

The modern technological world of work and the fast-paced lifestyles either coaxed from or forced upon us by modern Western society serve only to distance us all continually from our primal ancestral roots. Our psychological connection with the great outdoors, for which we were biologically and physiologically designed, has fractured. With this in mind, it makes sense at this stage of our guidebook to pause and examine our ancient origins, from both a social and a physiological perspective.

Thousands of years ago, our ancestors lived together in tribal groups of approximately 150 people. They spent considerable time outdoors, foraging and working the land, all the while learning to respect and navigate nature's elements and the cycles of the seasons. Collectively, our ancestors' survival relied on team work. Each individual undertook specific roles, depending on their competency or skill (carpentry, forging weapons, weaving, basketry, etc). Their diet (as yet untarnished with the addictive sugar and salt supplements that flood modern processed foods), physical lifestyle and psychological disposition meant they didn't suffer from many of the stress-related illnesses associated with today's lifestyles.

This isn't to assume, however, that our ancestors didn't encounter hardship or adversity. Their challenges were physical ones involving endurance, survival, extreme manual labour, travelling on foot to hunt and gather food, building shelters, and working the land, all the while remaining constantly alert so as to look out for each other's safety. The group tackled the trials and tribulations collectively, with a deep sense of purpose, trust and belonging – which are essential for survival.

We only need to study the engravings of the stars that our ancestors left in sand and rock to reveal that their lives weren't just about survival but also about living rich, cultural, spiritual and meaningful lives.

As night fell, the tribe would come together around open fires to retell mythical stories within which tales of bravery and adventure are embedded. It was during these ritualistic gatherings that our ancestors breathed life into their senses of spiritual connection, ritual, awe and cultural identification. As they gazed in quiet contemplation at the mysterious cosmos above, they pictured the sacred and unseen forces that orchestrated order and union in their lives.

Jump ahead to the twenty-first century and consider just how removed many of us are from these primal but fundamental experiences within which the rhythms of Mother Earth are embedded.

Scientific and technological progress define humanity's greatest achievements in the modern world (medicine, agricultural mechanisation, global transport, satellite communication, etc.), but it's also important to consider the urgent struggle millions of people are experiencing to fulfil a deep sense of meaning, emotional stability, holistic connectedness, and a sense of inner peace or fulfilment while living and working within modern society.

Many people find themselves suffocated and isolated, working for long periods at a time operating technological equipment or systems within artificial environments that deny natural sunlight, green space or fresh air. This existence is so far removed from any meaningful connective experience (which was fundamental to the survival of our ancient ancestors) centred on working in harmony alongside nature's elements.

Furthermore, many people's work habits are contrary to the types of activities that support well-being and the development of strong immunity levels: exposure to outdoor sunlight (vital for the production of vitamin D), regular physical exercise outdoors, and sufficient social interaction working within a team that's fulfilling activities to achieve a common good. Modern work often encourages bad dietary habits – such as snacking between meals, consuming fast food and rushing meal breaks – in order to finish a work task before the close of the day.

The pace of modern life also makes it increasingly difficult to detach, switch off and regulate work-based commitments outside office hours. The texts, emails, forums and virtual networks stored on our smartphones and devices follow us home and even accompany us to bed! Having a screentime fixation and reading on smartphones before retiring to bed prevents the mind from winding down – ultimately, creating poor-quality sleep. Quality sleep is vital for maintaining optimum health and well-being.

For many people, finding time to just 'be' and taking care of themselves holistically – whether it involves mindfulness, contemplation, or opportunities to fully switch off and relax – are simply far too impractical or onerous to squeeze into the pace of modern work life.

You may be familiar with something Richard Bach said: 'Remember where you came from.' It might be useful to remember this quote when you find yourself falling victim to that inner voice of frustration – the echo from your ancestral past that occasionally beckons: *I wish I knew why I find so many things stressful. Is there something wrong with me?*

Ancient past vs twenty-first century

Contrasting our work and lifestyle activities operating in the twenty-first-century world of work with that of our ancient ancestors makes interesting reading.

Skill requirements for working and surviving in our ancient past

- Physical agility and fitness
- Tracking/trapping animals, fishing, scavenging, hunting and gathering; knowing what natural locations to avoid; finding drinking water; and moving water with gravity
- Using weapons, such as archery or throwing a spear or stone; crafting and using tools to farm the environment or build a shelter; constructing a perimeter for security; and building a well
- Knowing which herbs and wild plants are edible and when best to harvest them; making bread, cheese and butter; making food from scratch and butchering animals; saving seeds and preserving foods; keeping animals and bees; having knowledge of plants to treat illnesses and wounds; purifying water; and passing wisdom down through the generations
- Working in harmony with the patterns of nature and the seasons, understanding topographical clues to locate water

or provide natural defences, and enduring walking long distances using navigational and spatial awareness skills

- Making clothes, doing leatherwork, and building and lighting a fire to stay warm

- Appreciating deeply and practising cultural bonding; leaders prioritising the efforts of the community to better serve the group's needs

- Practising group storytelling where connection is built through sharing experiences; respecting the group's elders and learning from their wisdom and experience

- Spending considerable time outdoors working the land in a range of weather conditions, retaining high levels of immunity and physical endurance, and managing short bursts of the stress response and then recovery (running away from a fierce wild animal)

- Delivering trust, support and meaning through the collective; survival relying on the group working together

Skill requirements for working and surviving in the modern world of work

- Thinking expertly and creatively using skills developed through lifelong learning; embracing new skills (IT skills, critical thinking, etc.)

- Pulling many aspects together in complex systems; working smoothly in teams to solve problems, having the ability to ask the right questions to create innovative solutions and executing these solutions!

- Being a great communicator, using the skills of novelty, story and intrigue to engage others while getting a point across

- Using digital technology creatively to extend your message and engage others (product launch, slide show, blog, report, etc.)

- Knowing how and where to use e-based research statistics responsibly; being ethically responsible when using e-resources

- Using adaptability and resilience to embrace multiple careers in a lifetime

- Focusing on goals and the ability to organise and prioritise, being self-reliant with good time management skills, and having high levels of self-leadership

- Attaining a high level of emotional intelligence and using these skills to engage, lead and create lasting relationships; having the ability to handle prolonged mental stress

- Having a global awareness and an in-depth understanding of how best to communicate with other cultures

- Knowing your 'why'; providing solutions that solve problems specific to the twenty-first century (environmental, technological, sociological, etc.)

Stress busting techniques

As Lead's coaching progressed, Dael was able to form a more-objective review of his life and describe with greater transparency the times in the past when his behaviour had spiralled uncontrollably into long periods of worry and depression. Immersed in these states, everything in the outside world felt harsh and oppressive; problem circumstances were beyond his control.

With Lead's help, some of Dael's old habits and attitudes – such as continuously worrying or moaning about what was lacking or missing in his life – began to ease. The two friends often found themselves laughing hysterically about some of the ridiculous disempowering behaviours they'd adopted in the past, which did nothing to improve their circumstances. For example, allowing their worries concerning a dreaded upcoming event to hold them emotionally hostage and deflated for weeks on end, only to vanish once the event had passed. Dael had adopted one of Lead's affirmations to help temper this emotional response the next time he faced a similar situation: 'Hold on. What am I focusing on right now and is this thought serving me?'

Dael had even mustered up the confidence to explain to Lead that he suffered occasionally from oversensitivity. Because of this disposition, he often felt detached socially from his colleagues at work, and he couldn't help feeling this was a huge disadvantage in terms of being able to focus and get on with his tasks in hand.

Lead immediately reassured her friend, explaining he was certainly not alone and many a jungle creature shares his temperament.

She went on to explain that being oversensitive does have its advantages: 'Being sensitive just means you process physical, emotional and social stimuli – such as bright lights, crowded spaces and loud noises – at a deeper level. Although this can cause a little physical discomfort, being sensitive allows you to pick up subtleties in social situations, which is a huge advantage when solving problems or making sense of complex group disputes. Sensitive individuals are generally more compassionate, reflective and hardworking. They often develop into wonderful leaders or conflict-resolvers because they observe circumstances through a broader 360-degree perspective, from which they can gather a diverse range of information.'

Dael took some time to ponder this information to reframe his disposition. Maybe he wasn't quite as out of touch or at odds with everything in his outside world as he'd first thought. Indeed, maybe he had a lot more to offer than he first realised!

In order to stretch their legs, Lead beckoned her friend to join her on a short walk to a nearby pond in which many of the jungle turtles lived. When they arrived, they sat together on a boulder overlooking the pond to observe what the turtles were doing. Dael remarked how relaxed the turtles looked as they were simply sunbathing on the rocks, each with their head and legs tucked neatly inside their shell. He then contrasted their relaxed demeanour with the feelings of suffocation and exhaustion he felt when navigating long periods of stress during his working day. He explained to Lead just how immersive his stress levels were, which prevented him from thinking straight. His condition even affected his *energy levels and satisfaction in life, which occasionally resulted in periods of mild depression.*

The two friends continued to watch the turtles until Lead remarked, 'Under normal conditions, when we're relaxed or in a state of flow, the many regions of the brain communicate in tandem – much like the various instruments in an orchestra. The frontal part of the brain – which is called the "medial prefrontal cortex" and is responsible for focused, decision-making or problem-solving thought – works harmoniously alongside the "posterior cingulate cortex", which is at the rear of the brain and is responsible for generating speculating emotions, creative inspiration and memories. This relaxed and balanced state of mind is referred to as the brain's "default mode".

'When we're immersed in states of anxiety or stress, this default mode is disrupted and we can't think clearly or creatively, as the brain's activity is focused on dealing with the immediate threat that's disrupting our performance.

'However, the sensation of stress is a natural survival by-product from our primitive, reptilian ancestors that's actually designed to help us adapt to our surroundings and grow stronger. The purpose of stress is to prepare the body physically to react quickly to escape danger (such as falling into a river, fighting a battle or running from a predator). This automatic response is designed to heighten and tense the body in preparation to respond to a threat, but only in short bursts of energy, after which we can rest and recover.

'In the modern lizard-world, the circumstances that trigger stress are far more complex and prolonged, and they're driven by psychological pressure, rather than temporary predatory danger triggering a physical response. These new stress triggers that accompany our modern world include oppressive work environments, deadlines, money pressure, technology drain, competitiveness, overly busy schedules, low self-esteem, debt, mental exhaustion and poor work-life balance. To make matters worse, many lizards gauge their worthiness by comparing themselves with others continually and reaching conclusions such as "The grass is always greener on their side" or "I'll never be as good as them!" These pressure valves ultimately lead to a fight or flight response being felt

within the body, which then produces heightened levels of anxiety or a feeling of being on edge. When this type of psychological stress is allowed to continue for long periods of time, the physical body is placed into a constant state of tension, which can eventually lead to fatigue, worry, headaches, social withdrawal, anxiety, resistance, inaction, exhaustion and even disease.

'The key hormones released during periods of stress are cortisol and adrenaline. High levels of cortisol contribute to insomnia, increased blood pressure, accelerated heart rate, potassium mineral loss, vitamins B1 and D loss, inflammation within the body, lower immunity levels, brain fog, and a fixation on specific problems. Prolonged chronic stress can even contribute to bone and muscle loss, as well as poor digestion and kidney filtration. There are circuits within the brain, composed of millions of individual brain cells, which perform a range of functions. In order for the brain to operate correctly, these cells must operate together harmoniously. Prolonged and intense periods of stress can damage these circuits. A state of worry stimulates the amygdala at the base of the brain, which is responsible for regulating the emotions of fear and aggression. A state of being continually on your guard is created, resulting in a constant state of apprehension, panic and fretful thinking, which inhibits calm rational or objective thinking.'

Lead drew Dael's attention back to the turtles: 'Have you ever had one of those stressful days when one overriding, worrisome thought simply won't go away and continually wears you down, both emotionally and energetically?'

'Many a time!' he replied.

'Then try remembering these quirky facts concerning turtles next time this happens:

'1. Contrary to popular belief, turtles can't leave their shell.

'2. The sea turtle cousins of these little fellows we're watching have a great sense of direction, like a GPS [global positioning system].'

Dael looked baffled.

However, Lead was prepared: 'I know; it's another quirky lesson, but please let me finish.

'Begin by reminding yourself that worry only serves a purpose if it's held as a short-term state that, ultimately, encourages you to create a solution. However, continual worrying without actually formulating a solution to your problem never gets you anywhere. You can't think straight in this state. Some refer to the feeling as "having a foggy brain".

'So here's a solution. When you find yourself trapped in a perpetual state of stress and worry, recall the first turtle fact I've just shared – turtles can't leave their shell – and remind yourself it's similarly impossible for you to wriggle out of your current state of worry immediately, but you can initiate the following two-stage process toward a steady recovery:

'1. Just like the unique GPS skill possessed by the sea turtle, you too can apply your own GPS to help you formulate a more-objective evaluation of your position or circumstances.

'2. If there's nothing you can do in that present moment to actually solve the problem, pause and redirect the focus of your thoughts toward a more constructive or goal-driven activity.

'Focusing your mind in this manner helps alleviate the chaos within and ignites the frontal lobe of the brain, which is designed to focus on one thing at a time and prioritise thoughts; in this case, these thoughts are now being directed toward a more constructive or purposeful activity. If you continue with this approach, you'll be surprised just how liberating it feels. For example, you may decide to go for a run, dig the garden over or clear out a cupboard, which is far more purposeful than simply sitting around worrying. The key lies in giving yourself permission to reframe your situation, think yourself free of your circumstances, and refocus your energy on formulating short-term solutions that actually serve your predicament.

'All of us have the ability to concentrate in this manner, much like the will power we can exert in flexing a muscle. You can develop willpower (one of your six mental faculties, along with imagination, intuition, memory, reason and perception) by taking time out to light a candle and study the flame for ten minutes at a time. By staying present and completing this exercise correctly, you've achieved a level of mastery by purposefully redirecting the mental energy previously wasted on worry.

With practice, you can release anxiety and self-doubt and approach the rest of the day with a clearer head.'

Lead pointed to a particular group of turtles submerged in shallow water alongside the bank of the pond. 'Here's another clever behaviour that these turtles practise. Do you see those two turtles lying in the water? The water is very shallow there and has been heated up all day by the sun. These turtles know that lying in hot water reduces their stress hormone, cortisol, by a third! This might be something else you could try Dael – taking a long, hot soak in a shallow pool under the midday sun.'

'I love your ideas!' he said with a laugh.

Lead suddenly thought of another tool to share with her friend: an acronym to help manage stress. She took hold of Dael's hands and held them up at arm's length in front of his face and explained, 'The next time you feel stress building, hold your hands up like this, with your palms facing outwards and thumbs touching, and imagine the phrase "Help at hand" spread out across your hands, with each letter occupying a different finger or thumb. Holding your hands up in this manner and reading from left to right the letters on each finger or thumb also create an amazing symbolic act of defiance. You can imagine striking this pose when those around you are expecting too much or forcing you to submit to unreasonable demands.

'Reading from left to right, recall each letter and practise this stress recovery technique. She let go of his hands and picked up a stick to write out these words in the earth beside the boulder they were sitting on:

HELP AT HAND = Hold back, Exercise, Lists, Process,
Agility, Talk,
Happiness, Ambient music, Nature, Diet

'We'll start with the first letter on the pinkie of your left hand: H. H stands for "hold back". At the first sign of stress building, picture yourself putting your hands up, with your palms facing outwards in recognition of what's happening, and push back. You can seize control and you have the power to apply the brakes. Recognise and accept you are where you are: in a state of stress. Simply giving yourself permission to label and *observe the situation in this manner provides you with a more-objective and level-headed approach to formulating counterbalance solutions that can put you more in control. Even a slight shift in establishing greater control makes a difference to your overall mindset. Now continue to work through the following steps.*

'The next letter on your fingers, E, stands for "exercise". You'll disperse mental stress and improve your mood, self-respect, quality of sleep, relaxation and mindfulness by taking regular gentle exercise. Exercise doesn't need to be complicated. Consider the more obvious natural forms of movement, such as stretching, walking or gardening. Exercise floods the body with cleansing oxygenated blood and helps release trapped tension within the muscles and nervous system. It also provides the body with a break from harbouring tension and redirects its focus back to its correct level of homeostasis – namely, physical and mental ease and agility. You'll also feel better about yourself because you're executing a positive response as a counterbalance to a negative situation. Exercise will also improve the quality of your sleep and release feel-good chemicals within the brain, which are called "endorphins". Remember that quality sleep is very important in helping the body repair itself, build immunity and re-energise. During sleep, waves of cerebrospinal fluid wash in and out of the brain, which helps clear out toxins. The downtime you experience following exercise is a perfect opportunity for the brain to recharge after the rush of oxygen it's received. It's important to remember that it's not just our muscles that get tired following physical work but our brains also suffer from fatigue, and so they require care and attention too.

'Next, comes the letter L, which stands for "lists". Having time to relax and switch off is important, but it's worth noting that too much procrastination can actually add to more stress. Grouping and prioritising tasks written on a to-do list is a great way to mentally offload, as the paper – rather than your memory – takes over the ownership. Furthermore, the act of simply crossing off each accomplishment with your chosen pen can prove highly satisfying, and it helps convince your subconscious mind that there's some form of order, stability or routine in your life, which in turn alleviates any further build-up of stress.

'Another list you can generate as a means of helping alleviate the build-up of stress is called a "gratitude list". It's impossible for a lack, a limitation or stress to take centre stage when you take a break from the hustle and bustle and choose to immerse yourself instead in a deep state of joy, gratitude or thankfulness for what's already working in your life. This one habit alone will dramatically change your perspective and ease any preoccupation with feeling sorry for yourself.'

'What do you mean by "generate a gratitude list"?' Dael questioned.

She clarified, 'Take a large piece of paper and write out a list of twenty things in your life that you're truly thankful for. Don't stop until you complete all twenty – this is very important. Note how easily your mind wanders and how your ego will try to persuade you this activity is a waste of time. Your ego will want to return you to a state of self-importance or pity, as it loves crisis, comparing and fault-finding.

'It may take some time to finish, but it pays not to rush or cut this process short. When you do finish, sit back and note any slight changes in your mood or state of mind. As you step back into the world, you may sense a renewed desire to remain more present or connect with people with higher levels of empathy and support.

'It's such a simple task, but it's one of the most powerful tools at your disposal! But here's a bigger truth: when you develop this approach as a habit, you'll soon discover how the outside world will draw your attention to even better things to be grateful for that were previously below your radar. Finally, you'll enhance your senses of well-being and purposefulness as you continue to remain alert for more opportunities to feel blessed.

'Next is P for "process". Apply a process approach to improving your stressful situation. Begin by writing out the particular circumstances in your life that are causing you stress and move steadily toward observing them more objectively. You can do this by practising the following three-step process:

'1. Soothe a challenging experience with the statement "I'm feeling stressed. I know stress is a natural response left over from my ancient past. Assessing the meaning behind my emotions is okay. I now feel immediately more in control by recognising what's actually taking place inside me."

'2. Affirm this: "I'm going to step back now and view myself from a distance as if I'm a separate entity or observer. This higher self has the ability to replace my current stressful feelings with more neutral or balanced emotions. Choice is my greatest power. No one person or thing has power over me unless I choose to let it in. I'm going to nip stress in the bud and imagine what thoughts and actions I could lose myself in right now that would lead me to greater ease and acceptance."

'3. Take slow, deep breaths, matching the length of each inbreath with each outbreath, and return your focus back to your physical body. Celebrate the fact that you've regained control by exercising an elevated level of awareness. Affirm this: "I can incrementally advance my perspective. I'm doing okay. I have the power of choice. There's no point beating myself up. The mental chatter is undirected and ignorant noise inside my head, and it will pass! What has happened in the past has nothing to do with where I decide to go next with my thoughts and actions. Everything is simply energy. Where do I wish to direct my energy?"

'Next is A for "agility". It's important to remind yourself that you were created with physical and mental dexterity in order to advance your intention and interact with the physical world. In short, you're designed to move, and when we flex or stretch our bodies adequately, we alleviate the build-up of muscular tension or fatigue. This can involve practising a series of low-impact activities that improve muscle conditioning, core stability and balance (yoga, Pilates or tai chi). These forms of physical activity can help alleviate an overactive mind and help redirect attention back to a more holistic, spiritual or whole-body experience based on greater harmony and flow. Take a leaf from nature's book and observe how the octopus, with such ease and dexterity, adapts and morphs its body to fit a recess in the rocks. Observe the manner in which water effortlessly fills and takes the form of the space into which it's poured.

'The next letter, T, stands for "talk". Remember to ask for help! During times of stress, it's okay to reach out and connect with those you trust and respect most to help you tweeze out any issues that are preventing you from thinking with clarity, balance or perspective.

'Lizards like to help each other – it's in our nature. I've often turned to one of my friends for help or support during troubling or stressful times, and more often than not, they've shared a really useful nugget of wisdom – sometimes based on personal experience – which has really helped me. Making eye contact and sharing relaxing catch-up time with a friend also helps release oxytocin, the feel-good chemical housed inside the brain. If we feel better about ourselves, we're far more likely to approach our challenges with greater confidence and mental agility.

'H stands for "happiness". It sounds obvious, but cut yourself some slack from time to time. Create more balance in your life by giving yourself permission to do things that make you feel happy. This may simply include hobbies, relaxation, time with a loved one or an escape into the countryside. An activity that stimulates a range of senses can prove particularly effective at easing tension or stress (listening to your favourite music, looking at positive images, stroking your pet, basking in the sun, smelling and tasting your favourite meal, etc.).

'A stands for both "ambient music" and "ancient arts". Listening to calming, meditative music is an incredibly powerful tool that can help to combat stress. The limbic area of your brain is the emotional centre, and it becomes activated when you listen to upbeat music or joyful singing. Alternatively, to help encourage creative thinking or relaxed concentration, listening to theta-wave-frequency-based music can prove particularly effective.

Many of the ancient arts – such as meditation based on specific breathing exercises, fasting, chanting a mantra, walking barefoot and acupuncture, to name just a few – deliver considerable benefits that relieve stress. Above all, the simple act of allowing yourself the time to wind down and reflect at the end of the day enables your mind to empty and prepare for relaxation before retiring to sleep.

'N represents "nature". Spending time outdoors releases some obvious stress-busting benefits, including breathing fresh air and increasing cardiovascular activity. The perhaps less-obvious benefits of spending time outdoors include the lowering of the level of the stress hormone cortisol and more opportunities to experience mindfulness, clear-headedness and self-reflection. Gardening can help you feel less self-absorbed, releasing the perfectionist within, as nature rarely conforms to strict precision. It also releases the feel-good chemical serotonin within the brain. Tending a garden creates a sense of purpose and respect for living things. Connecting with nature helps us become less self-absorbed and eases depression.'

Suddenly, Dael jumped up enthusiastically. For the first time since meeting Lead, he felt compelled to share his interest in botany: 'Oh, I know all about this. My hobby is collecting and studying the health benefits of plants. Did you know that gardening outdoors also boosts the immune system and strengthens bones? And it improves both fine and gross motor skills, as well as improving coordination and balance. I've recently been studying the sensory benefits of spending time in nature. Did you know that focusing on the subtle noises plants or trees make as you touch them or when the wind blows through them helps stimulate your hearing, which in turn can release pleasant memories? Plants have a variety of textures that encourage us to want to feel them, which in turn can offer a sense of serenity. Smelling plants can trigger fond memories, which produce a variety of calming emotions. Nature's colours can also stimulate a range of emotions. Soft tones of lavender blue can prove restful for people feeling agitated, while bright reds and oranges can fill the observer with joy and energy. Tasting vegetables and herbs that have been grown and tended at home can allow a person to acquire a sense of achievement. Growing and harvesting vegetables and herbs, and then consuming this produce later can create a unique sense of satisfaction, as well as a mindful eating experience. I've been experimenting with the effect indoor plants have on air quality within enclosed spaces such as offices. Many of us work in very artificial environments full of dust, mould, bacteria and chemicals released into the air from furniture and machinery. You can help clean this air pollution by introducing snake plants, peace lilies and spider plants.'

Lead was somewhat taken aback by Dael's sudden exuberance, and she smiled. 'I've never seen you so animated and excited. This is great! We must talk more about this later. Meanwhile, let's examine the final letter: D.'

'D stands for "diet". Are you starting the day with a nutritious breakfast that will fuel and replenish your body? It makes sense that maintaining a balanced diet will help your body and mind function smoothly. You can help combat the build-up of stress by drinking water, eating plenty of green vegetables that are rich in minerals and vitamins, and limiting your caffeine and alcohol intake. Some consider fasting to be an approach to combating stress and even helping the body heal, but I'd always recommend seeking expert guidance first.

'It's important to consider the following questions if we want to undertake an honest review of our dietary well-being:

'Which foods do you regularly consume, and have you considered what effect these foods might have on your mood, concentration and alertness?

'Do you hydrate your body adequately throughout the day?

'What food do you consume to kick-start your day?

'What do you snack on throughout the day, and are these foods really what your body requires?

'Do you grow your own fruit or vegetables outdoors?

'When was the last time you actually prepared a meal consisting of fresh produce that you grew and cared for from seed?

'Do you skip lunch breaks and continue working? Could this habit contribute to how you feel later in the day (in terms of your energy levels and quality of sleep)?

'Finally, have you considered the difference it makes to your health and well-being when you choose to take the odd lunch break outdoors surrounded by nature? This simple practice can help boost your mood levels and support your concentration throughout the remainder of your day.'

Before the two friends said their goodbyes and pencilled in the next meeting in their diaries, Lead shared one last personal story related to the topic of worry and stress: 'My dearest Dael, I have one last true story to share to help add some perspective to the issue of tackling the state of worry. Very often our problems' solutions that we so earnestly crave the most can actually lie right under our nose. If we add one little letter

– I – into the middle of the word "nose" we can create the word "noise"! With this in mind, the story I'm about to share is entitled "Noise"; let me elaborate.

'The other evening, I'd reached my wits' end concerning a particular worry I was harbouring, and I decided to exit my house and take a long night-time walk. I hoped the cool, crisp night air and open spaces would provide some deliverance.

'Walking briskly through the jungle, under the stars, I waited patiently for some form of guidance or wisdom to enter my consciousness. At first, nothing particularly unusual or enlightening sprang to mind. I began to conclude that my hasty decision simply to take a hike outdoors, rather than trying to figure it all out, was somewhat foolish. Have you ever had that experience, Dael? You know, the sudden need to step outdoors in search of inspiration or solace, even though you've got so much to do and the ego is constantly reminding you that you can't really afford to waste this time.'

'I think we all do from time to time,' Dael agreed.

Lead continued, 'But here's the thing: inspiration and wisdom arrive if you're patient.

'Let me explain. Suddenly, my mindful walk was shattered. First, a vulture soared overhead, screeching with petulant ferocity. Next, an ear-deafening thunderclap shook the jungle. To top it all off, I walked past a group of hyenas laughing hysterically at the tops of their voices. It was so loud I had to put my fingers in my ears for protection. In a rather intimidating manner, they deliberately shuffled to be right in front of me and blocked my path. Rather than reacting and kicking up a fuss, I simply paused with my fingers still placed firmly in my ears. A few precarious seconds passed before they eventually lost interest and ran past, still laughing and kicking up great waves of dust across my path.

'In that moment, the answer I'd been so diligently searching for suddenly presented itself: noise – just too much noise. I was allowing too much noise and distraction to rumble around inside my head, but I had the power to put my fingers in my ears and simply choose to let it pass rather than fighting the route out of the problem!

'It was in that moment I recognised the universe had provided me with the perfect answer! All the worry, doubt, fear, frustration, argumentation and confusion was just that – noisy chatter inside my head – and the outside world had perfectly mirrored this predicament and then gone on to provide the solution. You see, Dael, when we get trapped in cycles of negativity, it's important to soften that noise by relocating to somewhere peaceful or quiet, so we can free ourselves from the ego that's always trying to perpetuate chaos. You free yourself when you silence the noise, stand back and respond to circumstances with a calmness of mind rather than simply reacting!'

Invoking a stress-free state by working alongside nature

The whole of creation exists in you, and it is your destiny to become increasingly aware of its infinite wonders and to experience ever greater and grander portions of it.

Neville Goddard (2010, p.40)

Many people accept a degree of affinity or respect for nature, but they simultaneously regard themselves as the superior being. As far as we know, humans are the only species that have the ability to articulate a deeper sense of consciousness, imagination, intellect and self-awareness. This personal sense of *I-ness, self-realisation* and *desire to leave an impression or a statement on the world* can take the form of art, creativity, literature, philosophy, and scientific or technological achievements. Complacency, however, is another human characteristic, and disregarding our responsibility to respect and work in harmony with the natural world makes all our notions of superiority somewhat shallow or meaningless. Today, more than ever, humanity is aware of its growing responsibility for the protection and preservation of Planet Earth. At the very least, we're aware our survival as a species relies on it. We all have our own unique part to play in learning how to develop greater care and appreciation for Mother Earth. We're tenants on this planet, not landlords.

How often do you create space in your life to practise acts of reverence or awe for the natural beauty around you? When we lose the ability to appreciate nature's intricate cycles, patterns and beauty, we inhibit our ability to access higher levels of creativity, emotional sensitivity and happiness. Nature is always your nearest neutral reference point to help you reset, ease stress and anxiety, and help deliver clear-headedness or inspiration.

Walking and stretching the body within nature has obvious physical benefits as well as stimulating and revitalising the senses. Brisk walking in nature, maintaining good posture and breathing in fresh air is a wonderful simple form of rejuvenating exercise.

Cultivating vegetables outdoors can encourage us to appreciate or reconsider our dietary intake. When we take a break from eating highly processed foods (which are designed and manufactured simply to overstimulate our taste buds and create an addictive response) and switch to consuming fresh, close-to-source, nutritious fruit and vegetables, we're gifting our bodies with what they truly need to thrive, which in turn affects our mood and sense of well-being.

The following are some nature-mindfulness suggestions that can serve to alleviate stress:

- Plan opportunities into your work routine to stop and be present in nature. As you breathe in fresh, oxygenated air, picture this air circulating and bathing the cells of your body. Reflect on and review your day so far while noticing the patterns or natural rhythms nature has to offer. This activity will recharge you, ease depression and help you to become less self-absorbed. Focusing on distant natural objects releases a sense of freedom, perspective, clarity and possibility.

- Gardening outdoors or caring for plants indoors helps soothe the perfectionist inside, as precision is rarely achieved in nature. Touching and caring for plants also reduces stress. It teaches us acceptance and heals the challenges we all face from time to time. Gardening provides us with the opportunity to experience biophilia (the vital well-being connection humans have established over thousands of years with planting and working the land). It helps lift our mood and reduce the amount of the hormone cortisol, which in turn lowers stress levels and increases serotonin (the mood-regulating hormone).

- Practising mindfulness while walking or resting in nature (simply stilling the mind in the present moment) allows you to listen to your inner voice of intuition, and then invite inspiration, guidance or peace. One useful exercise is to focus on the varying sensations around and within your body, then ground yourself by imagining your feet growing roots that burrow deep into the earth below you.

- Transform your working environment into a space that supports your well-being and productivity by allowing as much natural light as possible to bathe your work area. This will help you feel more energised and alert. Positioning indoor plants near your workspace will boost your productivity, absorb carbon dioxide and clean impurities from the air. If your work environment is stressful and confining, create time throughout the day to step outdoors, breathe fresh air and discover what nature has to offer close by. Nature is a wonderful mirror that can faithfully reflect to you subtle warning signs about how out of balance or self-absorbed you might be. For example, when you stepped out of your door this morning, did you notice the birds singing or were you so preoccupied with the day's agenda that you failed to pause and appreciate the present moment?

When you do find yourself alone within nature remember the acronym AWE, where A stands for "appreciate", W stands for "wonder" and E stands for "everywhere". You could try repeating, 'Beauty in front of me, beauty behind me and beauty to the sides of me,' as a means of acknowledging your acceptance and appreciation of the points made earlier.

Liberate *your perception of self*
and unlock the control of your emotions,
and then you'll achieve your desires.

Excursion Two

The E in LEAD
EMOTION

You can no more avoid assuming a feeling than you can avoid eating or drinking. All you can do is control the nature of your assumptions.

Neville Goddard (2010, p.58)

Route Guidance Twelve
Change = an inside job!

The mood decides the fortunes of people, rather than the fortunes decide the mood.

Winston Churchill (Goddard, 1969)

Choose your thoughts wisely

One morning, Dael sensed a dramatic shift in the direction of Lead's teaching as she arrived armed with a peculiar green parcel.

Lead rested the parcel on a nearby rock and asked Dael a question: 'Now, Dael, tell me this: what have you learnt from our meetings so far? Just give me what you've got!'

As Dael replied, he counted off each of his ideas on his fingers: 'Well... I now realise the type of limiting thoughts that so many lizards automatically replay in their minds, like a habit, which prevent them from truly thriving or gaining lavage over their hopes and dreams. I've learnt about some of the soft skills – sorry, I mean critical competences – that can help you thrive in work life. I've become more aware of just how incomplete my school curriculum was at equipping me with the skills I needed to realise my full potential. I'm aware of the five aspects of well-being, and I've explored some new terminologies that, before meeting you, I knew very little about. I realise why so many lizards find it hard to work and live in the modern world, considering how our ancestors evolved working and surviving alongside nature's elements. I've learnt about the importance of reconnecting with nature, managing stress, overcoming fear and building greater resilience. I've filled a whole notebook full of tips and techniques that I can use to regain my power when faced with everyday challenges.'

'Umm... excellent,' replied Lead. 'Are you ready for the next stage?'

Dael didn't hesitate and nodded enthusiastically.

She therefore went on: 'Wonderful. Now I'm going to give you a secret message written in the form of a question inscribed on a small piece of slate. The slate is wrapped securely in a banana palm leaf and bound in jungle twine.'

Lead drew Dael's attention to the green parcel on the rock beside them. 'The inscription on the slate contains the secret to happiness! You must promise not to remove the palm leaf from around the slate until tomorrow. Keep it safe and close by you during your working day. Every hour throughout the day, carefully unwrap the palm leaf and study the question inscribed on the slate. It's important to then record in your notebook, at that very moment, an honest response to the question. Bring all your notes to our next meeting.'

With a glint in her eye, Lead gently handed Dael the concealed slate, then turned to leave.

Dael didn't notice Lead's hasty departure, as he was unable to pull his attention away from the curious prize he was turning over in his hands. Slate was extremely rare in the jungle, and there was only one place it could have come from: the deep bed of the perilous Oncondo River, hundreds of miles away. Had Lead really travelled all that way to find such a precious and unusual gift? Coupling this fact with the intrigue Dael now felt rising up within him meant he could hardly contain himself.

The next morning, during his lunchbreak, Dael carefully untied the twine from around the slate, peeled off the banana leaves and began meticulously searching the surface of the slate for the hidden message. To his surprise, there was nothing inscribed on the surface of the slate! He wondered if Lead was playing a trick on him or if he'd maybe been given the wrong rock sample. Dael decided, however, to honour his friend's instructions and continue to study the slate every hour at work in the *manner that Lead had requested. Maybe the message on the slate would somehow magically appear later in the day.*

Dael continued to peek at the slate every hour, but nothing changed. By the end of the day, he felt somewhat irritated and bemused by Lead. What purpose did an old piece of slate serve anyway?

The following morning, the two lizards met as usual, but Dael still felt cheated and confused. He wanted to cut to the chase and have it out with Lead for making him look such a fool.

However, she took the initiative and asked, 'So, my friend, what answers did you record?'

'The slate was blank. I'm afraid I can't see the point,' explained Dael.

'Exactly,' Lead stated, exultant. 'And every day for the rest of your life is just the same – a blank slate just waiting for you to write a response about how you choose to be emotionally! The reason so few lizards truly thrive in modern work life is because they stop asking the following question: how could my day unfold with improved ease and flow? Or to take it a step further: how do I wish to create my day so I experience greater joy and harmony?'

'What?' spluttered Dael. 'Is that it?'

'I haven't finished. Everything you experience in life is actually communicated through feelings, and feelings are dependent on one thing only: your habitual emotions! Learning to modify and select the right emotion is your ultimate point of power – the one aspect of your existence you must master to truly liberate all aspects of your life. Let's be clear, however: I'm not suggesting you deny or hide a negative emotional response to an unfortunate event that may come your way, but what I'm saying is remain aware. Choose your thoughts wisely and realise you also have the ability to monitor and select empowering emotions at the drop of a hat, which can help create your day!

'Creating positive change in your work life is primarily an inside job, my friend! We can blame the outside world for how we feel, we can make excuses or even incriminate ourselves, but ultimately, all are experiences of life held in some form of emotion or another. Everything just is! It's the meaning we associate with so-called 'things' (as quantum science

informs us that matter is 99.9% energy in varying degrees of vibration, rather than solid material) in our outside world that really matters. But I have a question for you: who or what is really in control when it comes to determining and monitoring our emotions?'

There was a stunned silence as Dael looked even more perplexed. He had never heard anything like this before. After some careful consideration, he thought about some of the difficult people he worked with and remembered some of the unfortunate events in his life that had made him feel miserable and powerless. The outside world did indeed feel like the big villain and root cause of so many of his past low emotional states.

The power in 'I am'

After allowing Dael a few moments to reflect, Lead continued, 'All of us only ever seek certain things or outcomes because we believe that acquiring them will make us feel better. Let's examine the habitual way in which we assign our release of positive emotions dependent on certain favourable experiences manifesting in our outer world (buying a new home, a trip overseas, treating yourself, winning the jungle lottery, etc.) We assume shiny things out there in the world will deliver the fulfilling glow we earnestly desire deep inside. It's for this reason that so many continually chase certain goals, acquire new things or frivol their life away trying to be someone or somewhere else.'

'I don't fully understand what you mean.' Dael was bewildered.

'You're experiencing the world outside by being fed information (news headlines, gossip, your progress report, your work appraisal, your bank statement, etc.) continually through your senses. You then form opinions or judgements on what's happening out there and immediately marry this up with some form of feeling. From this perspective, we construct our unique sense of I-ness.'

'What do you mean?'

'When life throws us a curveball of misfortune or an unfortunate setback we didn't plan for, we form an emotional judgement immediately and then articulate our feelings about it by declaring: "I'm fed up, I'm

stressed, I'm confused and I'm sick of this." You see, you feel and respond to a plethora of rich and intoxicating sensations in life, which are expressed through an "I am" declaration. Never underestimate the creative power contained within your "I am" statements. Much like with the analogy of "Which came first, the chicken or the egg?", can we be sure that an emotion arrives first and then produces an "I am" statement, or could it indeed be the other way round?'

'What? That's ridiculous. Slow down; this is mind blowing!' blurted Dael.

'Yes, but hear me out. Even if you can't comprehend my last point, these "I am" statements are important because they create the perception and meaning you associate with the outside world, as well as a sense of self-worth.'

Creating your reality

Lead went on to clarify this: 'Let's look at it another way. Your emotional state causes your feelings, which in turn influence your thoughts and subsequent actions. We could therefore conclude that our current state is always a by-product of a previous emotion. This subsequently creates a lens through which you forge opinions or assumptions about the people and events in your outside world, which in turn determines your behaviour or reaction toward these things. Ultimately, you can conclude that the manner in which you observe the world outside also has an effect on the things you're observing. Or to put it another way, what if the outside world created a feedback message, like a mirror, that validated where you were emotionally?'

'Go on... I think I can see where this idea is leading,' he said.

'Consider the experience of being in love. In this state, your outside world is filtered through a romantic, colourful lens (your emotional state at that time) that magnifies and brings into clarity the sensations of excitement and joy. Figuratively speaking, you see stars and love hearts wherever you look. When we change the emotional lens through which we view the world, we attract different people and circumstances into our life.

'If the outside world reflects our inner world, then our state of being creates our reality. What if you regarded your emotions as the cause substance that subsequently trigger the resulting "things" in the outside world that are reflected to you? This is what is meant by the statement "You create your own reality."'

Dael sat back, perplexed, before responding, 'Hold on, Lead, I just need a little time with this. Clearly, you've been living your life in this manner for a long time. I'm not sure if I'll ever be able to reframe my view of the world like you have.'

Lead took hold of Dael's shoulders and said defiantly, 'Yes, maybe not straight away, my friend, but remember that I had to start somewhere! Oh, and by the way, you never fully master this. The learning never ceases. I'm not saying this is all easy and we never stop reacting to what's out there in the very real world. I still feel emotionally scattered when visiting the jungle dentist or filling out a tax return, you know!'

Lead laughed, but then went on: 'The important point is to be aware, to endeavour to manage or prepave your emotions as much as possible, and to watch what happens in your life. As with any skill, it's all down to practice!'

'I'm sorry, but I don't understand what you mean by "prepave",' Dael responded a little sheepishly.

'Oh, sorry. Prepave means to clear the way or make room psychologically for new experiences to enter your life by changing mindsets, beliefs or assumptions about your worthiness, how the outer world operates and your place within it. This might include rekindling an awareness of your unlimited potential to allow more goodness and plentitude to enter your life. For example, to prepave the experience of receiving greater abundance, you might reconsider your definition or assumption about what abundance means to you exactly, the ease at which it naturally surrounds you, and the variety of avenues or exciting opportunities through which it can find you.'

Emotional states

She went on to explain, 'We can instantly trigger certain sensations or *reactions within the body (a cold shiver, clammy hands, butterflies in the stomach, an adrenaline rush, tension, insomnia, a cold sweat, etc.) simply by thinking about a particular past event (either pleasurable or unpleasant) that deeply impacted us emotionally at that time. In this state, the body has become a slave to an emotion that, in essence, is a form of trapped energy. Since energy can't be created or destroyed (according to the law of perpetual transmutation of energy), the body inexplicably absorbs strong emotions and stores them like a memory.*

'Maintaining your focus on such memories results in you becoming even more sensitised emotionally. These emotions flow back into the body, creating a feedback loop. If this momentum is rehearsed long enough, we create a habit and get stuck in an emotional state. Some of our reoccurring, emotionally engrained habits can often be traced back to experiences that took place decades ago, and they can be very difficult to break.'

Strategies to control emotions that disempower you

She added still more detail: 'To summarise, every experience in your life is actually taking place internally, projected against the backdrop of your marvellous imagination, like a movie. Within this film, you're both the actor and director, but I'll explore that more later. For now, remember that nothing in the outside world, as relayed and filtered through your five senses, actually means anything until you attach emotional identification and meaning to it.

'When you select a particular film to watch at the cinema, you'll often make that decision based on the emotional experience you'd like to entice (thrill, terror, excitement, comfort, joy, etc.). Do you think it's possible that you could adopt a similar approach in creating your day?'

'I don't get what you mean,' he declared.

'Can you think of a reoccurring theme, a topic or aspect of your life right now that automatically triggers within you a series of negative emotions centred on a lack, disharmony or worry that rumble on week in, week out? Consider how easily these negative emotions ride on the back of that theme, so much so that they swamp you, take you over and

almost become an identity in themselves. It's probably the case that these negative emotions are well rehearsed, yes?'

'Yes, I can think of one annoying situation that's been on my mind for some time.'

'I now want you to imagine a large gold coin that represents symbolically the particular theme you just recalled. Imagine one side of the coin represents the negative emotion you've automatically assigned to that theme. Returning to the idea we explored earlier, during our discussion on resilience, now flip the coin over and picture, if you can, it embodying an emotion still linked with the theme but having the complete opposite feeling – the sweet spot or preferred emotional state.'

'I'm still not sure exactly what you're getting at.'

'For example, let's pick up the coin entitled "my level of vitality". Let's imagine your experience of this theme is far less than perfect. One side of your coin represents all the emotions associated with feelings of frustration, despondency or fatigue that you may currently be perpetuating. This could look like poor work-life balance, inappropriate rest or an unhealthy diet. On the other side of the coin reside the feelings of joy, effortless ease, energy and abundance, each of which you could imagine as an inherent emotion linked to a scene in which you're bouncing through life, full of zest, completing fulfilling and purposeful activities. Do you see how every topic – whether it's finances, health, relationships, prosperity or a sense of meaning – is bound by the law of opposites?'

'When you put it like that, Lead, I can sort of see the logic in that.'

'You see, the opposite emotions are faces belonging to the same coin. You can't have one state without the other. It's perfectly natural when you're trapped in a negative emotional state to assume that the only way you could reverse this condition is by experiencing an opposite scenario; that is, a dramatic positive shift in outward circumstances. But we have to be smarter than that because living a life wishing for things to simply change, out of the blue, is rather short-sighted. However, when you become fully aware and engage two of your greatest mental faculties – will power and imagination – you have the ability to master your emotions by choosing how you wish to think. From this higher state of consciousness, you're applying a force that, if used responsibly, can quite *literally change your reality – especially if you believe the idea that your inner state influences the circumstances that show up in your life.*

'Let's look at it another way. The actor and director are both committed to delivering a successful performance, but they hold very different roles, even though they share a position alongside each other on stage at times – like the two faces of the same coin. They're both part of the same screenplay; however, the actor behaves subservient to the lines contained within its script, but the director – while reviewing the script – can act with great freedom or autonomy and even make changes to the way a scene is organised or portrayed. In any situation you're in, Dael, ask yourself what part you wish to play in your life – the actor or director.

'I'm now going to share a process that's so unique I even attached my name to its title. It's called the "Lead emotion process", and once you've mastered it, you can apply it at any time to regain self-control, shift up a gear emotionally and, ultimately, influence your outside world.'

Lead then went on to talk Dael through her process...

The Lead emotion process to transform your state

First, stop, become profoundly present and observe the emotion you're immersed in. Try labelling the emotion as if it were an entity outside you.

Next, check this emotion and ask yourself, 'Is this emotion pulling me up or throwing me down?' If it's pulling you up then remain in that vibration, if not, read on.

Imagine the coin or the actor-and-director analogy covered earlier and consider the law of opposites. What emotional states could reside at the negative and positive extremes of the circumstances you've assumed have triggered your emotion in the first place?

Then apply your willpower to flip the coin and focus on your preferred choice of emotion.

Enhance this exercise by imagining yourself as removed from the drama of the circumstance you find yourself in and try to observe it objectively. Try not to get wrapped up in attempting to remove a negative emotion, because you'll simply add more momentum to the feelings you don't want. Instead, focus on the ideal state – the other side of the coin. What would that feel like? With this approach, you'll begin forging a new emotional pathway through which the outside world has to begin slowly mirroring your preferred state or assumption.

Finally, round off the process by repeating this Émile Coué quote: 'Every day, in every way, I'm getting better and better!'

Somewhat taken aback, Dael stared thoughtfully into the distance while attempting to digest everything Lead had just shared. 'I get what you're saying, but what about the times when you feel thoroughly paralysed emotionally and the noise in your head makes it almost impossible to adopt the Lead emotion process?'

Lead listened intently, resting her elbows on a tree branch and placing her fingertips together as she formulated the perfect response.

Tumbleweed moments

She then explained, 'Imagine tumbleweed relentlessly rolling across the desert in the wind. It's an image often employed by a film director to introduce a sense of foreboding or a desolate opening scene in a movie. You can picture that scene, can't you, as the tumbleweed is thrown helplessly hither and thither?'

Dael nodded enthusiastically.

'Have you ever experienced tumbleweed moments like that in your own head, Dael, when your thoughts rolled helplessly from one negative focus to another?'

'Indeed, I have', he replied. 'Sometimes, I've lain awake for hours at night worrying about a particular issue in my life and knowing all too well I was perpetuating still-darker emotions, triggering yet more despair. I then end up with this storm rolling around inside my head that can last for days. It's horrible.'

'Yes, I understand, my friend. These negative and catastrophising thought habits create negative emotional states that are very hard to escape from. It feels like you're being held captive, doesn't it? Think about it – just like the tumbleweed is cursed to roll around the desert relentlessly under the control of the wind, you're negative emotion is only behaving in a similar manner.'

It was at this point that Lead climbed up on to a branch overlooking a narrow stream and looked down at her friend. 'I've now taken this elevated position on this branch to make an important point. You see, to solve the problem, we have to look at this dilemma from a point of elevated awareness or higher consciousness. I'm about to provide you with some further ideas. You may want to make notes.

'First, imagine yourself standing in that desert, observing the tumbleweed. How would you prevent it from rolling around in the wind?'

Dael thought for a moment, feeling slightly under pressure as he was unable to provide an answer immediately.

Lead broke the awkward silence. 'Now, you can't stop the wind, but you could put a foot on top of the tumbleweed so it stands still. So, going back to the situation you described, you could try asking yourself these questions:

'What image am I rehearsing in my troubled mind right now, and is it becoming more turbulent now it has been hijacked by negative momentum?

'Has the thing I'm worrying about happened yet?

'Can I recall a similar time in the past when I came through okay in the end?

'What am I surrendering to allow this momentum to continue?

'Who's the ultimate authority with the control to stop all of this?

'Your answers will allow you to separate out the knee-jerk emotional reaction and detach it from the momentum. In this sense, you've put a foot on the tumbleweed and applied the same primary point of power discussed earlier: choice! You can then use this affirmation: "I have a choice to hold this tumbleweed in place, even though the wind may still *be gusting around me. I'm taking back control!" You've now asserted the higher awareness within you – the neutral observer or ultimate wisdom within.*

'Next, with your foot on the tumbleweed and your back to the wind, you have the ability to find greater balance or perspective. From this position, imagine the tumbleweed's rigidity lessen as it's crushed under the weight of your foot. It can't go anywhere now and it's under your control. As you do this, you turn your attention to the storm around you, and then picture the wind dissipating slowly. Now you can observe your immediate environment with greater clarity. Think of it as taking respite, occupying a fresh space outside the eye of the storm and coming up for air! You can then affirm this: "I'm free and capable of choosing my emotions. I'm aware the state I'm in is simply a thought held captive by misaligned energy. I do have the choice to stop and appreciate, even for a few seconds, that there are alternative avenues to which I could switch my focus. I can change my perspective incrementally. I am where I am, but one thing is for sure: all this will change, and I'll be in another place before too long."

'So Dael, repeat back to me what you've just learnt.'

'By working through the preceding steps, you've identified the tumbleweed (representing the worry or negative emotional state) and the wind (representing the momentum energy inside your mind) as two separate entities. By separating the two, you sever the link one has over the other and dissipate the energy.'

Lead clapped her hands together in excitement. 'Excellent, my friend. Now remember that we're not trying to make problems go away or escape our responsibilities, but rather, we're resetting our thoughts and escaping the paralysis in order to make clearer or more-objective decisions.'

Raising your emotional state in your everyday work life

Dael didn't want the discussion to end as he'd never heard anyone explain ideas like this before, or in such detail, when it came to the topic of combating emotional entrapment. He pressed on with another question: 'Just to take the focus away from dwelling on the more extreme emotional traps we can find ourselves in, what about the more general or insignificant circumstances in life when you're not necessarily struggling emotionally but just wish to experiment raising your emotional state to demonstrate to yourself you can actually exercise this uplifting power?'

Lead response was rather abrupt: 'First of all, no day in your life should be regarded as insignificant!'

'Of course. You're right. I'm sorry.'

'Going back to your question, I once worked with a tree frog called Erawanu [what does that spell backward?] who spent her working day at an office desk. Now Erawanu was a good student of mine. She avidly studied the knowledge that I've shared with you so far, but she naturally progressed to the stage where she wanted to put into practice everything she'd learnt while studying under my mentorship. She did this so well that she not only transformed her experience at work but also her whole perspective on life.'

'What did she do?' asked Dael. 'I'm intrigued.'

'Well, she admitted to me that she felt somewhat indifferent or uninspired at work, occasionally getting stuck in despondent thought cycles or low emotions, and this really bothered her. She felt the only time her mood lifted was outside of work, during the evenings or weekends. I challenged her by asking her why she was assuming that her time spent at work wasn't the appropriate environment in which to also raise her spirits.

'We worked together on visualising her work environment as if we were bystanders observing a movie scene in which we could see her going about her day in a more buoyant and uplifted manner. We embellished this scene by imagining the rewarding emotions this new state of being would deliver. I encouraged her to rehearse this power statement whenever possible: "I am where I am, but I bear the power to choose how I feel!" Followed by this: "All I ever have is the now! What do I wish to experience emotionally, even in quite ordinary, everyday circumstances?" We discussed the sorts of feelings that jungle animals experience when they're fulfilled and happy – such as gratitude, joy, connection, energy and empathy – and then examined how she might incorporate them.

'She understood she couldn't instantly switch her reality from one rather negative state to another more positive one, so instead, she exercised a stepped approach.

'Her first step was to begin her day over breakfast by listing ten things in her diary that she felt grateful for. She also rehearsed in her mind's eye her ideal day, feeling the sensation of joy from connecting with and supporting the people around her. She imagined herself finding opportunities within normal, everyday conversations to demonstrate greater connection, empathy and warmth with the people she worked with. She saw herself going about her working days finding opportunities to compliment, support or uplift her customers and work colleagues.

'Eventually, she was ready to implement the new behaviour into her day by taking tangible action steps in the outside world. This wasn't as difficult as you'd imagine, because she'd rehearsed her preferred new emotional state so many times within her imagination that she'd already developed her new state into an emotional habit. She actually got a buzz from stepping out the door in the morning, because she realised her well-rehearsed emotions could create her day, rather than the day determining her emotions. She maintained her focus, behaving in accordance with her intention, and subsequently, her working days unfolded with a greater ease. A deeper sense of fulfilment, self-respect and meaning took hold of her days.

'Her new behaviour had a dramatic effect on the people she worked with. Apparently, some of her work colleagues even turned down better-paid promotions working at other companies and chose to stay where they were simply because they didn't want to lose the feel-good ethos that she'd created in the office. Within the year, her job role had changed following her appointment to a new work position, and guess what? Her new role involved leading and supporting her fellow employees.

'Here's the important point: the change she witnessed didn't occur as a result of merely hoping or wishing for a change in her outward circumstances or by applying huge force to the manipulation of people or things, but it came about by getting emotionally involved with her imagined ideal scenario. She'd created a world within that felt so real and familiar that it eventually became her outward reality. She had mastered the art of emotional leverage.'

Lead jumped down from her tree branch and immediately began rummaging around in the bank of the stream. She stood up eventually, clutching a ball of moist earth, and declared, 'Aha... here's some. Look, Dael, what's this?'

'Is that clay?' he queried.

'It is... now, look!' Lead began to manipulate the clay gently between her hands. Although the clay was rather firm at first, with patience, she was able to warm the clay with her hands, making it more malleable. There was no extraneous haste or force required, just a little patience, until Lead was able to shape the clay into the letter g.

'She explained, You see, by kneading the clay carefully and slowly, you can produce quite intricate forms, and it's just the same when it comes to originating emotions to help create your day. It takes a little time and patience, but nothing that's any good comes through force and haste... It's all about steadily moulding the right sorts of images within your mind!'

'What's with the letter g?'

'Oh, it represents the perfect lead into my next idea, but let me put this back where it belongs first.' Lead reformed the clay into a ball and carefully pushed it back into the river bank. 'As the clay belongs back in the ground, and we're studying the topic of regulating or managing our emotions, I call the following process the "emotion-grounding exercise" (hence the letter g) and it's another perfect but simple technique you can practise for a few minutes each morning to help you create your day.'

She went on to talk Dael through the exercise...

Emotion-grounding exercise

When it's safe to do so, take a moment to stop and focus on your breathing. Concentrate on any tension or unfavourable sensations you can feel within your body.

Next, focus on the sounds you can hear around you. Separate the noises into nearby and distant categories. Can you differentiate between noises that are natural or mechanical, or calming or intrusive?

Now that you're present, work on slowing down time by focusing on your position relative to the environment around you. Check how your body is positioned. Relax any muscular tension and close your eyes for a few seconds.

Open your eyes slowly, and then relax your observation of objects around you so you reach a point of calm, non-judgemental detachment. Right now, all is good – and you're good. The outside has released its hold on you.

From this general, more serene state of being, fall gently into an imaginary zone of peace and serenity, suspended within the void of space, and ask yourself what emotion you wish to immerse yourself in right now. Is it a state you wish to take back out into the world and share with others, or is it just for you to enjoy in the present moment? There's no right or wrong answer.

Begin teaching your body what it feels like in this new state. How would your body react if it were playing out these emotions fully right now (such as a shiver of excitement; deep, focused breathing; butterflies in your stomach; or a rush of energy)?

Finally, although this isn't always the case, note any waves of inspiration or insight that may enter your space.

As you return to your daily affairs, act as best you can from the preferred calm, centred and elevated emotional state you evoked during your meditation. Ask yourself how your immediate environment is being coloured by the emotions you're harbouring right now: warmth, love, compassion, connectivity, empathy, joy, gratitude, etc.

By carrying out this exercise, you've taken yet another vital step toward emotional empowerment. You could imagine you possess the ability to mould a new reality or hop across to a parallel universe that's more congruent or aligned with your true self.

Upscaling emotions one step at a time

The two friends decided to stretch their legs and walk for a while. All the while, Dael continued to ponder the range of ideas shared that morning. Lead could see her student needed more help and beckoned him to follow her along a narrow path that led deeper into the forest.

'Where are we going?' asked Dael.

'Hold on,' replied Lead, 'I think the place I'm looking for is just around this corner... ah, here we are!'

Lead had led him to a forest opening flanked by tall palm trees. As they stood watching the trees sway in the breeze, Lead announced, 'Ah, here they come, right on cue. It's lunchtime!'

'Who's coming?'

At first, Lead didn't say anything as her attention was fixated on the movement emanating from the shrubs that enclosed the clearing. Lead's voice quietened to a whisper. 'Ahh, there they are. What do you see, Dael?'

Emerging from the shrubs and scurrying on all fours were a group of about five primates.

'Monkeys!' cried Dael. 'Shouldn't we hide? We'll scare them off.'

'Don't worry.' Lead chuckled. 'They're far more preoccupied with what's concealed at the top of those palm trees than worrying about us!'

As the friends huddled together behind a Bougainvillea shrub, Lead explained quietly: 'You see, at the top of those palm trees there's the most delicious fruit that our jungle provides. These monkeys are one of only a few skilled types of animal who can scale those tall trunks to access this bounty.

'For now, I want you to think of the fruit as their goal. The top of the tree is where all their joy and success lies.'

Gradually, the monkeys began scaling the trees. The route looked precarious, but they applied serious skill in ascending the tree trunk in a precise and regimented manner. With great dexterity, each monkey defied gravity, advancing upward by alternately sliding upward one hand and then one foot. Their technique was clearly well rehearsed.

Lead clarified, 'If you look closely, Dael, you'll notice that the surface of a palm tree trunk is made up of a series of equally spaced horizontal rings, like narrow steps. The fibrous surface of each ring isn't dissimilar to that of a coconut husk. Imagine each of those rings represents an emotional state, with the most negative or mundane at the bottom of the tree trunk, rising up sequentially to the most empowering and enlightened at the top. For example, we could imagine emotions such as depression, unworthiness, worry and frustration at the bottom, rising up to hopefulness, fulfilment and joy nearer the top. Of course, in between them, halfway up the trunk, would be the more general emotions, such as boredom, indifference and contentment.

'Let's imagine the monkeys are influenced by some mysterious force that causes them to halt their advance and remain stuck on whichever ring matches their current emotional state. The monkeys are also unaware that there are other emotions etched on the tree trunk above them and ignorant as to why they're being prevented from climbing further. Do you get the idea?'

'I think so', replied Dael. 'Please go on.'

'Let's picture a particular monkey who finds his climb halted mysteriously halfway up, while he's fixated on the emotion of discouragement. What if we were to ask the monkey why he was experiencing that particular, rather negative, emotion? Let's imagine he began describing how he felt emotionally, using words such as "worthless" and "disillusioned". He then elaborates, justifiably blaming his state on an incident that had happened earlier in the day when he received a barrage of criticism and rejection from his work colleagues. Now we know that nothing in the outside world actually means anything until we attach a particular meaning to it, but the monkey doesn't possess this awareness.

'What if we invited the monkey to climb down from the tree and sit with us on the ground for a while and view his predicament from a more enlightened perspective? We could direct the monkey's attention toward the full range of emotions now clearly visible rising up the tree trunk. We could explain to him that, in order to free himself from his current position, he had to raise his awareness, study the law of opposites and apply the power of choice to ask himself "Is that thought serving me?"

To help the monkey to flip the meaning he was attaching to his current experience at work, we could explain that the opinions of others are just that – their opinions or viewpoints. But this doesn't determine whether something is necessarily right or wrong, or indeed, what the reason you should doubt yourself is. It would also be of benefit to explain to the monkey that the rejection of an idea isn't the same as the rejection of the person owning the idea.

'When the monkey internalises his emotion in such a manner and then reframes his current emotional state, he has mastered the art of "neutral observation". The monkey, now unblinkered by the emotional paralysis concerning the so-called "unfortunate circumstances" in the outside world, is free to return to his original position on the tree (a state of discouragement), reconsider his position and slide up to the next preferred emotional state or step on the tree trunk (hopefulness). If he continues to embody this approach to evaluating the circumstances of his life, he'll find he moves steadily closer to attaining his ultimate prize, which is waiting for him at the top of the tree. With this awareness, the monkey will indubitably notice some of his friends are preoccupied with their emotional positions at various stages up the tree trunk. He may choose to warn them that, remaining stuck in their positions on the tree could lead to them growing weary, perhaps losing their grip altogether and sliding downward, resulting in injury and disarray.

'Before we send the monkey off to begin scaling the tree again, we'd just need to remind him that, now he's embodied this new level of awareness, he has a responsibility to remain attentive and not negate his attention with respect to refining his tree-climbing techniques, remaining present and concentrating on what's immediately in front of him, so he appreciates the journey. There's no fast-track approach to reaping the jewels of fulfilment, I'm afraid. If the monkey takes his focus off these things, he risks losing his grip altogether and falling. This is why all the great mystics have replied with the same one-word answer when asked what the meaning of life is: attention!

'Finally, it would help the monkey further if we encouraged him to invest in seeking support from a mentor, in the form of daily encouragement, as it's not always easy to do all this alone. The monkey needs to accept there will always be fluctuations in his progress, as no one is perfect – but it's the general upward trend that matters. You're aiming to assimilate higher emotional states, creating new habits without having to think too hard about it or diverting your gratitude from the present moment. It's very important that this inner work is carried out in a relaxed manner. Force negates! Remember what I said before: you are where you are! What's really important is that you make a decision about where you wish to go emotionally. With practice comes confidence. One thing's for sure: once you fully endorse this new approach, life will never be the same again!'

Dael broke Lead's flow by asking, 'You mentioned that it would be important to remind the monkey not to abandon its climbing technique; will you elaborate on the process of shifting yourself from one immersive emotional state and transforming it into another?'

'Observe how the monkeys climb the tree. Before they can move upward, what technique must they execute using their hands and feet?'

Dael carefully studied the monkeys scaling the trees. 'Well, they slowly release their grip with the hand below their outreaching one, and then switch roles.'

'Exactly. So, to answer your question, it's actually a process of releasing old emotions steadily, then replacing them with slightly more elevated ones. In this way, you advance up the emotional scale little by little while retaining your grip on the present moment, if that makes sense.

'No one is exempt from existing in some form of emotional state or other, but we have to identify with the observer inside us who has the power to step out and view our circumstances more objectively. A good method for maintaining this self-reflecting form of objective observation is to ask yourself occasionally how you feel about other people or circumstances in your life, as this will highlight how you feel about yourself. Your only role is to manage your own emotions, not the lives and intentions of other people, and to grow more aware that the outside world is, fundamentally, you pushed out. Come, Dael, we must eat. All this lively talk has made me hungry!'

Liberate your perception of self
and unlock the control of your **emotions**,
and then you'll achieve your desires.

Excursion Three

The A in LEAD
ACHIEVE

Calmness of mind is one of the beautiful jewels of wisdom.
It is the result of long and patient effort in self-control.

James Allen

Route Guidance Thirteen
Mastering the faculties of the mind – the key to achieving success and fulfilment

For as he thinks in his heart, so is he.

Proverbs 23:7 (New King James Version)

The ideas that changed everything for Dael

Achieving more by understanding how the mind works

One afternoon, as the two friends hiked up a secluded jungle path into the mountains, Lead picked her moment to surprise Dael by handing him two very unusual gifts that she'd hidden in a hollow in a tree at the foot of the mountain pass. Working in secret for days on end, away from prying eyes, Lead had prepared the gifts to mark the next important chapter of Dael's learning journey.

The first gift was a pale-grey conch shell on which she had etched a peculiar diagram. The second gift was an extraordinary plant, potted in a split coconut shell and flaunting burgundy plumage that resembled a brain – a cockscomb celosia!

Lead chuckled to herself as she handed Dael the plant. 'I immediately thought of you, Dael, when I found this in the jungle. It fits perfectly with today's lesson, which focuses on the mind. It's just a bit of fun – a reference point, if you like. Of course, plants can't grow new brains, though we can, but more about that later!"

Next, Lead drew Dael's attention to the drawing on the conch shell. It was a simple profile of Dael's head with a line running horizontally through the middle, defining two areas that were shaded in different colours, with the lower area slightly larger than the one above.

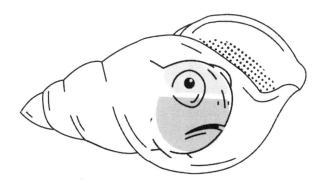

'When did you prepare all this?' he enquired.

'Oh, over the last two weeks or so, when I realised you were finally ready for the next phase of tutorials. The information I'm about to share is really important, but very few lizards in this jungle have the opportunity to be exposed to it, let alone master it. It's a little involved, Dael. Are you okay if I press on?'

'Yes, yes; please go on,' insisted Dael. 'We've come so far and learnt so much, it would be crazy to stop now.'

'Okay, here goes. Imagine that the shaded areas I've drawn on the image of your head represents your mind. Of course, your mind contains a plethora of complex components, including the six mental faculties we explored earlier, but for today's lesson, we're going to examine just two key parts of the mind, which I like to refer to as "lizard aware" and "lizard stored".'

Lead pointed to the shaded area at the top of the diagram. 'This area represents the lizard-aware aspect of your mind. This is the centre for logical or problem-solving thought activity, concentration, speculation and decision-making. For example, if you decided to focus your attention on thinking about how you might decorate or rearrange your study, solve a difficult calculation, or organise a trip using a map, then you'll predominately be applying the lizard-aware region of your brain. Incidentally, it may seem incredible, but you have tens of thousands of lizard-aware thoughts a day. Of course, it's impossible or unnecessary to recall all the thoughts you have throughout the day, but I'm merely sharing this fact with you so you'll realise just how active and dynamic your mind is.

'It's worth noting that, for most lizards, problem-solving or sustained concentration is best carried out early in the day when the mind is most alert. It's for this reason that I always put aside the more mundane tasks until the afternoon, when I know my brain is somewhat sluggish. Our brains gradually wind down still further in the evening, but this can allow more-holistic or more-open communication between all regions of the brain, and I find this is the best time to be creative or invite inspiration.

'Now let's examine the other aspect of your mind, which is represented in the drawing by the lower shaded area entitled "lizard stored". This is the part of the brain that operates automatically, deep behind the scenes, if you like. For example, it's responsible for that urge we lizards have from time to time to bask in the sun so we keep our body temperature regulated between twenty-nine and thirty-two degrees Centigrade. It's also responsible for making our heart beat quicker to pump blood around our body faster so we reach our ideal body temperature more effectively. Lizard stored houses a vast amount of information – including your beliefs, habits and emotions – but you'd find it quite difficult to unpick all of this. You see, the lizard-stored aspect of your mind communicates through the language of symbols and imagery.'

'What do you mean?' asked Dael.

'When you sleep at night, with your senses closed down and lizard aware disengaged, lizard stored has free rein to communicate through your dreams. Certain obstacles, deep concerns, repressed memories or emotions – which you might be unaware of or even deny during your waking day – can be rehearsed and explored through dreaming. It's within this state that lizard stored also has an opportunity to explore other possibilities or other versions of you. Didn't your teachers at school share any of this with you?'

Dael shook his head.

'Hmm, I thought so.'

Dael began to share his experience of school. 'The only thing I can remember about school is my teachers telling me I'd never amount to anything. I think I was put in the bottom set in every subject. They told me I didn't have it in me – whatever "it" was. I always believed that our potential was based on genetics and that intellect and talent were things you were just born with! Some get lucky, and some don't, I suppose.'

Suddenly, Lead drew closer to her friend, shifted her focus to staring deep into Dael's eyes and spoke in a resolute manner. 'If your will and imagination are strong enough, you can create a whole new mind and whole new reality!'

Achieving more by understanding neuroplasticity

Lead took hold of the cockscomb celosia plant and pointed to its brain-like foliage. 'A word I want you to become familiar with is "neuroplasticity", meaning that the brain isn't fixed but is a malleable, evolving system that's amenable to suggestion – hence the term "plasticity". There are neuro pathways within your brain that serve to reinforce and consolidate the emotionalised beliefs and habits you rehearse frequently over time. They can rewire and harden, if you like, stimulated by new information to create new connections. Likewise, redundant neural pathways can weaken and diminish over time.'

'What do you mean?' he queried.

'Think of it like this. The mountain footpath we're currently on only exists because others have travelled up and down this route and beaten down the jungle vegetation to form a compacted-dirt track. In the same way, if you keep rehearsing a certain thought or behaviour, it creates a neuro route that eventually becomes a hardwired learnt response within the brain. We've learnt from our previous lessons that emotionalised thoughts are the most powerful neuro-route builders, as they carry the greatest intensity. This is why sustained stressful living, worry, self-condemnation or pessimism is so damaging to your health and well-being.

You're quite literally teaching your mind to expect more of the same. Understanding the process of neuroplasticity allows you to revaluate or monitor some of your habitual repetitive thoughts, to consider the effects they might have on your health and performance, and to start making some changes.'

'If you habitually repeat empowering thoughts over a long period of time, can this have the same effect of creating new neuro pathways?'

'Indeed they can, because the brain is a chemical factory. Feel-good chemicals, such as dopamine and serotonin, can be released throughout the body simply by picturing a familiar thought that feels exciting. These new signals generate new thoughts, which then generate new expectations, and these, in turn, alter your perception of reality. Do you ever consider what thoughts you're choosing that might trigger a positive neuro-chemical response?'

'Oh yes. Certainly, Lead. Just the anticipatory thoughts and expectation I have before meeting you each day to learn new and thrilling things fills me with a rush of excitement.'

'Very good, my friend; that's also a fantastic example of a well-rehearsed neuro pathway you've taught your brain to hardwire. It's these thoughts that contain the biggest benefits for your health and well-being, as they'll energise you and generate a sense of gratitude,' she responded.

'Going back to examining the impact these less-favourable thoughts have, if they're repeated long enough, they can develop into entrenched limiting beliefs and habits. This is important because our beliefs are critical in determining the meaning we attach to certain circumstances in the outside world and our performance within it.

'Every thought you have matters. Even at a microscopic level, the cells in your body respond to the energetic field you generate when you're emotionally immersed in a state. Do you ever consider the power your thoughts and beliefs can have over your recovery from minor illness, increasing performance, vitality and the capacity to develop greater resilience?'

Achieving more by mastering your subconscious mind

She continued, 'Coming back to the diagram and the lizard-stored aspect of your mind, I know it's a rather crude representation, but note how much larger the lower shaded area is. What does this tell you?'

Dael thought for a moment. 'The shaded parts of my mind are disproportionate in size. I'm sensing you're going to suggest that this is significant when it comes to explaining how best to achieve certain results?'

'Exactly, and this is the perfect opportunity to delve deeper into explaining why we don't always do the things we say we're going to do or achieve the kind of results we wish for. It's not that one aspect of your mind is actually physically larger than the other, I've simply used this diagram to highlight where your true powerhouse lies, which is in controlling your beliefs and actions. What I'm about to share is only really understood by one in a thousand lizards.

'To truly transform your life, you have to engage with and convince lizard stored to get on board.

'Here's a good example to expand this idea. One of my students decided to leave a highly respectable teaching career after twenty-five years of hard work and dedication, to risk everything and live off a minimal wage to focus on developing a new business idea. It took four years and considerable financial challenges before their idea finally materialised and they attracted high-paying clients. When I first began coaching my student, they articulated with much enthusiasm how they'd desired a quick transformation into an entrepreneurial role, but under the surface, a more powerful and silent motivation prevailed within them.'

'I don't understand. What do you mean?' asked Dael.

'I haven't finished the story. You see, the overriding foundational drive embedded within their lizard stored was actually a desire to slow down, to create more free time to probe their creativity abilities fully (which included writing their first book) and unearth greater fulfilment after spending so long caught up in the rat race. This deep emotional desire or intention implanted in lizard stored was what ultimately governed their fate over that four-year period. It's always worth remembering *that the silent and invisible force pulling your strings from the inside can sometimes override the good intentions and plans you think you're enacting on the outside!*

Achieving insights into why it's hard to change

She continued, 'Here's another example. Don't take this personally, but let's say you decided to stop wasting every evening lazing about by the pond catching fireflies, but chose instead to spend that time exercising at the jungle gym – say, twice a week. This act could fulfil the yellow "zest" category of health and vitality that we studied earlier. If you fail to implant this new fitness regime idea – embellished with the emotion of pleasure or reward – into lizard stored, your old default mode or habit would simply take over and deliver a host of reasons why it's best to skip the visit to the gym and continue with what you normally did before. This is called a "paradigm", and it resides within you, continually trying to keep you grounded in your safe zone. Unless you're extremely strong-willed, it's the reason why it feels so daunting to have to put the effort into travelling to the gym, especially after a long day at work. Eventually, you'll put it off to another day or conclude that you don't think it's really for you or you don't have it in you.'

Dael politely raised his hand and asked, 'Umm... this new term "paradigm" – will you explain it a little more?'

'A paradigm is simply a set of commonly accepted or established beliefs, theories, modes or models of thought, consensuses, or basic assumptions that all force us to remain fixed in certain behaviour patterns. When these assumptions are challenged and altered, this is referred to as a "paradigm shift". Paradigms can exist in society, education and even within the world of science. For today's learning, we're examining paradigms in the context of the mind. One of the most powerful paradigms that holds so many back from achieving real growth in life is the limit they apply to themselves in terms of their true worth and potential.'

'We're not so much lazy but more misguided creatures of habit, aren't we?' he chipped in.

'You could think of it like that, but now I've taken the lid off this Pandora's box, do you see how this new information is so empowering once it's understood and internalised? Do you feel like, excuse the expression, you're getting under the bonnet of what really controls some of your thoughts and actions, which ultimately control your destiny?'

'But hold on,' protested Dael. 'Going back to the gym example, I don't understand why my paradigm would stop me from doing something that would ultimately serve me – namely, achieving greater health and fitness?'

'Ahhhh...' replied Lead, beaming. 'Our habits and paradigms fulfil a necessary role of helping us tick along within the safe and familiar "known" environment. As long as what you're doing doesn't unsettle or create a huge deviation from the norm, the paradigm will feed you the message that it's completely reasonable to continue as normal. Remember that all of life's lessons, including the ones that taught you to adhere to caution, have brought you safely to this point, so it feels quite natural not to rock the boat and instigate bold decisions that could potentially disturb your natural homeostasis. We also inherit deep, primal risk-evasion instincts that go way back to our ancient past when we were dinosaurs. Doing anything out of the ordinary back then, such as satisfying your curiosity by wandering off the beaten track during a hunting trip, involved risk and could ultimately result in an attack by a predator or even death!'

'So what you're saying is that, in order for real improvement and change to take place, we have to face this wall of resistance with steadfast commitment, smash through it and reprogram lizard stored?'

'Yes, exactly, Dael; it's imperative that you regard lizard stored as your servant, with you at the helm as captain and master! For most of the animals of the jungle, feelings of fear, lack, negativity, indecision and apathy rule their lives, and as hard as it may sound, this behaviour is engrained and perpetuated automatically within lizard stored. Many creatures know they should each make changes to their life and occasionally take action to correct certain matters, such as setting a New Year's resolution, but they're fighting a losing battle because the've failed to understand the role of lizard stored. To create real change, you have to remove the veil from your mind and study what's really going on beneath it.'

Dael jumped up suddenly, clearly distressed. 'This is terrible... I mean, no one tells you about this stuff at school. If I hadn't met you... oh, it just doesn't bear thinking about. Your explanation makes me draw only one conclusion: unlike lizard aware, which relies on the senses to create a version of reality, lizard stored quite literally creates its own certainty. You're right; it's lizard stored that truly governs our lives, isn't it?'

Lead rested her hands gently on Dael's shoulders and calmly helped him settle down on a tree branch. 'Ohhhh... that's only half of it, my friend!'

'What? You mean there's more?'

'Do you trust me when I say, "Intention declared or affirmed equates to power"?'

'What do you mean?'

Achieving more by applying empowering affiramtions

She explained, 'There's a solution that will enable you to get behind the curtain, so to speak, and ensure your lizard stored is working in harmony with your conscious desires and intentions.

'I want you to picture the lizard stored as fertile soil in a garden, waiting for any idea to be planted. Just like the role the soil plays in a seed's growth, lizard stored provides the perfect conditions for a vision that's emotionalised with desire and passion to germinate and take form!'

'Furthermore, it can't tell the difference between what's imagined vividly (positive or negative) and what's real. This is why it's so important to use your imagination in the manner for which it was originally intended.'

'What do you mean?' Dael needed clarification once more.

'You have the ability, by applying your will, to hold any vision or idea within your imagination until it seeps into the storehouse of your lizard-stored mind, where it builds into beliefs that transform into actions that create changes in your outside world.'

Dael interjected, 'In other words, it bridges the gap between intention and manifestation in the outside world.'

'Precisely,' she replied, 'but remember that the lizard-stored part of your mind faithfully reflects exactly what you frequently imagine into it, good or bad and regardless of whether you're aware of it or not.

'At first, it doesn't even matter if you don't necessarily believe the things you feed it, as repetition over time will steadily transform these commands into their physical counterparts. This is why repeated affirmations, embellished with intense feeling and imagery, work so well.'

'What do you mean by the term "affirmation"?' asked Dael.

'An affirmation is a short phrase or statement you repeat to yourself, either inwardly or out loud, to reprogram any limiting belief patterns or to reinforce specific qualities or attitudes that are ultimately transformed into positive changes in your self-image, behaviour and actions. They can also be used as a means of self-encouragement or to improve focus and concentration.'

All of a sudden, Dael remembered something. 'Oh, hold on. My friend Lufetarg used this type of approach to evoke greater appreciation and gratitude in her life. She was aware she had become too immersed in fault-finding regarding the people and circumstances in her life. It had become such a problem that this habit prevented her from finding enjoyment in even the simplest of things. One day, she found this amazing book entitled Stand Back and Count Your Blessings to Receive Greater Fulfilment by... oh, what was the author's name...? A strange name... Gorfesiw, I think. Anyway, it had such a profound effect on her life that she applied one of the key ideas in the book, which was writing out and then speaking aloud a daily gratitude affirmation.'

Lead replied, 'This, of course, is a great example of using an affirmation in a positive and empowering manner, but for many jungle creatures, their habitual affirmations or self-talk prophecies are often directed toward worry, fear, doubt or catastrophising (for example, "I never have enough money!"; "I'll never figure this out!"; "Nobody loves me!"; "Why is my physical ailment taking so long to heal?"; "Why is life so hard for me?"; "I'm no good at..."; and so on). Consistently applying affirmations intended to reverse these types of negative thought habits takes considerable willpower, but with practice, it does get easier.

'The immediate thoughts and feelings you affirm as you rise in the morning are paramount in creating your day. A powerful affirmation delivered at this time can keep you grounded and focused when uncertainty reigns all around. I wake every morning and say out loud, "I'm so lucky I've been granted another day alive when millions last night ceased their time living on this earth." This is a great example of a grounding affirmation rooted in a profound state of gratitude. Openly acknowledging the gift of life can build motivation, self-belief, faith and resilience. A state of gratitude can support the immune system and help contribute to a healthy mind-body connection.

'You could think of a positive affirmation as a motivating friend who's always by your side, whispering the right messages in your ear. I always say to my students, "You have to be your own best friend and motivator, rather than looking to somebody else to do everything for you! You must look within for certain answers, but it's equally important to allow these answers the space through which to communicate, even if the message is hard to bear."

'The more feeling you can wrap around your affirmations, the better, as this helps embed them into lizard stored. I enjoy repeating my motivational affirmations while looking at my reflection in water. This isn't an egotistic exercise, but it's an opportunity to enhance the affirmation process and make it more memorable for my lizard stored. This involves observing my lips moving as I say certain words and noting the subtle changes in my facial expression.

'How you phrase your affirmations is also very important. Repeat "I am," rather than "I'm going to," as this places your affirmation in the present tense. This is vitally important because your lizard stored responds best to affirmations presented in this manner, as it pictures events as if they're happening now.

'You can also use affirmations to prepave your day and help evoke a more productive outlook on life. For example, you might use affirmations like these: "I'm really enjoying this meeting today with people I haven't met before"; "Ideas keep flowing"; "That's so pleasant"; "I'm getting so much done today in this state of ease and flow"; "Everything works out ideally"; "I'm so happy that I'm completing these tasks effortlessly"; and "Everything today works out perfectly."

'Certain words are extremely powerful when it comes to transforming your state. For example, try repeating the words, "Joy, joy, joy," at any time and, with practice, you should notice yourself feeling more relaxed or in control. This one exercise can also evoke a surge of optimism or renewed expectation.

'To further embellish everything we've covered on the topic of affirmations, I like to picture what happens when a pebble is thrown into the middle of a pond. Can you picture that, Dael?'

'Yes, I can,' he confirmed. 'As the pebble hits the water, it produces ripples on the surface that grow outwards in size until they collide with the banks of the pond.'

Lead nodded. 'Exactly, and one of my favourite visualisation techniques is called the "ripple effect". This is where I imagine my affirmation being dropped into the centre of a huge lake and producing ripples that radiate out to be received subsequently by the world (the shore of the lake). This creates an even stronger emotionalised image for my lizard stored, demonstrating that what I'm affirming isn't a drop in the ocean, but it's a powerful, enduring message that travels beyond the constraints of my imagination and out into the universe. Another reason why I like to picture the ripple effect is because it helps remind me of the best way to allow new ideas to flow into lizard stored – calmly and through relaxed waves of thought.

'Finally, you can enhance the power of your affirmations by applying certain kinaesthetic approaches.'

Achieving more by aligning actions with decisive thoughts

'What does "kinaesthetic" mean?' questioned Dael.

'Basically, this technique involves synchronising your learning with specific body movements to help hardwire the experience in the mind as a memorable sensation. This approach can make it easier to recall facts *or information from memory. Furthermore, when we integrate our fine motor skills with our learning, such as making intricate things with our hands or simply running our finger under a line of text as we read or study, it helps direct our attention and lock the experience into a memory. Your hands are also an outlet for the creative life force that flows within you, as it spreads out and is localised at the tips of your fingers. Our ancient ancestors knew this wisdom, of course. We can all acknowledge the creative energy that's delivered through, for example, the fingers of the potter's hands crafting the clay, the intimate caress from a loved one, or the healing power of Reiki or massage.*

'I apply kinaesthetic learning when I go for my evening jog through the jungle. I think about three things that went well during my day while repeating short statements of thankfulness that I embed into the rhythm of my jog. You can also try this idea just before you fall asleep at night. As you relax, take slow, deep breaths while recalling events from the day that fill you with gratitude, and then carry this energy into your sleep. Your last conscious thought of the day is always carried over into lizard stored, where it becomes solidified and embellished as you slumber. It's in this state that the mental cogs are put into motion, accentuating and developing the things that matter most to you at that time.

'Repetition is the mother of skill, so when you exercise any of these techniques I've shared so far, remember to stick at it.

'Here, my friend, have some of my affirmations to start off with. I carry them around with me everywhere I go. They're quotes, but you can rephrase them using the first-person voice. For example, change the word "yours" to "mine", "us" to "me", and both "you" and "we" to "I".'

Lead rummaged around in her jacket pocket and handed Dael several schefflera (umbrella tree) leaves, which were small enough to fit into a wallet, with each one carefully inscribed with a short affirmation:

... the best, and all there is, is yours...[Behrend, 2013, p.91]

Thought is the only power which can produce tangible riches from the formless substance. [Wattles, 2007, p.17]

Tell the world what you intend to do, but first show it.
[Hill, 2009, p.216]

AS MUCH AS WE CAN BELIEVE will be done unto us.
[Holmes, 1998, p.38]

'Finally, here's one of my own. Just fill in the blanks with your intention.'
She wrote on a blank leaf:

I am [name your role].

I'm [describe what you're doing], which looks like [describe the subsequent effect or mark this role has left in the outside world; what is the world shouting back at you as it celebrates your manifestation?].

Achieving more by applying reverse psychology

'Finally, Dael, here's one more really cool idea that I found worked wonders when I wanted to attract a specific opportunity into my life.

'About a year ago, I had a strong desire to work with a vibrant team (which I knew must exist somewhere in the world of business) that inspired and coached young entrepreneurs. At that time, there appeared little indication that such an opportunity would present itself, but I didn't let this prevent me visualising my preferred reality. I pictured myself being approached by a team of business coaches who were asking me to contribute and share my expertise on their new apprentice-training programme. On this particular occasion, I decided to drop my usual method of applying a straightforward empowering affirmation, like the examples we've explored so far, and adopt a completely different approach by experimenting with reverse psychology.

'I wrote out "I'm not being requested to join an awesome team of business professionals inspiring and uplifting younger people, and I'm not being paid handsomely for my efforts." I wrote this message on a sheet of papyrus and placed it on display in my office. I also inscribed it on the side of a small conch shell that I kept in my coat pocket. I made a habit of pulling the shell out and reading the message on it as much as possible. Meanwhile, I carried on with my daily activities while trying as best as I could to remain in a calm and relaxed state.

'Do you know that, within a couple of months, I was approached by a team of business coaches asking me to contribute and share my expertise on their new apprentice-training programme? I was also rewarded handsomely for my efforts.'

Dael interjected, 'But hold on, I don't understand how an affirmation worded in this way can attract what you want.'

'Let's say, for example, I warned you, Dael, "Don't, whatever you do, notice yellow flowers walking home from work." What are you likely to do?'

'Look out for yellow flowers!' Dael chuckled.

'Precisely, and what's really interesting is that writing out an affirmation in such a manner can be highly effective in helping you create a positive change in your behaviour or interaction with outward circumstances, as it helps you relax into a more accepting, almost ambivalent attitude that attracts the inevitable outcome – the opposite of what you've written down. It helps you avoid falling into a state of desperation or neediness. The last thing we want to do is entertain our lizard stored with the thoughts of, Well, how on earth is that going to happen?'

'This method helps you get around that problem. It also means you're less likely to go about your days in a state of lack, preoccupied with what's missing in your life. Of course, this approach may not work for everyone, but nevertheless, a state of lack only leads to more of the same thing, so it's important that, when you create any affirmation, you're not unwittingly strengthening the sensation of doubt over the likelihood of any change happening.

'Another interesting observation I've made concerning the application of affirmations is that amazing things rarely come to us precisely as we expected.'

Dael needed more clarification. 'What do you mean?'

'Just like an audience sees a group of actors enter a stage, serendipity and good fortune have a habit of entering our lives from the wings, just outside our field of vision. Ironically, being obsessed and hoping and wishing for a manifestation to arrive in a precise way can actually slow *things down. A calm and patient state of expectancy is always the ideal means of attracting the perfect solution that's out there, simply waiting to find us! You have to want it, but not so much that you fall into a state of desperation. I've said many times that the secret of life is all about the application of ease and flow, rather than force and haste!'*

As Dael drew his attention back to the affirmations on the palm leaves, wondering how he might modify them, Lead prepared her next lesson.

Achieving more by crafting vision boards

'I'm wondering, Dael, do you have a vision board?' she asked.

Dael looked puzzled. *'No, I'm afraid I don't, but I think I've heard that phrase before.'*

'A vision board takes the idea of a written affirmation a step further into the realm of establishing a more concrete visual representation. This approach is highly creative and fully exercises your imagination. Creating a vision board can be great fun, but the process will often reveal many of your values and deep-seated beliefs about what you imagine is possible or what you think you deserve in life. When you design your first board, it's important to try to push these beliefs to one side. Rarely do we allow ourselves the freedom to think big and bold, so it will feel odd at first when you settle down with this exercise. Regard the exercise as a "nothing to lose" opportunity to try something new, especially if your past efforts to force your intentions on the world have repeatedly failed.'

'So, what do you need to do?' asked Dael.

'Begin by putting aside some quality time alone, free from distraction. All it takes to stop you in your tracks is one interruption from a critical bystander looking over your shoulder and asking what you're doing or reminding you that, perhaps, you're wasting your time.

'Next, use this time to explore some of your deepest desires, and then imagine how they could appear in the outside world. Ask yourself this: "What do I value most in life? How do I wish to live? How do I wish to serve or be remembered? What sorts of environments do I wish to work in and with whom? What would it feel like if my wish were to be fulfilled?"

'Try forecasting the fruition of your desires into a week, month or year from now, on the premise that no dream or goal is too big and you have the power within to choose any experience. Ensure you cover all aspects of life, including your health, family, career, hobbies and personal goals. Don't hold back, and think of this activity as an opportunity to spend a private, intimate time with your authentic self – a voice that's often drowned out by everyday conformity or busyness.

'As you address each question, ask yourself this: "Is this something that would truly make me fulfilled or aligns with my true self?" It's often difficult to provide immediate answers to all these questions, so keep coming back to this exercise until the process is complete.

'When you've finished your list, prioritise one or two ideas, and if it feels right, go on to refine them further. Next, draw or collect images from magazines or the jungle internet that best represent or epitomise each idea. For example, if you dream of meeting the ideal person, collect images that closely resemble what they'd look like. Where might this happen, and how would they greet you? If you dream of the perfect indoor environment to work in, what would the view out the window be like? What furniture would be in the room? What would the environment feel like? What ambient background noises might you hear? Who would be working with you?

'Do you get the idea, Dael?'

'Yes, I think so, but I may have to give it a go a few times as this is all so new to me!'

'Absolutely, my friend, and remember that your paradigm will deliver a cautionary voice, reminding you that life doesn't work this way, urging you to give up, or arguing that the process isn't likely to provide immediate and unequivocal results. Nevertheless, press on regardless, and as you study and familiarise yourself with each scene on your board, try to imagine what people might say about you if your wish were fulfilled. What does it look and feel like after living in your new lifestyle for six months? These "later down the line" images can be very powerful. Remember that there are no limits to your imagination. The only limits that exist are the ones you place on yourself. Your imagination can portray a preferred reality or scene you wish to attract into your life that's every bit as real as if it were happening right in front of you!

'Finally, glue the images you've collected onto something solid, such as cardboard or a wooden board. If you enjoy being creative, you can decorate the board and complement each image with a written affirmation, starting with "I'm so excited now that [fill in the blank]."

'Place the board somewhere you'll view it frequently, but – of course – not in an environment that requires 100 per cent of your attention remains on other things that could be dangerous if you're distracted from them. I like to put my vision board on the table next to the chair where I relax and read each night. Some creatures put their vision boards on their office table or even next to their bed!

'You've now taken the first step toward purposeful and deliberate creation. Don't waste time or energy worrying about how things will transpire! The "how" is none of your business! Remain in a state of calm and contented expectation. Focus instead on embodying an assured attitude, and don't lose your faith in the inevitability of your vision becoming a reality – which is the only attitude that matters. Go about your days taking the necessary actions that move you closer to your goals, but don't lose faith. Remember that you have to believe in yourself as a deliberate creator endowed with everything you need to witness your desires manifesting in your outside world.'

Suddenly, Lead paused and glanced anxiously at the sun, which was sinking low in the evening sky. 'Now there's a vision, my friend, that's telling us we really must get going. It's getting late,' declared Lead with a laugh. 'Have you seen the time? There's still so much more to share. Are you okay with what we've covered so far?'

'Yes, yes. It's all been very practical. I'm okay and, please, I don't want these lessons to stop!' Dael replied emphatically.

He had taken on a lot of information, but Lead understood, and she immediately put her friend at ease by wrapping her arm around his shoulders, delivering a hug and smiling. 'You need some rest. Come, let's meet again tomorrow morning, and we'll continue this conversation on the mind.'

Liberate your perception of self
and unlock the control of your **emotions**,
and then you'll **achieve** your desires.

Route Guidance Fourteen
Achieving mastery of the mind by establishing a new perspective on space and time

You are today where your thoughts have brought you; you will be tomorrow where your thoughts take you.

James Allen

When the two friends met the next day, Lead arrived clutching an avocado. She placed it carefully on the jungle floor and, with the tip of her tail, began etching the following words into the earth:

Past

Present

Future

Lead began her lesson. 'Have you ever tried to tear into an avocado to taste the delicious, soft flesh within?'

'Yes, many times. We lizards love the flavour of avocado flesh,' Dael confirmed.

'Good. Now I want you to visualise the process of peeling back strips of the avocado's hard skin to get to the soft flesh inside.' Lead chuckled. 'But beyond that, of course, is the seed at the centre, which can prove a rather slippery object to grapple with. We're going to relate the avocado to the concept of time. Think of the past as the seed: solid, fixed and permanent. Think of the present as the soft, delicious, malleable flesh and the hard skin as the future. Which is the most pleasurable?'

'Well, Lead, the tasty, soft flesh, of course!'

'Exactly, and which timeframe did I associate that with?'

'The present.'

'Yes, and it's here that you must focus your attention. It's only through a state of being truly present that you'll ever experience a heightened level of consciousness. Returning to the image of the avocado, the past is never insignificant, as it has brought you to where you are now. The avocado seed represents your past, and just as the seed is the solid form around which the avocado flesh grows, your past thoughts and actions create the concrete results and circumstances in your life right now.

'This doesn't mean, however, that your past conditions or circumstances should have any hold over how you plan to transform your thoughts, look ahead and create new pathways toward greater success and fulfilment.

'Let's examine the skin of the avocado. Have you ever considered that the skin stretches and grows outward, even changing colour and texture dependant on the expanding growth of the flesh within? Just like the avocado skin, your future solidifies, stretches and unfolds outward in a way that's directly related to how you nourish and nurture your present moments.'

Dael was again in need of further enlightenment. 'What do you mean?' he asked.

Lead thought for a moment. 'Umm, maybe my avocado analogy isn't working so well. I know, let's go to Green Pond, and I'll explain.'

Achieving the lily pad hop

Green Pond was well known to many of the jungle inhabitants. It had earnt its name on account of being covered in a carpet of lush, green lily pads. In the middle of the pond was a small, rocky island covered in moss and mango trees.

Lead took up a position perched on top of a boulder overlooking the pond. 'What you're about to learn is perhaps the most challenging perspective on life that any lizard can contemplate. Once mastered, however, you'll experience a joy beyond compare. For now, all I ask is that you remain open and receptive, and you join in with me.'

At that point, Lead beckoned Dael to join her at the edge of the pond. Dael knew this particular pond was extremely dangerous as the water was deep and dark. Many a lizard had drowned trying to balance on the thin and slippery lily pads while trying to catch pond skaters or water beetles. This had led to many parents preventing their offspring playing anywhere near the pond, even during the peak of the dry season when the water level was relatively low.

Lead cleared her throat. 'I want you to imagine that the island in the middle of the pond is that ultimate goal everyone wishes for in life; for example, the ideal job, the big win, a luxurious holiday or the perfect lizard partner to step into your life. You get the idea; it's the one outcome you'd associate with solving all your needs. Most lizards live their lives in a constant state of dissatisfaction, always looking ahead toward these sorts of escapes. They blatantly confess that their happiness and contentment will somehow be transformed once these goals have been achieved. To them, daily life is merely an annoying stopgap to endure, often with little or no relevance to their heartfelt wishes.'

Lead led Dael close to a large lily pad that hugged the bank of the pond. She took hold of his hand, and they both climbed onto its thin, glossy surface, balancing themselves precariously and swaying from side to side. She pushed the lily pad away from the bank, and the two friends began their journey across the pond.

Out of the blue, the edge of the lily pad began to buckle and lift slightly under the weight of the lizards' feet, which sank downward, pressing indentations into the centre of the leaf's fragile, thin surface. The balancing act was so precarious that Dael feared the water would soon spill over the edges and engulf their legs, causing the lily pad to submerge and tip them both into the pond. Frantically, he focused all his attention on his only salvation and point of safety: the island in the distance. He held his arms out horizontally over his hips trying to keep his balance. It didn't take long before Dael's leg muscles began to tire from the tension required to maintain such a difficult posture. Dael began to panic. It took several insistent commands from Lead before Dael prised his attention away from the island to look up at her face.

'Now observe our predicament,' puffed Lead. She pointed toward the island in the distance. 'I bet you'd rather be over there. Doesn't it look far more secure and solid than where we find ourselves currently? Unfortunately, there's no turning back. What do you suggest we do, my friend?'

Dael had a sudden thought. 'Hey, Lead, if we leap really quickly from one lily pad to another, we could get to that island and the safety of firmer ground.'

'We could, but many a creature has slipped and drowned in attempting such a feat. There is, however, a deep truth contained within our dilemma. Imagine if each of these lily pads represented one of the days that pass us by. You know what I mean: the days we count down from Monday to Friday, the countless days we wish away before the build-up to the weekend or an annual holiday where the real enjoyment of life begins. There is, however, an alternative perspective that deploys far less effort and angst. Wouldn't it make more sense to savour the joy evident in all we ever have – the actual reality of the present moment – and work outwards from that?'

He was so absorbed in Lead's words, that Dael drew his attention away from the island and his efforts to keep his balance through tensing his legs. Instead, he relaxed them slightly, then lowered his body so he was squatting, almost sitting down. Gradually, he stopped swaying from side to side. Peering between his legs, Dael found himself instead drawn to studying the slippery surface of the lily pad. It was covered in a glossy, translucent film that looked quite beautiful as it reflected the sparkling rays of orange light from the setting sun. As both lizards lowered themselves, slowly gaining greater composure and stability, the lily pad stopped swaying and rippling. Clutching on to each other's sides, the two friends carefully sat down in unison, side by side.

They gazed silently at the evening sun as it melted behind the mango trees on the horizon. In that moment of peace, Dael realised the significance of what had just happened. He was suddenly still and present – his panic and feverish behaviour had given way to silence and serenity. He was now safely sitting down, captivated by the simplicity of merely *pausing for a moment and reflecting as the lily pad floated effortlessly across the pond.*

Dael considered all his previous desperate efforts and exertion in trying to maintain his balance and composure, and he now felt rather foolish. The only balance he ever required had always been available to him, right under his feet and contained within the narrow space on the lily pad. If he'd only lowered his gaze from the island for one moment, he'd have realised a significant truth: sometimes, carrying out your acts in a calm and balanced manner, while simply appreciating what's in front of you, gets you to your goal far more effectively than frantic toil and haste alone will. Lost in the moment, he didn't notice the mysterious and almost subtle momentum that was carrying the lily pad slowly across the pond. As it bumped into another lily pad, the two friends carefully slid across onto the new one, only to watch the one they'd just travelled on submerge slowly into the darkness of the pond.

Lead gazed deep into the water, and then turned toward Dael. 'The great secret to life is realising that your journey is part of your destination or goal. Disengaging with what's directly in front of you and appreciating the small miracles that cross your path, the unfoldment of certain insights or serendipity, and the support or contribution special people make to your life serves only to detach you from the meaning inherent within your journey of unfoldment. Where you are now is also part of where you think you need to be in the future! This is why it's so important to stop and pay attention to what's happening in your world right now that's delivering an opportunity for you to experience gratitude. Only in this state can you truly experience the richness of life! This includes cultivating peace of mind in whatever you're doing, including your work. Even though your predicament on the lily pad was somewhat precarious, once you stopped panicking and became more aware of the balance and ease available to you on the lily pad all along, you became truly present. Furthermore, it was from this perspective that the ideal solution presented itself, and so it is with the process of life!

'Think about some of the more unfortunate circumstances from your past, such as certain mistakes you've made, opportunities you've missed, things you regret or failed ambitions. The one characteristic shared by all these past events is that they're fixed. You can't go back and change them, but many lizards hold themselves hostage by replaying negative memories that eventually place their limbic brain in a depressed state.

'Some lizards overthink their future, wondering if it's predestined or an ever-evolving story of endless opportunities and choices, all floating around in a state of flux – much like these lily pads – just waiting for you to select and shift from one world to another. The point being that continually dwelling on past or future perspectives is rather frivolous because you miss out on appreciating everything you have – where you are right now.

'The only thing that matters, my friend, is acting attentively right where you always are: the present moment.

'Then the next now.

'Then the next.

'Then the next... and so on!

'You're only ever in one place in the universe, and at one point of awareness and state of being: the present – the now! You can't feel happiness tomorrow because tomorrow isn't here now. You can't be successful, at peace, complete or fulfilled next year, next month or in five minutes' time with whatever or wherever you might wish yourself to be, because you're only ever in one place – now!

'Of course, there's nothing wrong in exercising your intention by setting a goal and picturing it playing out in the future using your vision board or an affirmation. We all need targets and goals to keep us motivated from time to time, but so many creatures spend seemingly endless amounts of time and energy being everywhere but in the here and now!'

Eventually, after hitching a ride on several lily pads, the two friends reached the island in the middle of the pond and began exploring it.

As they stood on an elevated knoll on the centre of the island, Lead turned to her friend and asked, 'What do you see looking back on the journey we've just shared?'

Dael's reply was immediate: 'Appreciation!'

'Yes, my friend. We must never lose sight of two crucial truths about life. First, everything that has happened in your life so far has happened for a reason and been necessary to get you to where you are right now. Second, life often makes more sense looking back than it does looking forward! We grow and evolve by engaging with certain learning experiences that develop our unique character traits and attitudes. We can then share these experiences with the creatures we work and live alongside to encourage them along their particular life journey, and by doing so, we contribute toward the evolution of mass consciousness and the evolution of the jungle ecosystem as a whole.'

Achieving more by developing better ease and flow in solving problems

The two friends returned across the body of water in the same manner in which they'd arrived. They then climbed a steep path that ran alongside a narrow stream flowing into the pond.

Lead paused to watch a hoverfly holding a stationary position in the air, just at head height. 'Dael, check this out! Do you see that hoverfly just in front of us? It reminds me of a story.'

'Go on,' he prompted.

'I once had this problem that was taking me ages to solve, and I was getting nowhere. I decided to take it outdoors and sit on my garden bench to chew it over, so to speak, as effort and force just didn't seem to be delivering any immediate solutions.

'As I sat pondering, a flock of geese soared across the sky, squawking and flapping their wings frantically. I didn't know where they were going, but they gave the impression they were in a hurry to get somewhere rather important, maybe to migrate or find a new feeding ground.

'This got me thinking. Whenever we set out to solve a problem or achieve a specific goal, there's always that urge within to try to find a solution as quickly as possible, as if having to wait were an inconvenience.

'We attach great value to the speed at which we complete a task and, very often, just like with the geese, this depends on how fast we can flap our wings. In other words, you're focused on getting from point A to point

B or from the start to the finish line as quickly as possible by exerting as much force as possible. We assume that the more effort we put in, the quicker we'll get to our objective. From this perspective, the space in between point A and point B is merely an inconvenience and something to endure.

'I understood this idea and wasn't disputing the need for inspired action and effort, but something felt incomplete. I sensed a larger truth. As I reflected on these ideas, a hoverfly zoomed immediately in front of me with its little legs folded and tucked under its belly and its fragile, tiny wings buzzing with effortless intensity. It held a perfectly silent and graceful stationary position in mid-air, as if it were checking me out. As it hovered, with serene accuracy, it occasionally swivelled slowly from left to right. I marvelled at its dexterity. Suddenly, a huge insight flooded my mind.

'Of course, this encounter was no accident. That little hoverfly had found me at just the right moment to help shed light on my predicament and remind me there was an alternative way of viewing my problem.

'As with any act of enlightenment, it's not so much about finding "this or that", "A or B" or "black or white" answers as quickly as possible; rather, it's learning to view the question from a different perspective or unleash an inner knowing. Perhaps this is what the human Albert Einstein meant when he said, "We cannot solve our problems with the same level of thinking that created them."

'My thoughts returned to the flying geese. The image of them flapping their wings was a perfect representation of toil and effort. I then drew my attention back to the little hoverfly holding its graceful stance right in front of me, flapping its wings effortlessly as if it were operating at a quantum speed, frozen in the present moment. With this image in my mind, there was no getting from A to B. In fact, that idea became irrelevant.

'Taking a leaf from the hoverfly's book, I revaluated my approach to solving my problem, realising it was less about trying to get somewhere and more about discovering solutions that already existed and were hovering right in front of me, if I only I remained present and alert while operating in a state of ease and flow! It's this perspective that separates infinite thinking that's embroiled in insight and inspiration from the toil *and effort of finite thinking. Sure enough, when it was ready, the solution to my problem presented itself.'*

Achieving a more present connection with the rock in your life

'I love hearing the wisdom contained in your stories!' exclaimed Dael. 'I bet you have so many.'

Lead smiled. 'Yes, I do, actually; ready for one more?'

Dael settled himself on a moss-covered slope and rubbed his hands together excitedly. 'Definitely!'

'Well, this story examines the power lying within us all that, once acknowledged and revered, can completely change your perspective on life.'

Dael urged Lead on, 'Oh, go on... go on.'

She was happy to oblige. 'Once there lived a maroon-fronted parrot who (in common with this species) decided to build a nest high up in a crevice on a sloping cliff face. The parrot crafted an intricate but robust cup-shaped nest using jungle twigs and twine. She lined the nest with moss so her nights' sleep and egg-laying activities would be the most comfortable any parrot could imagine. To protect her new home, she secured one side of her nest with a smooth, large, egg-shaped rock that protruded from the cliff face.

'Although you'd assume that, after all her hard work, she'd feel rather proud or satisfied with her creation, she instead secretly harboured deep feelings of lack and frustration. Although the parrot was proficient at building a home, she covertly longed for more meaning and adventure. She had dreams of building a huge structure from bamboo at the foot of the valley, in which she could start her own school to teach other birds how to sing and impersonate the calls of other animals, just like parrots do. However, all her plans and efforts seemed to fail and were fraught with setbacks and bad luck. None of the monkeys (the only animals of the jungle skilled enough to build bamboo shelters) would help her unless she had something valuable to exchange for their services.

'Rather than commencing with egg-laying duties, the parrot chose instead to sit for days on end on the edge of her nest while gazing down into the jungle valley below, lamenting her predicament.

'One day, a problem emerged that diverted the parrot's attention from brooding over her lost dreams. Each morning as she awoke, through no fault of her own, her nest was saturated with water. This infuriated the parrot as she had spent so long searching out the perfect location and toiling over her nest creation, so much so that she had assumed it being secured high up on the cliff would mitigate any risk of getting damp from the humidity of the dense jungle below.

'To make matters worse, her sleep began to suffer as she was plagued by endless vivid dreams in which strange and mysterious images and symbols flooded her mind, as if some hidden power were sending her messages.

'One evening, the parrot turned her attention to inspecting the large, egg-shaped stone that secured the side of her nest to the cliff face, just to see if it was playing any part in her predicament. To her astonishment, she discovered a tiny hole at the top of the rock. It was a spring! During the day, any trickle of water flowing out from the spring evaporated quickly under the scorching sun, but at night, when the jungle cooled, the water flowed out readily into the parrot's nest. The parrot couldn't believe her bad luck. She simply couldn't face relocating and starting all over again.

'Later that night, before retiring to sleep, she sat up, directed her attention to the rock and thought about how she might stop the water flow. She decided to put her beak into the hole of the spring. She sat patiently with the tip of her beak resting in the tiny hole, gazing at the surface of the rock while listening to the chorus of jungle frogs croaking in the distance.

'The longer she settled into the present moment, the more she began to appreciate a sense of serenity and calm. She began to notice tiny crystals embedded in the surface of the rock that sparkled under the moonlight. Lost in the moment, she brushed her wing across the rock's cool surface, transfixed by its timeless stillness and solidity. As she did so, she slowly let go of the stream of frantic thoughts based on feelings of lack and frustration. As these thoughts ebbed away, she found herself cradled in a moment of peace and acceptance.

'In that serene void, she felt strangely at ease. She wondered whether the flow of the spring water was perhaps a reminder to encourage her to pay more attention to being present. Perhaps the spring water that filtered into her nest bed at night had unsettled her sleep pattern, causing her to dream more. Maybe the purity of the cool spring water had somehow evoked the unsettling wisdom that flowed through her dreams – in some way trying to deliver messages she couldn't or wouldn't adhere to when she was awake. She allowed the moment of stillness to linger.

'Unexpectedly, she became aware of the duality of her existence. On the one hand, she was the nest planner, the builder and the dreamer who had exerted all her will and intention on building her home and dreams high up in the cliff face. But now she'd become more aware of the role the rock had in her life, she felt inseparable from its immutable presence. The solid rock on which her nest was anchored represented a far greater foundation and more security than she had first imagined while building her nest. The rock was far more significant than her, but somehow also no more important, as it was still part of her existence. The rock slowly took on an identity itself – an identity she was growing more aware of as an eternal, once-forgotten-but-never-lost guardian or foundation of her life.

'The stability and permanency of the rock ignited a deeper curiosity or inner knowing within her mind. For the first time in the parrot's life, she accepted her old ways of viewing the world weren't working – and only the complete abandonment of these habits would supply the freedom and rebirth she desired.

'With her beak still pressed tightly into the spring, two entities (the parrot and the rock) had harmoniously become one. It marked the moment in which the parrot truly discovered the joy of savouring the present moment.

'She sat for a long time, listening and waiting in a silent state of surrender, until she became so relaxed that she slowly released her beak from the hole in the rock. She lay back in her nest, simply accepting the fact that a backlog of water was now gushing out from the spring.

Meanwhile, the water flowed through and under her nest with such tremendous speed and ferocity that her nest was picked up and washed down the valley.

'Although startled, the parrot resisted the urge to fly to safety and instead grabbed hold of the sides of her nest, which had now become a raft on a river-rapids ride, possessed by unseen forces.

'The parrot was transported down magnificent gullies and deep, narrow gorges – some of which she'd never seen before – until her nest eventually came to rest by the edge of a huge lake.

'As she gained her composure, she noticed the lakeshore sparkled, as it was covered with rocks encrusted with gold nuggets and precious gems. The abundance that lay before her was more than enough to pay the monkeys to build not one but a hundred schools! Everything the parrot had ever wished for was now suddenly laid out before her.

'By letting go of control, remaining present and trusting a force far greater than will power alone, the parrot had been led to riches beyond her wildest dreams.

'This was a power that worked outside expectation, as if everything the parrot had ever desired were already written in stone! In just the same way that the rock had made a channel through which the spring could emerge, she too had now opened a channel within – a natural conduit through which could flow a far greater force, which was always willing and prepared to grow within and through her.'

Dael sat in silence as he allowed the wisdom contained in Lead's story to sink in slowly.

Before the two lizards said their goodbyes, Lead invited Dael to join her later that night for dinner, as she was expecting a very special guest and felt it appropriate that Dael should be introduced to them. With no hesitation, Dael agreed and put a note in his diary.

Liberate your perception of self
and unlock the control of your **emotions**,
and then you'll **achieve** your desires.

Route Guidance Fifteen
Achieving higher levels of consciousness

Then you will know the truth, and the truth will set you free.

John 8:32 (New International Version)

Later that night, as he scurried through the jungle to find Lead's house, *Dael found himself completely preoccupied by replaying in his mind all the adventures he'd had so far with his new friend. The encounter with the monkeys, the adventure on Green Pond and Lead's extraordinary stories merely left Dael thirsty for more. It now felt as if every day were a true opportunity to learn something new and break free from the shackles of the past.*

All this excitement meant Dael was oblivious to the fact that the jungle air had turned cool following a heavy storm, and he didn't even think to wrap up warm. He did, however, remember to bring his notebook and the conch shell Lead had given him, then he could share them with Lead's guest.

As he drew closer to Lead's house, Dael had a question nagging at his mind: Why is Lead so keen to introduce me to her friend and does it have anything to do with the next course of lessons?

When Dael eventually arrived at Lead's house (a hollowed-out dwelling inside the trunk of a huge Astrocaryum jauari tree, which is known by the jungle animals to be a great provider of edible fruit in the autumn), he could hear the clinking of wine glasses and lively conversation reverberating inside. He knocked on the door.

As Lead swung open her door, a rush of warmth and light gushed out, bathing both lizards in a luminescent glow. Lead's greeting was equally inviting: 'Ahh, Dael. It's wonderful you could make it. Please, come in from the cold; you must meet Gorfesiw.'

Sitting on an old, brown leather armchair near the fire in the corner of the room was a very old tree frog clutching a particularly large glass of mango wine. Lead handed Dael a glass and led him over to her guest, who stood up rather awkwardly. Taking hold of Dael's arm with one hand and reaching out with his other, the old frog delivered a firm and enthusiastic handshake.

'It's a pleasure to meet you, Dael; I've heard so much about you,' said Gorfesiw, still avidly shaking Dael's hand. 'Lead has told me so much about all the fascinating adventures you've been having. Please come and take a seat by the fire as it's customary that we engage in some enlightening debate before dinner. Isn't that right, Lead?'

Dael felt a little uneasy and somewhat perplexed. As Gorfesiw had taken hold of his hand to greet him, he had received a rush of tingling energy that ran up his arm as if he'd been given a mild electrical shock. He didn't want to cause any concern and ruin the meeting, so he settled into his chair as best as he could and rubbed his arm discreetly, hoping it might ease the sensation that was now dissipating slowly throughout his entire body.

Lead suddenly interjected, 'Actually, I introduced Dael to the concept of emotional conditioning the other day, as well as information about lizard stored, timeframes, affirmations, paradigms, appreciating the present moment and reconnecting with the greater presence within. It seemed to go down quite well.'

Gorfesiw cleared his throat. 'Ahh yes, very good. Has Lead shared the idea of **manifestation, the universal subconscious mind, and primary and secondary causation?'**

'No, I don't believe so,' replied Dael. 'If it's as good as the last set of lessons, I'm all ears!'

Gorfesiw laughed. 'That's actually quite amusing for us reptiles because many of the other creatures in the jungle think we don't have ears – since they're not visible!'

Gorfesiw turned politely to Lead and asked, 'Do you mind if I take this opportunity before dinner to elaborate on what you've covered with Dael so far?'

Lead smiled enthusiastically. 'Oh yes; yes, please do. You tell it so well!'

The two lizards pulled their chairs closer to the fire and, like moths to a flame, found themselves drawn into Gorfesiw's enchanting allure.

Gorfesiw sat up straight, finished his wine and began. 'Many ask me whether it's possible to create real change in the outside world through the power of thought alone. In essence, they are, of course, referring to the process of manifestation. We're going to take this really slowly, one step at a time. You must stop me, Dael, if I lose you.'

Dael looked puzzled and politely raised his hand. 'Sorry, but what does "manifestation" mean exactly?'

Achieving the art of deliberate and purposeful manifestation

Gorfesiw cleared his throat once more. 'Basically, unlike the more obvious process of goal setting, which I'm sure you're familiar with and in which you focus your thoughts and actions on bringing about a desired outcome, "manifestation" describes the process of formulating an intention and co-creating it with the universe at a spiritual level, in a state of harmony, ease and flow. This is certainly not a new idea. It's been practised and written about for thousands of years. It can involve you deploying a variety of approaches, such as acts of visualisation, immersing yourself in the feeling of the wish being fulfilled, mindfulness or meditation, but all the while working in harmony with universal creative laws. There are many laws of creation, some of which I'm sure Lead has touched on, such as the law of vibration and attraction. We'll examine more of these laws as we go on. For now, with respect to the topic of manifestation, it's worth considering the following points:

'1. We grow up accustomed to the idea that, to create real change in our circumstances, we have to assert force or manipulation on ourselves, other individuals or things within our physical environment. There's nothing wrong with this approach, of course, and many would leave it at that, but the application of force alone is bound by certain physical constraints and limitations. Any such application of force requires movement through space, which will always create the sensation of time passing.

'Let's contrast this familiar form of creation with the idea of holding an intention within your mind, rehearsing specific images that evoke feelings of the wish having been fulfilled, and then stepping out into the world and acting in accordance with this preferred state. You still need to take action, but the difference here is that it's measured and inspired action.

'2. We're manifesting all the time, moment to moment, regardless of whether we believe this or not. Behind every manifestation is a set of intentions or beliefs we're not always aware of. We can manifest unfavourable conditions in our external world just as easily as favourable

ones, being unaware that our lizard-stored mind is fuelling the situation behind the scenes, as it were. Sometimes, we only become aware of this process when our physical bodies suddenly reveal specific illnesses or physical conditions.

'3. Our thoughts, emotions, beliefs and assumptions represent our state of being. Ultimately, these forces are energy, and energy can't be destroyed. Energy has to go somewhere. Mental energy or thought in motion continually formulates an image, which in turn is transmuted into an outwardly manifested form. In this sense, who you are is connected with everything in your outer world.

'4. You can't change the law of manifestation, but you can learn to perfect your use of it by becoming more conscious of how and what you think, moment to moment. As you grow to appreciate the subtle link between the nature of your thoughts and what turns up in your world, the more you're able to master the circumstances of your life and freedom from servitude!

'5. This may sound contradictory, but manifestation isn't really about adding something into your world; rather, it's about discovering and selecting what's already there in the unified field of energy! I'll explain more about the notion of time and the term "omnipresent" later.'

Achieving more by understanding the creative link between the individual and universal subconscious minds

'Now let's examine the gateway through which all this thought energy permeates, accelerates and transforms into form. You remember Lead's lesson on the brain and the terms "lizard stored" and "lizard aware", yes?' Gorfesiw queried.

'I do,' confirmed Dael. 'It's the idea that the real powerhouse that governs the extent to which we truly change our behaviour, conditions or circumstances is contained within lizard stored. It's here that our emotionalised beliefs and attitudes are solidified and gain momentum.'

With an air of approval, Gorfesiw leant back in his chair and announced jubilantly, 'Bravo. Very good, and nicely put, if you don't mind me saying? Has Lead explained the metaphysical relationship between your individualised lizard-stored mind and the concept of the universal subconscious mind?'

Lead interjected, *'No, we haven't got that far yet, although I've shared the drawing with Dael.'*

Dael immediately scrabbled around in his pocket to reveal the conch shell Lead had given to him, and then he passed it to Gorfesiw.

Gorfesiw carefully studied the drawing etched on the shell, then he looked up and declared with even greater delight, *'Ahhh... very good. Do you mind, Lead, if we use the correct terminology, and replace "lizard stored" with the term "subconscious mind" and "lizard aware" with "conscious mind"?'*

'Absolutely not,' she replied.

Gorfesiw held the shell out in front of Dael and pointed at the diagram of Dael's head. *'Working from top to bottom, the correct scientific language for the two aspects of your mind are actually "conscious" and "subconscious". I want you to imagine, if you can, that the lower half of your mind, lizard stored – sorry, subconscious mind – is one and the same as a universal subconscious mind.'*

Dael looked puzzled. *'The same as a universal subconscious mind? Sorry, I don't know what you mean.'*

'Alright, look at it this way. Can you picture a drop of sea water placed on the palm of your hand? Although you hold only a minute element, it contains all the properties of all the oceans of the world? I sometimes use the expression "chip off the old block" to describe this idea. You know, when, in essence, something small resembles all the characteristics of its parent. In the same way, your individualised subconscious mind shares all the characteristics of an infinite universal subconscious mind. This includes all the power and means through which it operates. You could think of our subconscious mind as an individualised, smaller extension of it.'

'Right. Now you put it that way, it helps a little.'

'Good. But unlike your subconscious, this universal power isn't individualised – it just is. It operates in the same manner as a lens or

mirror, taking thought energy and translating it into the most convenient physical equivalent, but it has no preference or will of its own. Think of its purpose as forming a spiritual mould from which a physical equivalent must manifest in the outside world. This universal power is omnipresent – it exists in all places at the same time. The scientist may refer to this as the "quantum zone". The mystic may refer to it as "the void", "infinite intelligence" or "the realm of infinite possibilities". Whatever term you use, it was there at the beginning of creation and will operate into eternity, transmuting all thought energy or intention into the physical equivalent forms we see around us through an ongoing process of creation.'

'You mentioned an ongoing process of creation. I don't understand that either.'

'The creative process is perplexing and mysterious at times, but it doesn't require any effort or force from you once you've embedded an originating desire within the "soil" of the subconscious mind.

'Creation is bound by the law of perpetual transmutation of energy. In just the same way that tiny shoots from a seed always find their way to the surface, so too will any idea infused with passion or fear find resolution in the outside world.

'When an idea is repeatedly emotionalised and envisioned in mind, it's bound by spiritual laws. Time and space are irrelevant. It's a done deal!

'Are you beginning to sense the immensity of the silent but creative force within you?'

'With your encouragement, I'm certainly keen to understand more and to try to embody this new level of awareness in my life.'

'Good,' declared Gorfesiw, 'Success in life is really about navigating your way forward with a foot in both worlds: the physical and the spiritual. You'll grow to appreciate the way in which your silent prayers, disguised as "I am" affirmations, are reflected in your outside world. For example, if you have a thought such as I wonder how I could develop that great idea I feel so passionate about. I'm sure there must be a way! you become immediately aware that both your individualised and universal subconscious minds will instantly start working behind the scenes, even while you sleep, to reflect on a response to that question *manifested as a physical result or a series of circumstances within the outside world.*

'*Another example might be thinking,* I wonder who I'll meet that will help me? I can feel that person stepping into my life as if they're already here! *Note how this question, at its heart, has the conviction and belief that, somehow, the solution is already waiting out there in the world, because there are endless possible solutions! This is faith in action. If you can hold it in your head, you can hold it in your hand. This event is just one of trillions already existent in the quantum realm; with repetition, you're allowing the ideal experience to find you. I know this is a fact, because I've experienced it.*'

Dael interrupted with, '*Quantum realm?*'

'*Ahhh, this is basically the idea that all possible events that could ever happen to you are spinning around simultaneously, unbounded by the limits of so-called "time and space". Originating thought is omnipresent – there's nowhere it isn't existing. You may have heard the term "quantum worlds" or "quantum entanglement". This is the idea that there are multiple versions of you living out very different lives in different worlds. It becomes interesting when we speculate whether we can jump between these different worlds to experience other versions of ourselves. In this sense, it's not so much about creating something new, because how can you create something original that already exists? Instead, we select a particular circumstance we wish to experience by embodying a preferred state relative to it, and then we allow it to materialise in our outside world.*'

Even though Dael still felt a little out of his depth, he pressed on with another question: '*You mentioned the term "universal laws" earlier. Are there universal laws concerning the manner in which we create the circumstances or conditions within our lives?*'

Achieving infinite possibilities with purposeful manifestation

Suddenly, the three friends encountered an awkward moment of silence. Gorfesiw paused his lesson and, deep in thought, began slowly running one of his webbed fingers in circles around the rim of his wine glass. Lost in the moment, he mumbled to himself, 'I can circle my finger slowly from one point on the rim of the glass and return to it again, thus creating the illusion of time, but the entire journey my finger takes is actually contained within the single rim of the wine glass. This too is our experience of the illusion of time!'

Lead and Dael glanced awkwardly at each other, not knowing how to react. Dael realised Gorfesiw had deliberately paused the lesson to see if he was comfortable before moving on to more-complex ideas.

Eventually, Gorfesiw broke the silence. 'Now, Dael, the information in this part of the lesson has the potential to revolutionise your whole perspective on life. I'm going to begin by introducing you to the idea of primary and secondary causation.'

Dael responded by hastily rummaging around in his pocket again to find his notebook. 'I'm so sorry. I must write all this down – just so I can keep up.'

'That's perfectly fine, Dael. Scribble away.'

When Dael was settled, Gorfesiw began. 'Let's start with the notion of causation. Basically, the word "causation" describes the impetus or starting point that produces a result or condition to appear in the outside world. Each possible condition can be traced back in time to a certain cause. We could refer to this originating spark or impetus as the "first cause".

'As today's lesson is centred on the power of thought, we have to realise that we're always applying some form of first-cause thought, whether we're consciously aware of it or not. Let's examine how most of us habitually function in a state of ignorance when it comes to understanding the causes and conditions in our lives. Now, don't take the word "ignorance" the wrong way. We're all ignorant or unaware when it comes to certain things. Quite naturally, most of our attention tends to be focused on external events or conditions in the physical outside world.'

'Of course, and rightly so as that's our governing reality,' stated Dael.

'Indeed, but our comprehension of whatever's actually out there in the outside world is essentially limited by our five senses and the manner in *which outside information is filtered through the mind. Do we ever truly know what's really out there? Can we really be sure that what's out there is always the primary cause that governs our experience of reality?'*

Dael looked confused. 'I'm not sure what you mean.'

'When we continually focus all our attention on external conditions as being the only driving force governing our reality, we automatically limit ourselves. Referring back to my previous explanation of the process of causation, if all your focus rests on these outward conditions, wouldn't you agree that these outward conditions also constitute the first-cause forms from which all our subsequent thoughts, beliefs, emotions and actions originate? These thoughts then serve to further reinforce and self-perpetuate additional antecedent thoughts, which in turn create even more circumstances related to the original condition you observed in the outside world. In other words, from this state, you perpetuate cyclical causation by continually reinforcing the limits formed by your mental images of what's already been observed in the outside world, creating more of the same.'

'I think I understand what you're saying.'

'Let's look at it another way. Imagine, if you can, riding on a spiral of thought energy that's moving outward from this first cause. In this sense, you're continually held captive, like a slave, to whatever external condition you observe and attach meaning to. Of course, it makes perfect sense to observe the world like this. You experience something in the outside world and you react. You then go on to process this experience with new thoughts, which become the entry points by which you can revisit the experience that's now held as a memory.'

Dael asked, 'May we go back to what you said about the fact that focusing all our senses and basing all our thinking on outside circumstances is limiting? I don't understand.'

Gorfesiw was happy to elaborate. 'It's not that I'm saying don't pay attention to things in the outside world; clearly, this would cause all sorts of problems. But what I am saying is that every circumstance or thing you're conscious of out there in the world forms a first cause from which subsequent related forms manifest. You can never initiate a complete and untarnished original thought based on observing what's already out there in your physical world. All these circumstances and things are merely mirrors or reflections of what has gone before. The great metaphysics writer, Thomas Troward, called this level of unguarded thought creation "secondary causation".

'Furthermore, our senses are programmed to seek contrast, attach meaning, draw comparisons or separate out information from the things we observe in the outside world. It's in this way that we form judgements or opinions. This explains why we often overanalyse or imagine all the potential hiccups, complexities or deviations that could occur when we plan an event that's important to us, such as organising a wedding or planning a long journey. In other words, overthinking or paying too much attention to what can be achieved or gained from the manipulation of external circumstances automatically triggers further thoughts or rationalisations of how things may not turn out in our favour.

'There's only one way to gain freedom from this mental bondage, so you can begin guiding the creative process in your preferred direction, and that's through the acquisition of knowledge and raising awareness. This is where the idea of primary causation comes into play: where fresh circumstances manifested in your outside world can be traced back to an originating idea you've become emotionally involved with that's held as an image in your mind, separate from external influences.'

'This is still highly confusing.' Dael's expression reflected his lack of comprehension.

'Ah, it will be, my friend, if this is the first time you've had to consider this type of language and information, but let me finish,' requested Gorfesiw. 'Primary causation means just that – you focus on creating in your mind the elemental, untarnished, pure idea in the form of thought energy that's not yet been passed into a manifested physical form, and thus is untethered to limitations or existing forms in the outside world. You carry out this process with the full understanding and faith that this too will birth subsequent outward conditions. Now, in applying this principle, we accept the idea that any originating idea or ideal held in the mind is the real substance, and all outward forms or conditions related to it are mere reflections of it.

'From this perspective, you reassign the proof you require that an idea has become a reality, such that it's not simply dependant on its appearance as some form of physical manifestation in the outside world, but on the premise that you can already see and feel it within your mind. It's here that your greatest power – imagination – plays a fundamental part.'

Dael raised a finger and asked politely, 'How might someone go about embodying these ideas in their daily life?'

'One word, my dear fellow: attention. When it comes to monitoring my thoughts or pursuing a particular idea, I always ask myself, "Is the thought I'm entertaining right now pulling me up or pushing me down? Is it based on an existing limitation or an opinion perpetuated in the outside world? Or am I thinking freely from the inside out?"

'Once you've formulated an originating ideal or idea, and you've identified it as a point of primary causation, knowing its already here, and you've focused all your will on energising it with passion, belief and faith, when you then step into the world, it's impossible for you to make any wrong decision in the pursuit of your goal or vision!'

'What do you mean?' Dael wanted to make sure he understood completely.

'As I alluded to earlier when I was running my finger around the rim of my wine glass, every idea that could possibly exist is already here – contained within the one! Every creation is finished and present simultaneously in all space and time. In other words, there's nowhere the idea isn't. Although you may assume you're originating an idea in your mind, the experience is an illusion because the idea already exists – you are, in fact, selecting your desire from the realm of infinite possibilities.

'If you truly believed your ideal or originating idea was already here, then how would you feel and behave, moment to moment? What vibration would you send out into the universe? Of course, this is a very powerful question to ask yourself.

'You have to become a conduit that works in harmony with the universal laws. One of these universal laws is the law of attraction, which is always at work delivering the circumstances in your day-to-day life *that reflect your prevailing state of being. The law of attraction is, in fact, secondary to the law of vibration. In other words, you attract into your life the people, things or circumstances that mirror your prevailing emotional or vibrational state. You see, everything in the universe vibrates, including your state of being. Remember, you can only experience that which you are being.'*

Achieving mastery of your infinite potential by recognising the power of 'I am'

'How can you assess your true state of being?' queried Dael.

'I apply a technique called "distant viewing" in which I imagine my higher self or spirit stepping out of my physical body and observing my predicament from a neutral or elevated perspective. From this observant perspective, you can notice the underlying state you're in. Ask yourself this: Is this a state of ease or stress? Is your focus on lack, limitation or abundance? Are you originating creative thought or lack and servitude?'

Dael looked confused once more. 'I don't understand how simply building this mental picture can truly help when life is really challenging or when your back is against the wall. All this focus on how we're thinking or being must surely pale into insignificance compared with the hard knocks that undoubtedly hit us from behind sometimes. These sorts of experiences are very real things.'

'My dear fellow,' Gorfesiw suggested, 'you need to write down these two very powerful statements in your journal:

'So as you believe, it is done unto you.

'Judge not by appearances.

'Your body may be finite, and yes, it feels real pain and heartache, but at times like this, it's vital to remind yourself of your true infinite ability and that your "I am" declarations are ultimately what create your reality.'

'I'm even more confused. What do you mean?' Dael hoped the penny would soon drop and he'd understand completely.

Gorfesiw slowly placed his wine glass down on the table next to him and struggled out of his chair. He shuffled over to an old stool that was standing to the side of Dael's chair and rather awkwardly sat down.

Once he was settled he gave a measured sigh. 'My dear friend, I'm so sorry I startled you earlier when we shook hands for the first time. I bet that sensation came as quite a shock, eh?'

Suddenly, Lead scurried forward, clearly agitated. 'Oh, I'm so sorry, Dael. I completely forgot to mention my old friend's party trick. Sorry. Gorfesiw, it's not a prank but more of a gift, wouldn't you say?'

The two friends laughed.

'You're forgiven,' replied Gorfesiw.

Dael blurted, 'I'm sorry, but you're both losing me here. I don't understand.'

'My dear boy,' Gorfesiw explained, 'we tree frogs all share an unusual peculiarity or gift, as some may call it, handed down from our ancestors. You see, I can tell a lot about an individual upon meeting them for the first time simply by grasping their hand firmly.

'It seems amazing, I know, but by applying this technique, I can sense their passion, their inner calling or the reason why they were put on this earth in the first place. Call it what you will – a sixth sense, intuition or telepathy – but I've always possessed it.'

'What happens to you?' Dael really wanted to know more.

'I achieve this flash of insight by first transmitting a surge of energy out through my hands into the body and mind of my recipient, and then I wait to see what message energy is returned. This may have felt like a slight tingle or glow that travelled up your arm, yes? I'm sorry; I didn't mean to alarm you, of course, and this process only lasts a few seconds, but for the process to work properly, I have to ensure I have a firm hold of your hand and concentrate at the same time.'

Suddenly, everything began to make more sense to Dael. He had sensed something was afoot when he first shook Gorfesiw's hand. His intrigue grew. 'What did you see?'

'It's more a case of what I didn't see. I don't actually see anything – it's more of a sensation that I'm after, which transfers to symbols and emotions within my mind's eye.

'In your case, my friend, I sensed beautiful flowers and plants. I sensed a passion and love for botany – especially an interest in the healing and medicinal benefits of plants. I sensed frustration that this desire couldn't be shared fully and was somewhat suppressed or held back by so-called "external circumstances".'

The tense atmosphere in the room was suddenly transformed as Dael jumped up with joy and announced, 'Yes, you're absolutely right – that's amazing!'

He turned excitedly to Lead. 'He's right, isn't he, Lead? You know all about this.'

'Indeed, I do, but rest assured I hadn't mentioned any of this to Gorfesiw – I promise,' she confirmed.

Gorfesiw returned slowly to the comfort of his armchair by the fireplace, relocated his wine glass and prepared to give his final presentation of the night. 'Earlier, you expressed some confusion regarding the power contained within the phrase "I am". I believe it's important to share complex information like this in a form that my students can digest, so to aid your understanding, I'm going to use certain imagery that you can relate to.

Daffodil: A story of spiritual reconnection

'I want you to picture a daffodil bulb. Can you imagine that? What do you know about daffodil bulbs, Dael?'

'Oh, I've read all about these daffodil bulbs in my global botany encyclopaedia. They grow in cooler regions of the world, and they're truly remarkable,' Dael explained. 'They can be stored for months on end without the need for moisture, soil or light. In a sense, they're self-contained flower factories, as everything they need for producing a flower is contained within them. I also know they plant themselves. By that, I mean each bulb has contractile roots that pull it downward into the earth until it reaches the appropriate depth to sprout its first flower stem through the surface of the earth. This growth may wither after the spring, but don't be fooled by the plant's apparent inactivity - it's still very much alive and active below the surface. Some bulbs produce little bulblets under the ground that can produce their own flowers. I always find this fascinating.'

Gorfesiw smiled. 'Excellent, my friend. Now picture a daffodil bulb nestled deep within the cool, dark earth. We could describe its appearance at this stage as rather unimpressive, existing in its dormant or suspended state without birth or death. We know, however, it's far from lifeless; it's a self-contained entity, bursting with potential.

'Planted and cocooned in the earth as it is, the bulb is inseparable from the universal characteristics of the earth's fertile soil. Because the essential qualities of soil are consistent at any point below and across the earth's surface, you could say the bulb similarly shares in ths interconnectedness. You could conclude that the bulb exists in all places of the earth at the same time. This is what is meant by the term an "omnipresent state of existence".

'Suddenly, the bulb stirs within itself and dreams what it must be like to free itself from the dark abyss of the soil, burst upward through the surface of the earth, and experience a world of sunlight, wind, rain and all of nature's marvellous forms. Curious and inquisitive, it can't predict exactly what this adventure into the world of light would be like, so it merely dreams about the possibilities.

'Although it exists in an omnipresent state in unison with the infinite blanket of earth covering the planet, it can never experience the finite or tactile physical world above unless, of course, it reaches up, takes on a finite form and interacts with it. This new form, however, can't be the same as the bulb, as finite and infinite conditions can't exist at the same time, so it decides to rebirth itself as a different entity – a daffodil flower – to learn and experience this new world. It's fully aware, however, that once it initiates this transformation, one of the conditions of this rebirth into the physical world is that it must also forget it's a bulb.

'Nevertheless, the bulb affirms "I am that daffodil flower," accepts the sacrifice, sends a tender shoot up through the surface of the earth and, at the very moment, sentences itself to a state of deep sleep in which it can only share the daffodil's experience as a dream. As it emerges from the darkness of the earth, the daffodil is bathed in the first spring sunlight and immediately transfixed by the experience of being immersed in the outside world, now completely unaware of its connection and true origin with the bulb below ground.

'Over time, the daffodil's bud opens slowly to reveal a flower, displaying an array of dazzling yellow petals that rival the brightness of the sun's rays.

'As it stretches and grows upward, relishing its new position in the finite natural world, it's visited by bees, swayed by the wind, blanketed in cool snowflakes and admired by the local animals, which reinforce its identity, making it feel worthy and proud to share the joy of colour, beauty and fragrant scent with the world.

'Weeks pass, but late at night when it's dark and still, the daffodil becomes conscious of a deeper, more peaceful state of awareness that resides within it. It's an awareness that observes from a timeless, all-knowing perspective. In this stillness, the daffodil reconnects and acknowledges its true origin of the bulb, which – although silent at first – was always the flower's true entity. The longer the daffodil savours the stillness, the more it realises it's less a flower becoming conscious of the outside world and more the bulb becoming aware of the world through the adventures of the flower.

'At first, the daffodil wonders why the bulb fell asleep following the flower's emergence through the soil, but it gradually learns that for the bulb to impose itself upon the flower would violate the law of freewill – which is an intrinsic aspect of existence in the finite world.

'With this new found awareness, the daffodil develops a deep reverence for the bulb and is now aware that it had not only gifted the daffodil with life but, for this to take place, it had also sacrificed itself by putting itself into a deep sleep. It's now aware that all its experiences have also been observed silently through a dream-like state of awareness within the bulb. The daffodil slowly acknowledges the bulb's primary presence at its core, sustaining its existence, but oddly, it never feels any less important, as if the two entities were one and the same.

'The daffodil also becomes aware that, if the bulb had any form of intention, it would be a singular focus on observing how the daffodil defines itself through self-examination. This self-examination causes the daffodil to discover that its true self is one and the same as universal awareness, and it's able to expand its awareness or self-definition by observing and interacting with the outside world.

'Over time, the daffodil releases its hold on receiving all of its fulfilment based purely on its preoccupation with the meaning it derives from the outside world, and it instead grows more appreciative of its true power: its sense of complete fulfilment and joy, which was always present within. It wonders how this acceptance may spill out into the world as it pictures new possibilities within itself.

'Over time, a greater synergy develops between the daffodil and the bulb. Slowly, the qualities of the bulb merge with those of the daffodil, which is compelled to demonstrate its own unlimited potential and completeness. It revises the manner in which it observes the world and realises this shift in perception has a direct impact on the circumstances the outside world reflects back at it.

'The daffodil realises that the only reason it was filled with joy in rendezvousing with the bees or being kissed by the sun's warm rays was that this was precisely the manner or assumption from which it had decided to observe, judge and interact with the outside world. In just the same way, the daffodil also takes responsibility for acknowledging that the only reason it was filled with discomfort and confusion after being covered in snow and hail was because that too was the manner or assumption from which it had decided to view or judge the outside world.

'The enormity of this truth causes the daffodil to transform its self-perception further, encapsulating the qualities of the bulb, and free itself from the lack and limitation of the outside world by refining its infinite capacities, going within and creating originating ideas.

'Endowed with joy and passion, it imagines – as if it were already fulfilled – a vision of producing completely new and original flowers on the screen of the world, and by doing so, it draws even closer to the qualities of the bulb.

'Mirroring the bulb's mode of affirmation, the flower declares, "I am that originator and producer of more flowers just like me. I don't require *an external force to validate my vision or help me plant these new seeds, because they already exist within me since creation is finished." The daffodil also declares, "I am that infinite creative entity effortlessly selecting my preferred experience, free from doubt or limitation. The only limits are the limits I impose upon my own imagination. My assumptions, faith and beliefs create my reality."*

'The daffodil remains faithful to its assumption, and before long, tiny bulblets begin forming and shoot out from the sides of the bulb. For the daffodil, it feels fitting that this creation should spring forth from the only true source of eternal creation from which it came – the bulb.'

Somewhat drained, Gorfesiw slumped back, resting his head on the back of his chair.

There followed a long moment of silence, broken only by the roar of the fire burning in the fireplace.

Inspirational leads

*Eventually, Gorfesiw spoke once more. 'When you fully appreciate and then embody the enormity of truth contained in this story, all the **inspirational leads** necessary for your complete unfoldment will come your way.'*

Gorfesiw leant in closer to Dael and, with a glint in his eye, smiled before whispering slowly, 'I know it's all very involved, but by studying the right information, you too will find your own way through. I've merely planted one or two seeds of curiosity that will hopefully blossom into further insights along your journey, my friend.

'Curiosity is one of the first keys for unlocking enlightenment and the first stage in transforming a life of limitation into one of freedom and liberty. The term "enlightenment" is actually less about arriving at a point of personal clarity or celebrating the end of a spiritual journey, but it's more about a continuing journey of awakening. Of course, this experiential, never-ending journey is interwoven into every aspect of your life, including your time at work or leisure, your interaction with other creatures, and – of course – the very act of simply resting here right now, sitting by the fireplace.'

Dael could see Lead looking slightly agitated, and he wondered if he should request an end to the lesson.

However, Gorfesiw had one more point to make: 'Finally, it's important to reiterate that you must continue to hone the only force within the universe required in manifesting your desires – your imagination! Everything you see around you – the table, the chairs, the glass you're drinking out of and even this rather excellent mango wine – began in imagination. When you exercise your imagination, you're engaging a process shared by the Divine that created the planets, the stars and the universe! If you can reach a state where you have your ideal scene or desire so well rehearsed in your mind that it replaces the actual need to have it physically, you've mastered the greatest power in the universe!'

Gorfesiw spied a pile of firewood stacked next to an axe near the fireplace. 'Remember what I shared with you; to coin an old phrase: you're an individualised chip off the old block!'

Eerily, at that precise point, a large log on the fire crackled and spat, the noise reverberating around the room.

Gorfesiw chuckled. 'Yes, certainly; we're all chips off the old block.'

It was at this point that Gorfesiw, transfixed by the glow of the fire, delivered his final quote, which encapsulated and drew the evening's lesson to a close: 'The real question is this: to what extent will you grant yourself permission to fully stoke the glowing embers within so they transform into a raging fire that might inspire and light up the outside world?'

As Dael flicked back carefully through the pages in his notebook, reviewing hurriedly everything he had gathered from the evening's session, he noticed the first page of his notebook was strangely still blank, but it provided the perfect location in which to record Gorfesiw's final quote.

Lead stepped forward and politely beckoned her guests to join her in the dining room. 'Come, friends... let's eat!'

Liberate your perception of self
and unlock the control of your **emotions**,
and then you'll **achieve** your desires.

Excursion Four

The D in LEAD
DESIRE

Start where you are. Use what you have. Do what you can.

Arthur Ashe

Route Guidance Sixteen
Fulfilling the desire to feel valued and empowered in the workplace

When companies make their people feel like they matter, the people come together in a way that money simply cannot buy.

Simon Sinek (2018, p.98)

Where Lead works – Dael's curiosity pays off

After participating in months of fascinating tutorials under Lead's careful mentorship, Dael became increasingly curious about where exactly his new friend worked. It transpired that Lead worked for a large organisation called Citrus, headed up by a charismatic, entrepreneurial peacock called Redael.

Dael couldn't stop wondering whether this environment was responsible for nurturing Lead's infectious attitude and deep sense of fulfilment. He was soon to find out!

Citrus designed and manufactured high-quality, nutritious health-and-fitness-related food and drink products that were particularly popular among the jungle's more active four-legged animals, such as the cheetahs, panthers and lions.

Redael was a rather charismatic manager with a reputation for consistently launching 'outside the box', innovative health products. Before turning her talents to business, Redael had begun her career as a teacher. She earnt the nickname 'Redael Magic' from the parents of her students, on account of her ability to achieve dramatic shifts in children's confidence and self-belief.

She had left teaching to start a new adventure setting up her own business, but she continued to develop her leadership skills, which she used to motivate and inspire young apprentices. She quickly gained considerable credibility by exemplifying many of the principles that underpin a value-based learning organisation: strong ethics and a focus on employee development and well-being.

Her bold ideas, however, weren't always appreciated or supported by everyone within her business community. There were those, such as managers and chief executive officers (CEOs) of more traditionally led organisations, who regarded her leadership approach with a degree of scepticism or even ridicule. They argued that her ideas concerning the development of employees were too far-fetched, unrealistic, time-consuming and unmanageable. Nevertheless, whatever was going on at Citrus, it was certainly causing a stir within the jungle, which only served to fuel Dael's curiosity still further.

After some careful deliberation, Lead arranged for Dael to visit her workplace early one morning to meet Redael. She explained to her student that meeting her leader (and coach) would prove a useful experience to embellish and broaden his learning journey.

To mark the occasion, Dael decided to take his trusty journal with him to make notes. To help structure the meeting, Lead had also handed him a list of subheadings inscribed on a palm leaf – all centred on the topic of leadership. She explained that the headings might prove useful for guiding the conversation and moving it forward, especially if he lost his flow.

The power of self-reflection

Eventually, the big day arrived, and Dael found himself sitting waiting rather anxiously outside the Citrus company boardroom. Dael sat himself on a chair directly below a framed portrait of Redael, which held a commanding position overlooking the waiting room. The title 'Redael – Founder and CEO if Citrus' was proudly inscribed in bold letters at the foot of the painting.

Dael's attention was then briefly drawn toward a large, ornate, gold-framed mirror that was hanging on the wall in front of him and was reflecting the portrait above his head. He found himself suddenly transfixed by the spelling of 'Redael' reflected in the mirror: 'leader'.

As he waited, he hoped his visit wouldn't prove too much of an inconvenience by taking up the time of such a renowned and respected individual as Redael.

Dael's concerns were brought to an abrupt end when the company boardroom door swung open all of a sudden, and he could see Redael sitting on a chair in the middle of a circle of about a dozen junior company employees, all engrossed in a discussion.

To his astonishment, she beckoned him to join them. As Dael stepped forward, the conversation in the room continued. He picked up on the atmosphere in the room immediately, which felt surprisingly inviting and relaxed. Although the exact nature of the conversation was unclear, there were certainly no airs and graces or tones of authority being exchanged between the participants, but rather it was a more frank and open conversation.

Somewhat awkwardly, Dael walked around the circle of participants and located an empty chair in the corner of the room. As the meeting resumed, it became clear Redael was sharing a story concerning a work challenge that revealed personal inadequacies and dips in her confidence she was struggling to overcome.

It was at this point that Dael felt compelled to offer his apologies and leave as swiftly as possible. He thought to himself that there had clearly been a mistake and it wasn't appropriate for him to join in like this.

To his relief, Redael noticed his sense of awkwardness and paused the meeting. She smiled, jumped up from her chair, skipped enthusiastically over to him and shook his hand. 'Ah, Dael, welcome. Yes... Lead told me you were visiting today. I apologise; this session was moved forward from the planned session tomorrow, and I didn't have time to inform you, but we're nearly finished now. We call this team-building exercise a "gifted circle", a form of reverse mentoring and we practise it regularly for about ten minutes in the morning with all our teams! Please remain in your seat and observe, and I'll be with you really soon.'

Fulfilling the desire to feel pyscholgically safe in the workplace

Redael returned to her chair as her colleagues resumed their questioning to gain clarity about her dilemma. The conversation was coupled with encouraging gestures of support and acknowledgement, as if the group were building camaraderie and empathy toward their leader.

As the meeting progressed, Dael began to piece together specific themes within the discussion that were centred on ways of forging greater resilience and a growth mindset. A consensus began to emerge among the members of the group on how best to help their leader, and they took turns in offering support or advice.

Was Dael witnessing a team demonstration of the open communication centred on authenticity and trust alluded to in Lead's previous lessons? He began scribbling down in his notebook the plethora of ideas suggested by the group.

Just when Dael thought the meeting couldn't get more intriguing, Redael moved on to share still further personal challenges encountered outside the workplace.

Redael was by no means a young peacock, and at this point in her career – when many would be slowing down or refraining from deliberately throwing themselves into new challenges – she behaved as though she had just stepped out into the world for the first time, infused with curiosity and enthusiasm.

She embellished her story of personal challenge by consistently referring to her values, vision and ethics, as well as the part these played in maintaining her focus and resilience through hard times.

The group conversation then moved on to evaluating a problem concerning a new Citrus product launch. Each member took turns to share their ideas, but these were always in line with the values and principles the Citrus brand encompassed.

Every member of the group had an opportunity to talk and listen respectfully to the views of others. There were plenty of smiles and good humour, as the group endorsed an enthusiastic, go-getting attitude. It was at this point that Dael experienced a huge revelation: there remained no doubt that he had peeped into the cultural heart of Citrus and witnessed a pulse and vitality driven by what Lead had once referred to as "a just cause" in that it was people-focused, trustworthy and transparent.

The meeting drew to a close, and everyone returned to their work feeling upbeat and energised.

Finally, Dael found himself alone with Redael. There followed an awkward moment of silence before he remarked, 'I don't know what to say. That's not what I expected first thing on a Monday morning!'

Redael laughed as she beckoned Dael to join her in her office. 'Here, take a seat. Do you want to try some of our new sample food creations, tropical juice or coconut milk? We're always eager to collect feedback from our customers.'

Eagerly, Dael took up her offer as the two of them settled into the meeting.

Dael gingerly produced the palm leaf from his pocket and selected the first heading at the top: 'Problem-solving'.

Fulfilling the desire to solve problems creatively

'How do you approach the issue of solving problems at Citrus?' asked Dael.

'You may have noticed, Dael, that on this particular occasion our meeting concluded without the necessity to agree on one final solution. This is intentional because, here at Citrus, we endorse the idea that innovation requires space and time in which to germinate. I prefer to seek expertise in particular fields related to a problem rather than go it alone before I come up with a solution. The gifted circle isn't intended to encourage hasty A-to-B solutions; instead, it aims to promote open and divergent thinking, where everyone is involved in truly understanding the context of the problem first.

'I prefer my employees to take ownership of a problem and remain adaptable. This approach tends to motivate employees more. Many leaders don't do this, and they waste valuable time on other things instead. The world we find ourselves in – particularly following the challenges associated with the great storm last year – will never be the same again, and it requires all of us to continually find new ways to think, act and work together. Ultimately, solving problems is not just about creating new technology but it's also about creating ways to translate skills to others, which will result in a better future.

'Our gifted-circle exercise provides a wonderful opportunity to foster greater trust and transparency, and it reduces the need for anyone to hide behind a façade. When we all have an opportunity to contribute openly and creatively, our organisation can flourish and grow. Trust and transparency allow for clear outcomes, and I like to create space for my teams to explore bold new ideas.

'Of course, as a leader, it's also true that sharing all your pains and woes isn't always beneficial; it's all about knowing where to draw the line. I do believe, however, that trust has to remain the basis of my role as a leader. I want to ensure that, when my teams need something, they feel comfortable approaching me. In fact, I'd go as far as to say that trust is the key behavioural characteristic of any great leader. Indeed, I find trust is more important than loyalty, authenticity and communication. That trust has to be built from the top and filtered downward. I'd like to think that my teams don't have to gain my trust, but that I'll freely provide it instead. It's up to me to either develop or lose this vital quality. When a team operates on a foundation of trust, the process of creating an open and creative approach to problem-solving becomes so much easier.'

Dael glanced at his palm leaf again and found 'Trust and transparency' listed halfway down. As Redael had just covered this topic, he proceeded to the title below it: 'Legacy'. With increasing confidence, he asked Redael for more clarity surrounding this topic.

Fulfilling the desire to leave a legacy

Redael answered, 'I believe legacy is intrinsically linked to finding purpose or meaning. In other words, is what you leave behind better than what you started with? Did you add value? Have you improved things for the greater good, and did you leave no stone unturned? Have you given others the opportunity to do the things you've done?

'My ambition has always been to develop a company that will inspire and thrive well into the future. When I first led the company, I began by breaking down my "what" and my "why", so everyone could understand where I was coming from. It was then up to me to demonstrate these values with my daily behaviour and actions. I want Citrus to be led with a bold vision and purpose that will encourage and pave the way for as many as possible to step up and continue the legacy long after I'm gone.

'Monitoring sales and remaining aware of the trends in the outside world are all well and good, but I believe our success relies on establishing a just cause that has authenticity and vision embedded within it. It's maybe a little clichéd, I know, but it's purely about creating a positive impact on the lives of those we serve. This is our lifeblood at Citrus!'

The next title on Dael's list was 'Giving back'. He asked, 'What do you understand about the meaning of giving back as a leader?'

Fulfilling the desire to inspire others to achieve their full potential

Redael explained, 'I give back for my own self-worth. If I can open three doors for someone who asked for only one, then I've succeeded.

'Some of my other friends who run companies feel really uncomfortable giving too much knowledge away to their employees or allowing them to get really good at a role. I believe my employees are the future talent, and you have to allow them to grow so much that they may jump career and leave to move on to bigger and better things. Don't forget that the average time a young employee stays put within one organisation is around two to four years. Actually, just the other day, I had to allow one of my best employees to leave, even though I'd spent months mentoring them. I could tell that they'd had itchy feet for some time, so I was honest when *they asked me what they should do and I replied they needed to jump, as this was the next part of their journey. In fact, one of the questions I like to ask a new employee is what their leaving date is. You see, this is one of the ways I'm able to assess or really get to know an individual.*

'Giving back also breeds innovation. I have a vision, which is shared across all my teams, that one day Citrus will help educate and provide more accessible health options for all of the creatures in our jungle. Not only that but also our success will enable us to fund a sustainable programme to provide free nutrition for less-advantaged creatures in other jungles. This global vison stretches and challenges me on a daily basis, but it also provides the impetus for everything I do.

'When I climb my ladder to success on this business journey, I like to take others along to travel with me. The worst sorts of leaders are those who climb to the top of their ladder and then kick it down afterwards so no one can follow.

'Of course, you want your team members to be dedicated and committed, with the ability to be self-policing. One of the ways I give back is to reward individuals for initiating acts of self-learning, and not always those related to things within our organisation, but within activities outside too. I like to think my teams believe working for Citrus feels more like a vocation than purely work alone. Of course, I still need to be aware that I have a responsibility to direct employees' learning occasionally, so it encompasses the activities and goals we're trying to achieve.

'Everything comes down to operating within an environment of adaptability and continual growth, both personally and as a business. This, of course, is what's meant by leading an agile business model.'

Sure enough the title 'Agile organisation' was listed on Dael's palm leaf, next to the title 'Competition'.

Fulfilling the desire to remain adaptable and resilient

'What does the term "agile organisation" mean?' queried Dael.

'Basically, this describes an organisation that actively fosters a culture that enables it to pivot and react positively to sudden change in the outside world. In order to form the foundations for developing an

agile organisation, it's vital that teams are connected and informed on the broader picture. It's essential to foster an open, honest, respectful, trustworthy and safe working culture. Agility within a business is an extra dimension through which space to grow is made. Communication, flexibility and remaining proactive are, of course, central to the way my teams operate.

'This also includes avoiding the pitfall of constantly fearing or reacting to our competitors and trying to outwit or outdo them. In fact, in today's modern world, it can be wise to regard your competitors as potential collaborators. Competition, per se, is healthy, and I believe you can be competitive and collaborative at the same time. You need to be mindful of your competition, but not so much that you let it affect your core values and focus.

'When you start worrying too much about what your competition is doing, you tend to make rash decisions, and that's never good. What really matters is that we operate congruently with our values, listen to our customers and endorse creativity at all levels. In this way, we'll protect ourselves from merely reacting to our competitors; instead, we'll lead, and they'll follow.

'It's about being proactive rather than responsive in the way you operate. We aren't afraid to evolve or make changes, and this means sometimes embracing a degree of uncertainty. We never lose sight of the abundant opportunities available in the jungle marketplace.

'When it comes to our vision, trendy slogans or mission statements are never enough. We want our values to be important to our customers as well. I believe you should continually open your eyes fully to everything you experience on a daily basis. I try to avoid prejudging, and for every idea my team present to me, I allow the opportunity to explore and expand it.'

Dael moved the discussion on to the next topic on the list, 'Employee confidence', as the ethos at Citrus was clearly radically different to his experiences at work. 'I found the gifted-circle exercise fascinating. What drives this approach, and how do you develop this level of confidence and employability skills?'

Fulfilling the desire to enhance the employability skills of others

'At Citrus,' began Redael, 'we'll always endeavour to develop a work environment that encourages the development of MQ, which stands for motivational quotient or motivational intelligence, among our employees. MQ quite literally determines the success or failure of a business that's grappling with sudden change or a challenge in the outside world. We're fully aware of this when anything new is introduced into the company that uproots the way people normally operate – new technology is a good example – and we implement a support programme called 'UTOPIA', the letters of which stand for 'understand the threat, opportunity to practice, and improve adaptability'. Every employee has a support buddy who listens sympathetically to their concerns or needs during any work transition and helps them discover the opportunity rather than the threat when trying something new. In this way, we create a safe and supportive environment for our employees by developing a growth mindset. It's vital they learn how to take ownership of their thoughts and actions.

'I'm always reminding my teams that our species have successfully evolved over millions of years due to the unique way we've adapted and learnt. We must never lose sight of this quality, and it's worth remembering that when you're faced with a challenge or sudden change in life. We help our employees uncover their greatest power to help navigate these types of situations – choice! By that, I mean choice in how to think!

'I believe you develop confidence in others by understanding everyone as an individual, and you have to change your approach slightly as you communicate, so you can relate. Just like problem-solving, where you have to familiarise yourself with the factors behind a problem, you have to get behind and understand the people you're leading. It's useful to consider that when you address a group of people with an idea, as it may trigger ten different opinions rather than the two you anticipated.

'I encourage everyone to operate as naturally as possible and be the best they can be within their role. Of course, it's vital that I lead by example, including the manner in which I deliver training, as this approach ultimately drives company momentum.'

'What do you mean?' Dael asked.

'Let me give you a perfect example. I was asked by the leader of a company that delivers health-improvement services to give a presentation to her twenty new apprentices on the topic of employability skills and confidence. Their leader was keen to inspire and support them with fresh ideas that could open up discussion on many of the ideas we've covered previously. This request is by no means particularly unusual; every leader within business is facing the same dilemma: rapidly shifting their employee's personal leadership capabilities and growth mindset, regardless of rank or position, toward a heightened level of awareness that unlocks MQ and a greater sense of personal meaning. Leaders are seeking new ways to support employees in achieving their best self so as to enhance their career. It's all about developing those core behavioural competencies and learning how to manage yourself. These are essential qualities to master in allowing individuals and teams to work effectively in a world of unprecedented transition.

'Let's be frank, this is one of the hardest types of seminars I have to deliver to employees, and I have to accept in situations like this that, whether I like it or not, I'm selling an idea – in fact, pretty much everything we do in the business world is about selling, Dael. Incidentally, a quarter of the jungle's economy is driven by sweet talk!

'I began my presentation by sharing some brief global statistics related to the gap in employee soft skills, fulfilment, meaning and EQ (which stands for emotional quotient or emotional intelligence), as experienced within the workplace, and the enormity of the challenge leaders face in supporting their workforces. I proposed that this search for personal meaning and peace of mind presents one of the biggest challenges of modern times, which had, of course, only been exacerbated as a result of the upheavals over the last two years during the great jungle storm.

'I asked the group to work in pairs to complete an activity. I provided them with three palm leaves – one labelled 'MQ', one labelled 'IQ' (which stands for intellectual quotient or intelligence) and one labelled 'EQ' – and one small conch shell with a rolled-up small piece of papyrus sticking out of the end. I knew this would cause some curiosity within the group, which is an essential aspect of delivering an engaging training presentation.

'I then asked the pairs to work together and place the palm leaves' headings in chronological order, according to when they were identified by behavioural psychologists. Following a short discussion I revealed the correct order: IQ, EQ and MQ. I then moved on to propose that there's an emerging fourth intelligence.

'It was at this point that I drew their attention to the papyrus sticking out of their conch shell, and I asked them to pull it out and read the message on it. The heading 'meaning intelligence' or MeQ (an abbreviation of my own) was revealed; this is the foundational roots that enable all the other intelligences to function comprehensively. To help conceptualise this idea, I shared a diagram incorporating a drawing of a tree.'

Redael pulled open a drawer in her filing cabinet, withdrew a piece of papyrus on which was a copy of the aforementioned image and handed it to Dael.

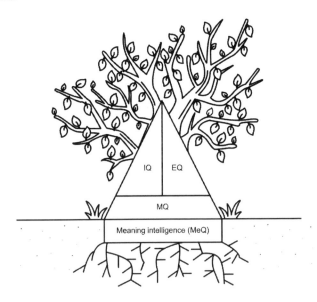

She continued, 'I then went on to make the case that the only way we can prepare ourselves for the dramatic changes in work and life ahead of us is by learning more about ourselves, breaking free of old limiting habits, and discovering we have the power to generate more self-confidence and unlimited resourcefulness. Once this discovery has been realised, it's possible – with the right mentoring – to create a sudden shift in self-belief and reach higher levels of awareness, which will ultimately impact your results.

'I summarised this part of the presentation with the following key points:

'1. Meaning in work is the burning platform for change.

'2. We all deserve the opportunity to access skills and knowledge that have the potential to improve our self-confidence and create a transformational shift in our behavioural competences.

'I went on to reiterate that this is especially needed right now following the unprecedented challenges of the last few years, the environmental state of the planet and the unpredictable future that unarguably lies ahead of us.'

This prompted Dael to ask yet another question: 'Creating this type of shift in people can be really difficult. How on earth do you achieve this?'

Fulfilling the desire to feel engaged and inspired

'You're right, of course,' Redael agreed. 'It's essential for any business to consider the issue of employee engagement if it's to keep up with the fast-paced world, but I also believe fresh ideas are required, both in terms of content and the manner in which training is delivered.

'Let me tell you what I do. I deliver my training in a style I call sequel – spelt c-e-e-q-i-i-l. It's a play on words, as it represents the "sequel" or the development of the themes I've just shared on the tree diagram.'

'May I ask why you chose those particular letters to spell that word?'

'The letters stand for creativity, engagement, empowerment, quirkiness, inspiration, imagination and liberation. When I was a teacher, this learning approach was the key to creating the shift in my students' self-belief, confidence and self-awareness. I guess I've just carried this approach over into what I do now.

'Intrinsic to this approach are the craft activities I deploy to help engage and empower people with fresh ideas. For example, with the session I've just shared, I focused on two topics that are highly relevant in *today's world of work: poor employee resilience and stress management. Instead of merely emphasising the negative effects these issues have on our well-being, I instead led the group through a series of practical activities in which they crafted models while imagining their future selves acting proficiently and confidently in these areas, both within and outside the workplace. As they completed their craft projects, I asked questions such as these: What habits and thoughts do highly resilient people exude? How would it feel to operate like that within your world of work? Can you imagine what others would say about you following this transition?*

'*I then asked them to apply the same approach relative to their management of stress.*

'*I want my participants to leave my training sessions feeling differently about themselves. Of course, they get to take these craft prompts away with them. I've heard about some employees who've placed them in their office or took a photograph on their smartphone as a useful visual reference point to turn to later.*'

Dael interjected, '*What were the craft exercises you just referred to?*'

'*One of the activities involved simply sticking together strips of papyrus to create a 3D model, which I've entitled "The resilience tree". This is a little table-top tree on which they record six of the less-obvious qualities necessary to build resilience. These titles are accompanied by short suggestions for developing resilience in everyday work-life situations.*

'*Regarding stress management, participants cut out a pair of hand shapes from thicker sheets of papyrus, and then they each write on the fingers and thumbs the letters "h-e-l-p-a-t-h-a-n-d", one on each digit. Again, this model serves the same purpose, with each letter representing a suggestion or prompt for combating the build-up of stress.*'

'*Oh yes. Lead taught me that one.*' *Dael selected another heading from his list:* '*Well-being initiatives*'.

Fulfilling the desire to manage uncertainty and reaching your full potential

'*How do you approach the wider issue of supporting the health and happiness of your employees?*' *he queried.*

'I believe this involves two crucial qualities as a leader: staying connected with the people you lead and listening to them. At Citrus, we fully embrace a "people-centred culture" in which I like to think of our organisation as one huge beating heart with our employees as the life blood, but just like in the body, this ecosystem requires the correct mental nourishment and agility to remain healthy.

'All our well-being initiatives are embedded into the things we do on a daily basis. We don't believe in simple tick-box exercises, once-a-year health workshops or token gestures. Our employees are intelligent, and they see through the façade.

'It's also worth considering that what constitutes well-being varies from one creature to another, and I think it's important to acknowledge this. It's easy for a leader to assume that providing a free meal out once a year for their team may tick a well-being box, but it's also important to appreciate that this idea may not excite everybody. For some, it's simply not their thing.

'Our employees love to come to work because it's a positive place to be, where everyone feels part of a team, with transparent roles and open environments that support healthy communication. Every member is recognised as a unique individual and isn't just a detached, small cog in a large machine. We empower our employees to grow personally, make decisions, and remain analytical and innovative.

'We have a unique development programme that enables every employee to have the opportunity to discover more about themselves through EQ. We offer everyone who works for us, regardless of their level of responsibility or role, the same benefits. This also includes access to and grants for education courses held within our own unique virtual learning zone. All our employees have equal opportunity to purchase shares and sit in on certain management meetings.

'Apart from the more obvious points we hear about in the media concerning the development of sound mental health – such as engaging in regular exercise and eating a healthy diet – I believe this state also relies on both developing the ability to manage personal failures and the obvious right to feel comfortable and proficient within your work role. This is why it's important to create a work environment in which *people feel safe before you can introduce more-testing situations to help challenge and stretch them.'*

Dael wanted to know more. 'How do you do that?'

'Put simply, by remaining as visible as possible. It's also about taking the time to have meaningful conversations with employees. If people feel supported, they're far more likely to open up and challenge themselves. If my team were sitting in a battle trench, I'd want to be there, right beside them.

'When it comes to creativity and sustainability, do you know what the biggest resource loss is within an organisation, which prevents it from thriving?'

'Sorry, no, I don't,' he replied.

'It's the misuse of the way people spend their energy, time and focus.'

'Yes, now I remember. I think Lead has told me about this before. You're talking about the way people hide from vulnerability, personal development and meaning?'

"Precisely, Dael, and here at Citrus, we obviously understand that our ability to reach our full potential as an organisation is directly linked to our employees' ability to do the same. That's why we developed a training programme that's committed to developing a workforce community with one key focus: to share how innovation nurtures everyone, or SHINE for short.

'If you get this approach right, it ultimately leads to improved employee retention, profit, performance and initiative. Our people are our greatest asset, and it's important they're led and supported at all levels. Did you notice the mutual support in the room during our gifted-circle meeting?'

'Yes, I did; that was so refreshing!' Dael declared. 'At my workplace, everyone is so gloomy. No one really talks to each other. I can't imagine ever feeling fulfilled and happy at work.'

As Dael continued to scribble down ideas hastily, Redael smiled and took the opportunity to lean back in her chair and allow her guest a moment for reflection.

Dael eventually looked up from his journal. 'You remind me so much of Lead's energy. It's truly refreshing and, may I say, very infectious, which brings me on to the topic of "Effective leadership".'

Fulfilling the desire to feel inspired and purposefully led

Redael nodded with approval. 'In terms of inspiring my staff, it's no accident that the words "leadership" and "learning" share the same first three letters! I believe these two words are synonymous. Having studied numerous great leaders, one key quality underpins their success, and it can be summed up with the phrase "Be a learner yourself"! You see, I think people respect you more if you remain open, approachable, authentic and curious. I often share personal stories with my staff about the approaches or mindsets I've adopted in the past to forge greater resilience during challenging times.

'It's important to help others feel confident and provide the tools to help them recover from setbacks. I'm consistent in my approaches, and I love to share with my employees any positive affirmations or remarkable, inspiring information gathered from classic books. I'm an avid reader, you know.'

Redael laughed. 'One of my past employees rather wittily referred to me once as being "built of facts", but it's true – I do love the idea of lifelong learning.

'Going back to my original point, I've spent years designing open workspaces and natural hubs for relaxation that allow my employees to feel free to innovate and work together. I believe the work environment can be a satisfying place to be in, which then helps to make it far easier to introduce challenges that can enrich employee experiences.

'You never get everything right, and it's important that you communicate this to those whom you lead. It's important to demonstrate how to lead with confidence and to defuse anxiety, through both good and bad times. Your followers need to believe in what you're doing. This comes down to my effectiveness as a leader in communicating my ambition and values. You'll find others will either get behind it or not. If not, it's my

responsibility to re-evaluate how I communicated my message and make the necessary adjustments.

'These days, I feel leadership isn't simply about things – for example, a product or service you provide – but is more about the quality of the chain of relationships established between the provider, employee and customer. Fundamentally, others have to believe in your mission. If that's clear, then people can get behind you.'

Dael drilled deeper with his questioning: 'How do you support those you lead in addressing challenges or embracing greater self-analysis?'

'There isn't a magic formula, but part of the solution is helping people move through uncomfortable feelings. Remember that a great leader understands the importance of filtering down from the top the appropriate behaviour in terms of morale and motivation. Inspiration plays a huge part in this. You have to set the example!

'Can you remember your favourite teachers at school? They were probably the ones who guided you through a challenge, helping you feel safe or more at ease, while bringing something out in you that you didn't know you had. I like to refer to these transformations as "critical shifts in a person's self-awareness"! This type of experience meant you grew to trust them implicitly.

'Really great teachers don't constantly remind their students about the big win at the end-of-year exams, but instead, they celebrate the growth, connection, meaning and learning evolving in the present moment. When we educate in this way, the student learns the true meaning of humility and resilience. If a young student is struggling to grasp a particular skill, a great teacher will take a risk, drop their assumptions, step out of their own comfort zone sometimes and get to know what truly motivates their student. They then develop the appropriate learning style that matches their student's persona. Later, when the student overcomes a challenge, the teacher asks them to articulate and share their approach, not just with the teacher but also with their peers; this positions the student in a place of authority, which in turn boosts their confidence, articulation skills and self-belief. This is when I've witnessed the critical shift most within my students.

'In just the same way, it's right and just that everyone within our organisation discovers their voice and the opportunity to feel differently about themselves. A great teacher will also get to know the sorts of things that interest or motivate their students outside the work environment. For this reason, I try my best to get to know all my employees and find out what makes them tick.

'Finally, the development of diversity awareness is a critical necessity for effective leadership. You have to think beyond the visible differences you see in other people, and this also includes taking into consideration less-evident factors that affect the way people work and the priorities they have. It's also my responsibility to develop more-inclusive environments that allow all my employees to feel valued and accepted, regardless of their rank or position. My goal is to create a working environment where everyone can operate with autonomy and confidence. Of course, it's also important that every individual is treated equally when it comes to expressing their talents.'

Dael located the next title on his list: 'Motivation'. 'What keeps you going? I mean, what motivates you?'

Fulfilling the desire to remain motivated and purposeful in work life

'It's all about motivation, Dael. In fact, you have to keep yourself motivated to be a motivator for others! Motivation comes through acting on your meaningful idea. Every step you take toward your goal builds momentum, but the most important of step, of course, is the first.

'Unquestionably, no one is perfect, and motivation can waver, but this is why it's important to continually develop greater resilience and self-belief. Your motivational energy can spill over and inspire others, and it makes a fabulous engagement technique. Never underestimate the positive effect you may have on others as you interact with them and go about your daily chores. This is something I've really grown to appreciate since taking on the leadership role at Citrus.'

'I've never thought of it like that before,' confessed Dael.

'I often remind my teams of the seven advantages of living a highly motivated life. When you're highly motivated:

'1. You discover that problems and setbacks are only temporary, and each one is an opportunity to foster greater immunity to defeatism.

'2. You stay focused on the task at hand and give it your full energy and concentration, which joins the dots that complete the full picture of what's intended or planned.

'3. You shut out the noise (distractions, nay-sayers, confusion, gossip, etc.).

'4. You realise there are limitless possibilities and huge depths to your creativity; the more you remain in this creative zone, the more likely solutions are to reveal themselves.

'5. You unearth limitless reserves of energy and a zest for life that help you endure and appreciate the joy of lifelong learning.

'6. You develop a deeper sense of fulfilment and self-respect from having stuck at something purposeful.

'7. You make an excellent companion and a more interesting person to be around.

'My only desire as a leader is that I inspire others to do what I do and continue this cause through applying an open mindset with respect to the necessity of embracing innovation.'

'How do you define "innovation"?' Dael asked.

Fulfilling the desire to create new ideas that add value to people's lives

'Fundamentally speaking, great innovation involves providing products, systems, processes and services that add value to people lives. I always feel there's a spirit of relentlessness embedded within the notion of innovation. It's that never-ending drive for improvement, much like the process of effective learning. The only reason anyone innovates is out of necessity.

'I believe innovation drives nations as well as helping prevent organisational inertia. These days, the continual emergence of new forms of business is usual – it's not a one-off!

'Innovation requires collaboration and the space or time to reflect and nurture ideas. In other words, you see a requirement or problem out there in the world, gather data or ask questions about why it persists and then bring people together to offer different viewpoints or perspectives. This is why we encourage networking, gifted-circle meetings, and open and free workspaces. These create ideal environments that encourage a synergy of ideas. You have to promote a creative culture from the inside out!

'Innovation also thrives when you choose to operate outside your familiar territory occasionally, as this encourages you to think differently. You see, Dael, you have to find opportunities to innovate – it won't come to you!

'Here at Citrus, we took the brave step of fully embracing the idea that reality is context dependant. This means that, when it comes to the topic of innovation, it's important to upgrade continually and unlock your own mind to new ways of thinking and evaluating the world outside.'

'What do you mean?' Dael questioned.

Fulfilling the desire to forge an open and growth mindset

'Recently, I've been studying a radically different way of viewing the world, and that's having a direct impact on the way I intend to create even bigger success for Citrus globally. In fact, only yesterday, I was explaining the idea to my junior apprentices, and it certainly created some lively discussion, I can tell you! I know time is short, so the best way to explain this radical thought perspective is to begin by looking back at your school years.

'Do you remember that rather stressful period of time as a young lizard when your parents had to select the right secondary school for you from a choice of, say, three or four contenders?'

Dael's response was immediate: 'Yes, I do. That's a critical time in any young lizard's life, and to some degree, the choice of school has a huge bearing on the direction of your young-adult life too!'

'So, looking back at that time, I bet I'm right in saying that you and your parents made a decision based primarily on what felt right. You may have perused countless school brochures, scrutinised exam league *tables or attended special induction events, but, ultimately, your and your parents' decision would have been based on a gut feeling. This intuitive choice was informed by picking up certain invisible messages about an establishment that were closely related to the idea of how the "hidden curriculum" was communicated.'*

'Oh, I know about that term. Lead covered it once during our meetings. You mean the sum total of attitudes, beliefs, culture, behaviours and ethos that an organisation communicates subconsciously to the outside world, which may be completely different from the rhetoric they broadcast publicly in selling their brand.'

'Precisely, Dael. It's a bit like the feeling of doubt you may encounter during an interview when you sense deep down the job isn't really for you. Even though you confidently press on answering questions and projecting the allure that you're enthusiastic about the new job, the actual messages you're communicating subconsciously relay an entirely different set of messages. Ultimately, it's this signal that others pick up, a bit like an invisible radio wave carrying a message.

'Bringing this idea back to the present, every business and organisation transmits to the outside world an invisible broadcast concerning their values, beliefs and assumptions. Just like the subconscious mind or hidden curriculum, these messages reveal their true intentions and are critical in determining the sorts of results they receive. So why's this important? Let's imagine that, under my direction, my leadership teams create a company vision for how we want Citrus to perform or be received in the world, but if this intent isn't epitomised in the thoughts and actions of every employee, then the mission fails! When you become fully aware of this fact, it forces you to reconsider how you communicate, listen and engage with your employees to bridge this gap. So, again, you can see where honesty, transparency and trust are critical leadership qualities that I must constantly keep on my radar to help to achieve this aim.'

It was at this point that, for a brief second, Dael's concentration wandered, and he thought back to Lead's earlier lessons on the power of the subconscious mind within the individual and how this compared to what Redael was now sharing.

'Now, that's the first aspect of what I've been studying. The second idea involves reconsidering completely everything we were taught at school about time, space and the essence of reality.' Redael chuckled. 'It's not an easy angle to grasp and, believe me, my new mentor – Gorfesiw – spent hours explaining this idea before it eventually settled within my own head. Oh, you've got to meet him one day!'

As exciting as it was, Dael resisted the urge to interject and share how he, too, had crossed paths with Gorfesiw. Redael was clearly in full flow – and now wasn't the time.

Redael went on, 'There's only one way to approach the ideas I'm about to share, and that's just to sit with it and get to know it on your own terms until it becomes your new norm with respect to the way you view the outside world.'

'I understand; so much of what I've been learning with Lead recently has needed to be that way. It's not information that can easily be handed over. Only you can get your own head around it,' suggested Dael.

'Indeed, that's true; anyway, here goes. Although things may appear solid, with time being experienced as a linear, evolving adventure comprising separate things and events, everything is actually just energy contained within a single point. With this in mind, the notion of duality or separatism becomes irrelevant. There are no beginnings or ends, and no rights or wrongs, just a cosmic soup, if you like, of an infinitude of potentials. Your role, as the interacting observer, is to imagine and select the preferred experience from a realm of endless possibilities. In this sense, you liberate yourself from the role of the victim, instead becoming the orchestrator of your circumstances. You do this by mastering your thoughts, feelings and actions – or state of being – to reflect the circumstances you wish to attract.

'So, from the perspective of my position as a company leader, my belief about how it is out there is vitally important when it comes to determining the success of my company. In other words, do I make the assumption that my company is growing more creative, innovative and agile, or that it's succumbing to the fear of vulnerability, limitation or insecurity?

'Whenever anybody approaches me for advice to help kick-start the big idea they're passionate about, I always respond by saying, "It's already here!" You see, the moment you picture a desire or create a vision of how you prefer your life to turn out, it's already yours because every possibility exists in the realm of potentiality. Your only role is to select it and live by it until you become it. You couldn't imagine it unless it were already here! There remains the illusion of time, in which a so-called "time lag" may appear; nevertheless, you've already named and claimed it! This is what I mean by working backward: maintaining a feeling that you're already living your desire.

'Going back to my point about getting people on board, you don't necessarily need to have every employee viewing reality in this way, but you do need to ensure they understand and appreciate that traditional A-to-B problem-solving approaches are always limited, because no matter how hard you try, by fixating on the problem, you're always subconsciously anchored to more of the same. For example, if I asked my teams to create a solution to get out of a negative situation or develop the opposite of something, what do you think would happen?'

'You'd get more of the same,' answered Dael, 'because you're associating even new thoughts with the original state of lack. In this manner, it can serve to exaggerate the problem because you're working from limited circumstances that already exist. You may patch up the problem for a while, but you only need to turn your back for a second and rapid change in the world will have caught you up, and before you know it, your solutions are outdated again.'

'Exactly! Now I'm not saying doing your research or adopting more traditional problem-solving routes have no place, because they do still work, but I am saying you have to think beyond this and remain open to the role that divergent originating thinking plays in creating solutions.'

Abruptly, Redael changed her focus, jumped up from her chair and beckoned Dael to follow her on a comprehensive tour of Citrus's operations, including packaging, food preparation and the research laboratories. Dael was greeted with warmth and interest by all of Redael's employees. He and Redael paused and sat together at one of the empty desks in the research lab.

Dael was compelled to delve deeper into the reasons why everyone appeared so upbeat and energised. Clearly, everyone he'd met so far loved working for Citrus.

He thought Redael must have been reading his mind when she enquired, 'Have you come across the terms "dopamine" and "oxytocin", Dael?'

Dael had to admit he was still unsure what these words meant, even though Lead had probably touched on them in earlier tutorials.

Redael explained, 'Dopamine is a neurotransmitter that's released in the brain to send pleasure messages to other areas of the body, as well as making the heart pump faster to increase blood flow. Since our early dinosaur origins, millions of years ago, the brain has evolved to reinforce certain feel-good sensations – such as receiving praise or acknowledgement – by releasing surges of dopamine that create a rush of expectation. This pleasure sensation is highly addictive and increases your desire to find more opportunities to experience similar sensations again. You know how conditioned we all are to that rush of anticipation when a "like" notification appears in response to a post we've shared on the jungle net or when an unexpected message appears on our smartphone from a friend? Of course, we yearn for more of these sensations, but the problem with this type of addiction is that it can lead to bad habits, such as not being able to leave your smartphone alone, imagining it vibrating when it isn't, checking it when your concentration should be elsewhere or even taking it to bed with you at night. At the extreme level, living a life of dopamine addiction can lead to an increase in headaches, tension, stress, antisocial behaviour and anxiety.

'There is, however, another feel-good neurochemical released by the brain, which is called "oxytocin", and that has far healthier benefits. It's released when we share, cooperate and support others. These activities can aid our sense of well-being and make us feel more energised, connected and fulfilled. This is why volunteering can feel so satisfying, and this holds true for both extroverts and introverts.

'A cooperative culture develops greater empathy, trust, productivity, purposefulness and creativity among individuals. So, it stands to reason that, if you create plenty of opportunities to develop these kinds of *experiences within the organisation you lead, the more purposeful and engaged your employees will be.'*

Redael's delivery was interrupted briefly as she left the room to take an important phone call. A young sloth entered the room and introduced herself as Rewollof, one of the newer apprentices at Citrus. She asked Dael if he required any further refreshments. Dael accepted, and he grasped the opportunity to test some of the principles Redael had just shared by asking her what made Redael such a unique leader.

Another viewpoint

The young apprentice was more than happy to elaborate. 'It's really quite simple – Redael inspires such close, supportive teamwork. I always feel as though I can express myself, including saying the things I may need the most help with. Everyone appreciates each other here, regardless of their position or years of service.

'When I first arrived here, I was a little nervous because my last boss spent all his time micromanaging everyone, and I lost my confidence and grew to hate my job. There were no opportunities for real personal growth or professional development, and I always felt demotivated as every step I made was scrutinised by my boss. To make matters worse he only gave lip service to diversity and inclusion issues within the workplace. As a result, so many of my fellow employees simply packed up and left. It's totally opposite here at Citrus. When I first joined, my line managers immediately instilled in me greater self-belief, and I trusted their guidance. I found this so inspiring!

'I love working here, and I've enrolled on several leadership courses. Learning always feels like fun and not exclusively linked to work. It's more about whole-person development. I know it sounds harsh, but I've learnt that no one really owes you anything when it comes to getting on in work, and this makes it even more special that everyone here is so supportive. It's out of choice, not because they're being told to. This style of leadership is so important right now, especially when you consider the fallout following the great jungle storm, when we were all thrown into early hibernation. During that period, it was really hard to maintain a

compassionate connection with other animals. My transition back into work was handled wonderfully here.

'Many of my friends are resigning from their old jobs to work for companies that take proper care of their employees. Some have gone solo and started their own small businesses. I think the great storm shook not only our way of life but also the way in which we think about work, choice and the values we wish to live our lives by.'

Dael enquired, 'What do your friends think about your experience here at Citrus?'

'One or two of my friends never stick at anything for very long before they get bored or decide to give up. I don't think they get my enthusiasm, but then they don't work here, so why should they? Many of them just want to do everything alone and on their terms, and this is fine, but when you're a young apprentice like me, when it comes to developing some of the broader soft skills – such as humility and honesty – how on earth are you expected to get everything right first time unless someone demonstrates what this looks like?'

'What do you mean?'

'Well, my leaders don't boast or take all the credit. They just set great examples. They applaud their teams and recognise all success as a team effort, rather than continually looking inward for gratification. It's almost like our collective goal at Citrus is bigger than our own egos! We're all provided with room to breathe, and favouritism is never really an issue. It's been a real eye-opener, that's for sure.

'They still ask for help – just like I do occasionally – but, of course, I'm still rather new here, so I ask different sorts of questions, which are more to do with familiarising myself with my new role. I've learnt there's huge value in developing humility and empathy. Humble people achieve very different results!'

Dael pressed on with his questioning: 'How did you get to this position? When you joined were there tests, exams or an induction process?'

'I had to submit my CV, of course, and during my interview, I was asked some unusual questions, but I think I did okay.'

'Will you explain a little bit more about that, please?'

'To my surprise, one of the first questions I was asked was what makes me angry or sad. I was encouraged to provide an honest answer. At first, I thought this question was rather odd, but I learnt later that it provided the interviewers with a far greater insight into my personality than simply asking what hobbies I had or what success I'd accomplished recently.

'They asked me to express my greatest weakness. I guess this revealed a lot more about my level of self-awareness and the degree to which I pursued lifelong learning actively. I was also asked to articulate what skills I needed to develop.

'Redael often reminds us to ask ourselves the same question at the end of each working day: "What have I learnt and done today that demonstrates I'm geared up for personal development?"

'Another strange question they asked was who my best mate is and why. I think this revealed more about me as a team player, the values I appreciate most in other people and maybe the extent to which I rely on other people.'

Carefully counting each one off on her fingers, Rewollof proceeded to deliver an extensive list of questions that she was presented with during her interview. 'They also asked questions/requests like these:

'Describe a condition when your work was most effective and least effective.

'When was the last time you completed something highly creative?

'What voluntary activities have you undertaken recently and what have you learnt?

'Does it frustrate you when your team members get all the praise?

'What does the word "humble" mean?

'What things do you do that are so much better than what other people do?

'When did you last demonstrate resilience or endurance in doing something new?

'Can you name a time when you truly received the credit for something?

'Name three recent points in your career where you celebrated openly someone else's ability to overcome a challenge?

'What are "authenticity" and "vulnerability", and which is the bigger weakness?

'Name someone whom you admire because they discussed openly how they overcame low points in their life.

'How often in a month do you meet with a mentor or someone you respect to receive advice?

'I later found out that how I answered these leading questions determined my level of EQ and MQ.'

Their conversation was interrupted as Redael came bounding into the room, smiling and waving her hands energetically. 'Ah... you've met Rewollof. How are you doing today? How did your sister's race in the jungle athletics tournament go?'

As they chatted, Dael took a moment to reflect. He was taken aback by the level of genuine interest Redael was showing in her new employee's news.

Redael laughed as she joked with her young apprentice. 'Have you been sharing all our trade secrets, Rewollof?'

'No, no; we were discussing my induction process,' replied Rewollof. 'Now I really must be getting on. It was great meeting you, Dael. Hope you have a brilliant day.'

Dael and Redael found themselves alone once again.

Redael used the opportunity to share her final point: 'Isn't it great to see our young apprentices shine with so much confidence? So many people simply hide their true selves at work, but here at Citrus, we like to recognise the whole person. Of course, we're all naturally inclined to protect ourselves at work, but I think it's important to explain to our apprentices the disadvantage of this type of behaviour. Instead, we actively encourage them to pursue one or two of our self-development courses. We believe knowing yourself is the key to growing yourself! We also invest heavily in developing our employees' soft skills. I like to think that this approach also helps develop our future leaders.'

'I've never really understood the term "soft skills",' remarked Dael.

'"Soft skills" is an interesting term, isn't it? Here at Citrus, we're beginning to get used to using the term "critical skills" instead as it's more accurate. We associate it with certain character, personality and EQ capabilities. These sorts of skills aren't straightforward or easily acquired. They can't simply be gained or ticked off from a list – you develop them through experience. Again, my role as leader is to do my best to demonstrate these skills as much as possible, as well as providing the sorts of experiences from which my employees can develop them.

'We live in such incredible times, Dael, and the challenges continue to grow. What's expected from us all in today's world is unprecedented. As a leader, I have a duty to equip our teams with the appropriate thinking skills that allow them to ride the challenges that will undoubtedly occur in the future.

'One of my favourite questions to ask my employees, regardless of their position or role within the company, is "What do you still need to learn?" It's a great question as it displaces them or catches them off guard, so they can't fall back into simply describing their role. Another fantastic question to ask is "What will have happened to you in ten years' time?" This opens up their imagination, and you can quickly tell if they've thought about their long-term goals.

'We're committed to encouraging honest and trustworthy communication; you witnessed that earlier, no doubt. At Citrus, you're always supported and never alone. Did you notice the excitement and energy at this morning's meeting?'

'Yes, I did,' confirmed Dael. 'But how can excitement grow from such an awkward and transparent display of authenticity?'

'Everyone these days is looking for happiness or fulfilment in the wrong places. A lot of creatures fail to realise that these qualities grow best when you force yourself to stretch beyond your comfort zone. However, growth isn't always without pain, challenge or frustration. You probably hear the term "well-being" being used a lot these days, but I'd go as far to say that a healthy state of well-being is intrinsically linked with the human need to grow, both emotionally and spiritually.

'In today's modern world, taking responsibility for how you think is the most important consideration facing every creature in the jungle.'

'Where do you start with such a huge undertaking?' questioned Dael.

'Just start!' answered Redael, laughing. 'You begin by inspiring others so they feel differently about themselves. Then you make a commitment to set an example. Finally, you have to strive continually to develop an intense curiosity for life. Sorry, listen to me going on. Enough about my passion. So, Dael, tell me about you. What's your drive?'

'Well, it's not so much a drive, but I love learning about the benefits of gardening and working with plants. It's more of a hobby, you see. It's not what I do at work.'

Redael's face lit up immediately, and she requested, 'Please tell me more.'

Dael composed himself. No one apart from Lead had ever shown such an interest in his hobby before, so he gave it his best shot. 'Gardening has taught me patience in a world where the opposite is very often the case. You can never be a perfectionist or self-centred when working in a garden, as plants operate in a completely different manner.

'Tending a garden is the perfect mindfulness solution that releases the inhibiting grip of emotions such as anxiety, stress, depression and sorrow. If I feel uptight, cross or bogged down, digging over soil or pruning hedges always does the trick. I love the way all my senses are stimulated when I get close to certain plants and flowers. I love the way houseplants purify the air indoors. I love the calming colours in flowers, such as lavender blue and purple. The scent of certain flowers really lifts me out of negative moods.

'When I'm tending to my garden, the sounds of birds or the wind blowing through a palm tree always reveal a sense of power and serenity that makes my problems seem less significant. Getting your hands into soil, planting seeds and touching plants brings me back down to earth. Even better is the joy of growing your own vegetables and then eating them when they've been freshly harvested the same day. I enjoy stretching and moving my body outdoors, and of course, there's the added bonus of just how good it makes you feel, as well as the boost to your immune system.

'I've actually developed several practical courses to teach others about all these benefits, but as yet, I've not had chance to expand on this. Like I said, this is more of a hobby, you see, but I'd love the opportunity to share all this knowledge and passion with others one day.'

Redael jumped up excitedly and announced, 'You'd be a great inspiration for our botanical innovation department. At the moment, they're looking for exciting, new ways to engage our younger customers in promoting a new herbal drink we're developing. In fact, we harvest the herbs here at our site. We're toying with the idea of running a series of outreach courses for local schools on the health benefits of growing your own plants and vegetables. If we could promote our story to a wider audience, that would be great.'

She thought for a moment. 'Hey, Dael, are you aware there's a new role opening in our horticultural education outreach department? You'd be a perfect candidate. You should apply.'

Dael immediately withdrew his air of confidence, lowered his shoulders and stuttered, 'Oh no, I'm sure there are better-qualified creatures than me out there.'

'Well, you'll never know unless you try. In any case, what's more important for you right now, particularly after everything you've recently learnt from Lead? Is your life going to be about trusting and acting on your passion and enthusiasm, and then discovering where it my lead, or about simply doing more of the same and submitting to the fear and servitude of self-doubt?

'I'll leave you with that thought.' Redael smiled. 'Now if you don't mind, I have to draw our meeting today to a close, but think hard about what I've just shared.'

As Dael said his goodbyes and strolled home, the idea that Redael had just planted in his mind gained momentum. Of course, once he shared this news with Lead, she didn't hesitate to encourage Dael to go for the job, especially as the new role at Citrus encompassed everything he felt most passionate about.

The perfect end with a new beginning

A week later, Dael applied for the job, and following two rather frantic weeks of interview preparation, to his surprise, he acquired the new position at Citrus. Of course, Dael's initial feelings of shock and disbelief at achieving such a radical change of fortune were eventually transformed into acceptance and then jubilation. He couldn't stop thanking Lead for all her help and encouragement, but this wasn't the end of their adventure together, as the two friends continued to meet each week at the Firefly Coffee House.

Despite all the excitement, Dael became slowly aware of an even greater sensation: gratitude. True to the law of attraction, everything that was happening in his life right now was merely a reflection of his new state of mind, which had been forged after weeks of study under Lead's guidance. It was as though everything he'd ever longed for had always been present and only required a shift of awareness for it to fully manifest. Lead had provided the perfect key to enable him to unlock his true potential by helping him liberate his emotions to achieve his desires. Dael felt as though he'd woken up from the dream of life.

Liberate your perception of self
and unlock the control of your **emotions**,
and then you'll **achieve** your **desires**.

A few months passed by, and then, one day, as Dael was travelling to his new work role at Citrus, a young salamander hurried past him, only to slip on some fallen wet palm leaves and slide awkwardly into a ditch. Dael helped the poor fellow up hurriedly and brushed the dirt from his jacket. The salamander looked somewhat baffled as if this were the first time that anyone had displayed such compassion. He introduced himself nervously as Ycagel and said he'd just begun an apprentice programme working with a new organisation at the northern edge of the jungle. A conversation ensued in which Ycagel shared more about himself and, in particular, the struggle he was having with managing his work-life balance.

So began a series of conversations in which Dael embarked on a fresh adventure where he was fulfilling a new role, not as the student but now as the mentor supporting another lizard's learning journey. The wisdom and support Dael shared in leading his new student toward the path of liberation would change Ycagel's life forever.

To be continued!

Conclusion

You've finally completed all sixteen route guidances and scaled the highest summits of wisdom and knowledge for navigating the path through the jungle of work life.

Now turn back and review the eight themes at the beginning of the introduction to your guidebook:

> » *Can you sense a slight change within you since first reviewing them, as if you're reading them through new eyes?*
>
> » *Does it feel like they no longer serve a purpose in actually helping you advance closer to your ideal?*
>
> » *Do you notice how emotionally debilitating these statements are? And do you perhaps sense an urge to resist them by asserting a steadfast attitude that will allow you to rise above the negative energy they convey and release the unlimited resilient and noble power within you?*

Simply viewing the world through a lens that only magnifies what's wrong or missing in life will ultimately serve to merely reflect to you the outward conditions and circumstances that exemplify everything you don't want.

Lead

If Dael were presented with these statements following everything he'd learnt so far about the power of embellishing a positive affirmation with the phrase 'I am', he'd undoubtedly rewrite each statement in the following manner:

1. I am filled with positivity, and I am experiencing financial security and job certainty.

2. I am confident, clearheaded and at ease, living a life in tune with my true values.

3. I am enjoying a holistic, meaningful, purposeful and fulfilling work life.

4. I am free and enjoy plenty of space to be respected by others for my opinions, expertise or support.

5. I am connected to wonderful people and have a packed social calendar.

6. I am independent, and I am being presented with countless opportunities that transform my appreciation of my unique learning journey in which freedom and liberation grow daily.

7. I am thrilled how I am honing my creative skills by using technology when and how I choose to and always in a state of flow and ease.

8. I am relaxed, and I am enjoying the harmony, serendipity and wonderful opportunities in my life that come my way effortlessly.

Now you've shared in Dael's adventure, prising open his door to liberation, all that remains is to ask yourself whether a similar doorway exists within you and whether you have the courage to throw the door open and step fully through it. The only limits preventing you from doing so are the limits you impose on yourself and the manner in which you apply your imagination.

With this in mind, if you do decide to step through this doorway, then your guidebook's final farewell message behoves you to heed the following command:

Judge not by appearances,
forever seek gratitude in the present moment
and guard your thoughts wisely.

Go now, step back into the jungle, share your truth with the world and lead the way!

> *'Dear Source,*
> *Can you recognise the wisdom and creativity*
> *being released right now that flows through me,*
> *although it originates from you?'*
> *With this remark, Source wakes up from the dream*
> *and replies, 'Yes, I can – now you've declared that!'*

Ttell am Y not 25.02.2023

Bibliography

Adrienne, C. 1999. *The purpose of your life.* New York, NY: William Morrow.

Allen, J. 2022. *As a man thinketh.* s.l.: Reader's Library Classics.

Begg, D. 2001. *Synchronicity: The promise of coincidence.* London, UK: Thorsons Publishers.

Behrend, G. 2013. *Your invisible power.* London, UK: Merchant Books.

Boldt, L.G. 1999. *The Tao of abundance: Eight ancient principles for abundant living.* London, UK: Penguin Arkana.

Breathnach, S.B. 1999. *Something more – excavating your authentic self.* London, UK: Transworld Publishing.

Bryan, M. 1998. *The artist's way at work – twelve weeks to creative freedom.* London, UK: Pan Books.

Burchard, B. 2014. *The motivation manifesto: 9 declarations to claim your personal power.* Carlsbad, CA: Hay House Inc.

Byrne, R. 2006. *The secret.* London, UK: Simon and Schuster UK.

Byrne, R. 2010. *The power.* London, UK: Simon and Schuster UK.

Cainer, J. 2006. *Cosmic ordering: How to make your dreams come true.* London, UK: Collins.

Cameron, J. 1995. *The artist's way: A course in discovering and recovering your creative self.* London, UK: Pan Books.

Cameron, J. 1997. *The vein of gold: A journey to your creative heart.* London, UK: Pan MacMillan.

Cameron, J. 2002. *Walking in this world: Practical strategies for creativity.* London, UK: Rider.

Carnegie, D. 2006. *How to win friends and influence people.* London, UK: Vermilion.

Chartered Institute of Personnel and Development, 2022. *Health and well-being at work 2022.* [online] Available at: https://www.cipd.co.uk/Images/health-well-being-work-report-2022_tcm18-108440.pdf

Choquette, S. 1999. *Your heart's desire: Using the laws of manifestation to create the life you want.* London, UK: Piatkus Books.

Coelho, P. 1995. *The alchemist.* New York, NY: HarperCollins.

Dale Carnegie Training. 2011. *Make yourself unforgettable: How to become the person everyone remembers and no one can resist.* London, UK: Simon and Schuster UK.

Das, L.S. 2000. *Awakening to the sacred.* London, UK: Transworld Publishers.

Deane, S. 2022. Fear of flying statistics, trends & facts (2022 Data). *Stratos Jet Charters.* [online] Available at: https://www.stratosjets.com/blog/fear-of-flying-statistics-trends-facts

Denny, R. 1997. *Succeed for yourself: Unlock your potential for success and happiness.* London, UK: Kogan Page.

Dispenza, J. 2012a. *Breaking the habit of being yourself: How to lose your mind and create a new one.* London, UK: Hay House UK.

Dispenza, J. 2012b. *You are the placebo: Make your mind matter.* London, UK: Hay House UK.

Dispenza, J. 2019. *Becoming supernatural: How common people are doing the uncommon.* London, UK: Hay House UK.

Dyer, W.W. 1998. *Manifest your destiny: The nine spiritual principles for getting everything you want.* London, UK: Thorsons Publishing.

Edwards, G. 1999. *Stepping into the magic: A new approach to everyday life.* London, UK: Piatkus Books.

Edwards, G. 2009. *Living magically.* Reprint. London, UK: Piatkus Books.

Evans, B. 2020. *How to have a happy hustle: The complete guide to making your ideas happen.* London, UK: Icon Books Ltd.

Farrimond, S. 2020. *The science of living: 219 reasons to rethink your daily routine.* London, UK: Dorling Kindersley.

Ferriss, T. 2017. *Tribe of mentors: Short life advice from the best in the world.* London, UK: Vermilion.

Gallo, C. 2014. *Talk like TED: The 9 public speaking secrets of the world's top minds.* London, UK: Macmillan.

Goddard, N. 1969. *The game of life.* [online] Available at: https://nevillegoddardbooks.com/neville-goddard-text-lectures/the-game-of-life

Goddard, N. 2010. *The power of awareness.* Scotts Valley, CA: CreateSpace Independent Publishing Platform.

Goleman, D. 1996. *Emotional intelligence: Why it can matter more than IQ.* London, UK: Bloomsbury Publishing.

Grant, A. 2016. *Originals: How non-conformists change the world.* London, UK: W.H. Allen.

Gray, J. 2001. *How to get what you want and want what you have.* London, UK: .Vermilion.

Hawkins, D.R. 2014a. *Letting go: The pathway of surrender.* London, UK: Hay House UK.

Hawkins, D.R. 2014b. *Power vs. force.* Carlsbad, CA: Hay House Inc.

Hendricks, M. 2019. *The No-BS Fitness Formula*. Manchester, UK: Compass-Publishing UK

Hill, N. 1996. *Napoleon Hill's positive action plan: How to make every day a success*. London, UK: Piatkus Books.

Hill, N. 2009. *Think and grow rich: The original classic*. Mankato, MN: Capstone.

Hillman, J. 1997. *The soul's code: In search of character and calling*. London, UK: Transworld Publishers.

Holder, J. 1999. *Soul purpose: Self-affirming rituals, meditations and creative exercises to revive your spirit*. London, UK: Piatkus Books.

Holmes, E. 1998. *The science of mind: A philosophy, a faith, a way of life*. New York, NY: Tarcher Putnam.

Houston, J. 1998. *A passion for the possible: A guide to realizing your true potential*. New York, NY: HarperOne.

Jones, J. 2009. *The magic-weaving business: Finding the heart of learning and teaching*. Cranage, UK: Leannta Publishing.

Kegan, R. and Lahey L.L. 2016. *An everyone culture: Becoming a deliberately developmental organization*. Boston, MA: Harvard Business Review Press.

Lenoir, O.L. 2016. Society should promote high self-esteem for children. *The Poly Post*. [online] Available at: https://thepolypost.com/opinion/2016/02/23/article_f15cfdbc-d9a9-11e5-8cb5-277a99095b74-5/

Klaff, O. 2011. *Pitch anything: An innovative method for presenting, persuading, and winning the deal*. New York, NY: McGraw-Hill.

Maltz, M. 1989. *Psycho-cybernetics*. New York, NY: Pocket Books.

Marr, B. 2022. The 7 biggest business challenges every company is facing in 2023. *Forbes*. [online] Available at: https://www.forbes.com/sites/bernardmarr/2022/11/15/the-7-biggest-business-challenges-every-company-is-facing-in-2023/

Martina Désirée, 2008. *Neale Donald Walsch – God says yes*. [video] Available at: https://www.youtube.com/watch?v=ZMPhTLez_Ck

Millman, D. 1993. *The life you were born to live: A guide to finding your life purpose*. Tiburon, CA: HJ Kramer Inc.

Moody, H.R. and Carroll, D. 1998. *The five stages of the soul: For everyone who has ever asked, 'Is this it?'* London, UK: Rider.

Moore, T. 1992. *Care of the soul: How to add depth and meaning to your everyday life*. London, UK: Piatkus Books.

Moore, T. 2003. *The soul's religion*. London, UK: Transworld Publishers.

Murphy, J. 1989. *The amazing laws of cosmic mind power*. Hoboken, NJ: Prentice Hall.

Murray, P. 1998. *You can always get what you want*. [audio cassette] London, UK: Hodder and Stoughton.

Murray, P. 1999. *The 49 steps to a bright life: A conspiracy for personal success.* London, UK: Hodder and Stoughton.

Myss, C. 2002. *Sacred contracts: Awaken your divine potential.* London, UK: Transworld Publishers.

Neil, M. 2013. *The inside out revolution: The only thing you need to know to change your life forever.* Carlsbad, CA: Hay House Inc.

Nightingale, E. 2013. *The strangest secret.* London, UK: Merchant Books.

Parkin, J.C. 2016. *F**k it – do what you love.* London, UK: Hay House UK.

Pink, D.H. 2006. *A whole new mind: Why right-brainers will rule the future.* New York, NY: Riverhead Books.

Pratchett, T. 1992. *Witches Abroad.* London, UK: Corgi.

Pritchett, P. 2012. *You²: A high velocity formula for multiplying your personal effectiveness in quantum leaps.* Dallas, TX: Pritchett, LP.

Proctor, B. 1996. *You were born rich.* Scottsdale, AZ: LifeSuccess Productions.

Redfield, J. 1994. *The Celestine prophecy: An adventure.* London, UK: Transworld Publishers.

Redfield, J. 1995. *The Celestine prophecy: An experiential guide.* London, UK: Transworld Publishers.

Redfield, J. 1997. *The Celestine vision: Living the new spiritual awareness.* London, UK: Transworld Publishers.

Redfield, J. 1997. *The tenth insight: Holding the vision.* London, UK: Transworld Publishers.

Redfield, J. 1999. *The secret of Shambhala: In search of the eleventh insight.* New York, NY: Bantam Press.

Redfield, J., Murphy, M., and Timbers, S. 2002. *God and the evolving universe.* New ed. London, UK: Transworld Publishers.

Riggio, R.E. 2023. 4 top leadership challenges for 2023 and beyond. *Psychology Today.* [online] Available at: https://www.psychologytoday.com/us/blog/cutting-edge-leadership/202301/4-top-leadership-challenges-for-2023-and-beyond

Robbins, A. 2001. *Awaken the giant within.* London, UK: Simon and Schuster UK.

Robinson, K. 2017. *Out of our minds: The power of being creative.* Mankato, MN: Capstone.

Ross, A. 2016. *The industries of the future.* London, UK: Simon and Schuster UK.

Schulz, M.L. 1999. *Awakening intuition.* London, UK: Transworld Publishers.

Sinek, S. 2018. *The infinite game.* London, UK: Portfolio Penguin.

Stevenson, D. and Farmer, P. 2017. *Thriving at work: The Stevenson/Farmer review of mental health and employers.* [online] Available at: https://assets.publishing.

service.gov.uk/government/uploads/system/uploads/attachment_data/file/658145/thriving-at-work-stevenson-farmer-review.pdf

TED. 2010. *Bring on the learning revolution!* | Ken Robinson. [video] Available at: https://www.youtube.com/watch?v=kFMZrEABdw4

Tolle, E. 2001. *The power of now: A guide to spiritual enlightenment.* 1st UK ed. London, UK: Hodder and Stoughton.

Trilling, B. and Fadel, C. 2012. *21st century skills: Learning for life in our times.* San Francisco, CA: Jossey-Bass.

Troward, T. 2014. *The essential Thomas Troward: Complete and original editions of the Edinburgh lectures on mental science, the Dore lectures on mental science, the creative process in the individual, the law and the word.* Scotts Valley, CA: CreateSpace Independent Publishing Platform.

Turner, C. 1997. *Made for life: A compelling story of the human spirit's quest for fulfilment.* New ed. s.l.: InToto Books.

Waitley, D. 1996. *The new dynamics of goal setting: Flextactics for a fast-changing future.* London, UK: Nicholas Brealey Publishing.

Walsch, N.D. 1999. *Friendship with God: An uncommon dialogue.* London, UK: Hodder and Stoughton.

Wasmund, S. and Newton, R. 2011. *Stop talking, start doing: A kick in the pants in six parts.* Mankato, MN: Capstone.

Wattles, W.D. 2007. *The science of getting rich: Attracting financial success through creative thought.* Great Yarmouth, UK: Destiny Books.

Wiete, A.K. 2013. *Leadership and emotional intelligence: The keys to driving ROI and organizational performance.* Human Capital Institute Research in partnership with MHS. [online] Available at: https://eqdevgroup.com/wp-content/uploads/2016/02/Leadership-EI_The-Keys-to-Driving-ROI-and-Org-Perf.pdf

Acknowledgements

When people ask me what I've learnt to appreciate the most during my incredible journey of entrepreneurism and resilience over the last six years, I always reply, 'It's quite simple: it's all about people, people, people!'

When you look for adventure and the possibility of meeting amazing, supportive people in the world, you'll find you'll attract the perfect circumstances into your life.

In no particular order, I would like to thank the following people:

I offer my thanks to Richard Hurst, who was right there at the beginning of my journey, and whom I first met during bizarre circumstances: I was dressed in a fancy-dress pilot uniform (it's a long story) at my school leaving party at the Mercure Parkway Hotel, Leeds, in July 2017. He approached me and asked where I was flying to, and I had to confess I was actually a teacher. He was undeterred and somewhat intrigued, and as he pressed further with his questions, I shared my vision and reason for leaving the mainstream education system. There followed an exchange of business cards, and then regular meetings in which Richard became my first mentor, sharing unique wisdom, energy, business advice and a deep appreciation of life. His key advice to me in the jungle was 'Tony... all that matters first is that you can stand on your own two feet, grow and create an income!'

Thank you, John Macintyre, for always believing in me and providing that critical 'go do' encouragement, insight and support (I think this book would still be on the drawing board if it weren't for you, John). His advice to me in the jungle centred on this: 'Tony, plan it and get it done!'

We all need a soul mate, and without Mike Hendrick's (fellow author) friendship, support and calm perspective, I truly believe my book-writing journey could have halted on numerous occasions.

Bless you, Mike! Mike's advice in the jungle was always 'So, what have you learnt?' and 'It's all gooood!' (pronounced very slowly).

Thank you, Denise Chong (who came bounding over to read my name badge at a business networking event, and we instantly hit it off) for your amazing emotional intelligence, impeccable global HR expertise, and grammar and proofreading support during the draft stage of writing this book. Her encouragement in the jungle was often this: 'Look at you! Isn't this great?'

A huge thank you to Alex Naylor for believing in me, taking me under your wing and taking the time out of your incredibly busy business schedule to mentor me and share your phenomenal humility and friendship. Alex's consistent advice to me in the jungle was 'This is amazing. Keep going!'

I'm eternally grateful to Roland Meredith (the voice of authority, critical thinking and truth) for agreeing to write the foreword for the book and for sharing endless wisdom, insight and vision concerning the future of education and how best to serve and empower young people. His advice to me in the jungle was 'Get it done – young people need your help!'

Thank you to Abigail and Chloe at Buttercrumble (the creative and talented people who helped make the images within the book come to life) for always being available for me to ask questions and for sharing warmth, creativity and hospitality (unique within the business world). Abigail and Chloe's advice to me in the jungle was this: 'You'll find that, if you stay true to yourself, you'll make it in the end.'

To Samantha and Joe Gaunt (the supportive and caring companions on my journey), thank you for your consistent authenticity, wisdom and business support. I'll never forget you both, especially as you said early on in my adventure, 'We'll always do anything to help you!'

I'm immensely grateful for Richelle Schuster (the door opener) for supporting me in the early stage of developing my business. You connected me with so many wonderful people within the

West Yorkshire business ecosystem and provided me with so many opportunities. Richelle's advice to me in the jungle was this: 'It's a difficult journey. Giving people the key to my networks can make a huge difference!'

Thank you, Lloyd Naylor (the wise, mystic Jedi knight and peaceful warrior with me on my journey) for always being there when I had a question related to the business world and, indeed, the challenges of life in general. Your thirst for lifelong learning and awesome leadership skills have been a huge inspiration to me. Lloyds's advice to me in the jungle was always 'Know your value and charge accordingly!'

I feel so blessed to have received both support and insight from Gordon Bateman, who's an incredible business leader, avid lifelong learner, event organiser and opportunity-maker with the greatest depth of expertise in engaging employees I've come across. Gordon's advice to me in the jungle was 'People invest in another's passion, genius – get going!'

It's impossible to convey how much gratitude I have towards my editor and coach Alexa Whitten, who expertly and patiently guided me through the whole book-publishing process. Alexa, you're the best! Alexa's advice to me in the jungle was 'A beast of a book, but a beautiful one – so get it done!'

As any successful author will tell you, enrolling the help of a first-rate copy-editor and proofreader is absolutely essential for ensuring that the text flows as smoothly as possible and without any errors. I believe I found the very best person for this role in Lindsay Corten. Thank you, Lindsay, for sharing your impeccable knowledge of grammar, sincere warmth and unwavering guidance throughout the final stages of bringing this book in to land!

To my friends Vanessa Campey and Rav Panesar, a huge thank you for sharing such wonderful friendship and support throughout (often over coffee or brunch).

Finally, endless gratitude and love for the silent, behind-the-scenes, wonderfully supportive and patient person – my dear wife

Debbie, without whom this book would never have seen the light of day!

Furthermore, for all you readers out there with a vision – only you can make it happen. And remember this: you couldn't imagine it unless you had the capability to realise it in the outside world!

About the Author

Tony Mallett is a Leeds-based leadership and resilience coach, a speaker, an avid lifelong learner, and an Ofsted accredited 'outstanding' teacher, with twenty-five years' teaching experience. Tony's teaching career has always focused on enabling young people struggling with learning barriers to foster new mindsets, transforming doubt into confidence and providing them with a vision for a different, sustainable and more fulfilling future. Tony's knack for unlocking deeper levels of self-belief in his students earned him the nickname 'Mr Mallett Magic' within his school's community.

Tony's passion for creating new and exciting ways to inspire young people to think big provided the impetus for launching his own leadership development and training business Inspirationalleads.com in 2017. It was at this time when Tony began developing the ideas and research that would later transform into his first book.

In 2019, he developed a highly innovative gamification micro-learning platform designed to help young people develop greater confidence in communicating and applying twenty-four critical competency skills to help support their transition from education into the dynamic and challenging world of work.

In 2021, his ideas earnt him a place on the MIT Regional Entrepreneurship Acceleration Programme (MIT REAP) entitled 'BUILD', which is run in conjunction with Leeds City Council; it focuses on building a more sustainable and inclusive future. This opportunity provided Tony with the opportunity to create wider connections and support within the West Yorkshire business ecosystem.

The guidebook you now hold in your hands evolved steadily throughout this busy entrepreneurial period. Tony's determination to embark on this project was fuelled by his desire to challenge the norm, evolve fresh and innovative ways to engage young readers, and create the holistic go-to resource that he always wished had been available early on in his own working career. Intrinsic to Tony's approach to creating content for his book is his commitment to remaining true to his four key values: inspiration, education, creativity and personal growth.

Tony is currently working on broadening the long-term vision for his business by developing a fully interactive, large-scale version of his gamification learning platform that can be used outdoors at business networking or investment events. He's also busy developing 'The Lead Foundation' – a long-term vision in which a percentage of the profit from the leadership training his company provides goes toward funding international environmental projects that focus on both the preservation of plants and animals within tropical rainforests and reducing climate change.

Tony loves being creative and is a successful published song composer, musician, aviation-magazine writer, model maker and artist; he has a passion for exploring the great outdoors, especially through jogging twice a week and pottering around in his garden allotment.

To find out more, visit Tony's website:
InspirationalLeadsBook.com

1